STATISTICS IN PSYCHOLOGY

MPC-006

For

Master of Arts in Psychology (MAPC)

Useful For

IGNOU, KSOU (Karnataka), Bihar University (Muzaffarpur), Nalanda University, Jamia Millia Islamia, Vardhman Mahaveer Open University (Kota), Uttarakhand Open University, Kurukshetra University, Himachal Pradesh University, Seva Sadan's College of Education (Maharashtra), Lalit Narayan Mithila University, Andhra University, Pt. Sunderlal Sharma (Open) University (Bilaspur), Annamalai University, Bangalore University, Bharathiar University, Bharathidasan University, Centre for distance and open learning, Kakatiya University (Andhra Pradesh), KOU (Rajasthan), MPBOU (MP), MDU (Haryana), Punjab University, Tamilnadu Open University, Sri Padmavati Mahila Visvavidyalayam (Andhra Pradesh), Sri Venkateswara University (Andhra Pradesh), UCSDE (Kerala), University of Jammu, YCMOU, Rajasthan University, UPRTOU, Kalyani University, Banaras Hindu University (BHU) and all other Indian Universities.

Closer to Nature We use Recycled Paper

GULLYBABA PUBLISHING HOUSE PVT. LTD.
ISO 9001 & ISO 14001 CERTIFIED CO.

Published by:
GullyBaba Publishing House Pvt. Ltd.

Regd. Office:	**Branch Office:**
2525/193, 1st Floor, Onkar Nagar-A, Tri Nagar, Delhi-110035 (From Kanhaiya Nagar Metro Station Towards Old Bus Stand) Call: 9991112299, 9312235086 WhatsApp: 9350849407	1A/2A, 20, Hari Sadan, Ansari Road, Daryaganj, New Delhi-110002 Ph.011-45794768 Call & WhatsApp: 8130521616, 8130511234

E-mail: hello@gullybaba.com, **Website:** GullyBaba.com

New Edition

ISBN: 978-93-85533-35-8
Author: Gullybaba.com Panel

Copyright© with Publisher
All rights are reserved. No part of this publication may be reproduced or stored in a retrieval system or transmitted in any form or by any means; electronic, mechanical, photocopying, recording or otherwise, without the written permission of the copyright holder.

Disclaimer: Although the author and publisher have made every effort to ensure that the information in this book is correct, the author and publisher do not assume and hereby disclaim any liability to any party for any loss, damage, or disruption caused by errors or omissions, whether such errors or omissions result from negligence, accident, or any other cause.

If you find any kind of error, please let us know and get reward and or the new book free of cost.

The book is based on IGNOU syllabus. This is only a sample. The book/author/publisher does not impose any guarantee or claim for full marks or to be passed in exam. You are advised only to understand the contents with the help of this book and answer in your words.

All disputes with respect to this publication shall be subject to the jurisdiction of the Courts, Tribunals and Forums of New Delhi, India only.

HOME DELIVERY of GPH Books

You can get GPH books by VPP/COD/Speed Post/Courier.
You can order books by Email/SMS/WhatsApp/Call.
For more details, visit gullybaba.com/faq-books.html
Our packaging department usually dispatches the books within 2 days after receiving your order and it takes nearly 5-6 days in postal/courier services to reach your destination.

Note: Selling this book on any online platform like Amazon, Flipkart, Shopclues, Rediff, etc. without prior written permission of the publisher is prohibited and hence any sales by the SELLER will be termed as ILLEGAL SALE of GPH Books which will attract strict legal action against the offender.

Preface

Most psychological research involves measuring observations of particular characteristics of either a population, or a sample taken from a population. These measurements yield a set of values or scores, and this set represents the findings of the research, or data. Often, it is impractical to completely measure the characteristics of a given population, known as parameters, directly. Thus, psychologists often focus on the characteristics of samples taken from a population. These characteristics are called statistics. The psychologist then uses these sample statistics to make inferences about population parameters.

This GPH book **"Statistics in Psychology (MPC-006)"** deals with various statistical methods that are very crucial in psychological researches and help to assess the meaning of the measurements they make.

The book is written specially in question & answer format to provide students the instant gratification of a correct answer. Solved Practical Problems are also given for practice. In this book, we have tried to solve all possible questions from the exams' point of view. Solutions of previous years question papers have also been included to help students to understand the unique examination structure.

An attempt has been carefully made to present this book more useful and meet the requirement and challenges of the course prescribed by IGNOU University.

We wish you a successful and rewarding career ahead. Feedback in this regard is solicited.

– GPH Panel of Experts

Acknowledgement

Our compliments go to the **GullyBaba Publishing House (P) Ltd.**, and its meticulous team who have been enthusiastically working towards the perfection of the book.

Their teamwork, initiative and research have been very encouraging. Had it not been for their unflagging support, this work wouldn't have been possible. The creative freedom provided by them along with their aim of presenting the best to the reader has been a major source of inspiration in this work. Hope that this book would be successful.

– GPH Panel of Experts

Publisher's Note

The present book MPC-006 is targeted for examination purpose as well as enrichment. With the advent of technology and the Internet, there has been no dearth of information available to all; however, finding the relevant and qualitative information, which is focused, is an uphill task.

We at **GullyBaba Publishing House (P) Ltd.,** have taken this step to provide quality material which can accentuate in-depth knowledge about the subject. GPH books are a pioneer in the effort of providing unique and quality material to its readers. With our books, you are sure to attain success by making use of this powerful study material. Provided book is just a reference book based on the syllabus of particular University/Board. For a profound information, see the textbooks recommended by the University/Board.

Our site **gullybaba.com** is a vital resource for your examination. The publisher wishes to acknowledge the significant contribution of the Team Members and our experts in bringing out this publication and highly thankful to Almighty God, without His blessings, this endeavor wouldn't have been successful.

– Publisher

Topics Covered

Block-1	**Introduction to Statistics**
Unit-1	Parametric and Non-Parametric Statistics
Unit-2	Descriptive and Inferential Statistics
Unit-3	Type I and Type II Errors
Unit-4	Setting Up the Levels of Significance
Block-2	**Correlation and Regression**
Unit-1	Product Moment Coefficient of Correlation
Unit-2	Other Types of Correlations (phi-coefficient)
Unit-3	Partial and Multiple Correlations
Unit-4	Bivariate and Multiple Regression
Block-3	**Normal Distribution**
Unit-1	Characteristics of Normal Distribution
Unit-2	Significance of Mean Differences, Standard Error of the Mean
Unit-3	One Way Analysis of Variance
Unit-4	Two Way Analysis of Variance
Block-4	**Non-Parametric Statistics**
Unit-1	Rationale for Non-parametric Statistics
Unit-2	Mann Whitney 'U' Test for Two Sample Test
Unit-3	Kruskal Wallis Analysis of Variance
Unit-4	Chi-Square and Kendall Rank Correlation

Contents

Chapter-1	Introduction to Statistics	1-49
Chapter-2	Correlation and Regression	51-100
Chapter-3	Normal Distribution	101-154
Chapter-4	Non-Parametric Statistics	155-190

Question Papers

(1) December: 2012 (Solved) 209-211
(2) June: 2013 (Solved) 212-214
(3) December: 2013 (Solved) 215-217
(4) June: 2014 (Solved) 218-221
(5) December: 2014 (Solved) 222-224
(6) June: 2015 (Solved) 225-226
(7) December: 2015 (Solved) 227-228
(8) June: 2016 (Solved) 229-234
(9) December: 2016 235-240
(10) June: 2017 (Solved) 241-247
(11) December: 2017 (Solved) 248-250
(12) June: 2018 253-254
(13) December: 2018 (Solved) 255-256
(14) June: 2019 (Solved) 259-260
(15) December: 2019 261-262
(16) June: 2020 (Solved) 263-265
(17) February: 2021 (Solved) 266-267
(18) June: 2021 (Solved) 268-269
(19) December: 2021 (Solved) 270-277

Introduction to Statistics

An Overview

Statistics can be defined as an applied science, which deals with collection, compilation, analysis and interpretation of data. By using it, one can infer about population characteristics on the basis of the sample observations.

Statistics has its roots in the idea of "the state of things". The word itself comes from the ancient Latin term statisticum (collegium), meaning "a lecture on the state of affairs". Eventually, this evolved into the Italian word Statistik, meaning "Collection of data involving the State". Gradually, the term came to be used to describe the collection of any sort of data. Later on, statistics was defined as the branch of Mathematics, which deals with numerical data. Now, statistics is emerging as an interpretation of data obtained by conducting research. Statistics is used in all those area where data is generated. Since the data contains lots of hidden information, the knowledge of statistical tools helps the researcher to extract information from the data more easily.

Q1. Define the term parametric and non-parametric statistics. Discuss their assumptions.

Or

Discuss non-parametric statistics.

Or

Write various assumptions of parametric and non-parametric statistics.

Or

What are the various assumptions underlying Parametric and non-Parametric Statistics? [Dec-2014, Q.No.-1]

Ans. Parametric Statistics

Parametric statistics is defined to have an assumption of normal distribution for its population under study. It refers to those statistical techniques which have been developed on the assumption that the data are of certain types. In particular, the measure should be an interval scale and the scores should be drawn from a normal distribution (Stratton and Hayes, 1999).

There are certain basic assumptions of parametric statistics. The very first characteristic of parametric statistics is that it moves after confirming its population's property of normal distribution. The normal distribution of a population shows its symmetrical spread over the continuum of -3 to $+3$ SD maintaining a unimodal shape as its mean, median and mode coincide. If the samples are from various populations then it is assumed to have same variance ratio among them. The samples are independent in their selection. The chances of occurrence of any event or item out of the total population are equal and any item can be selected in the sample. This reflects the randomised nature of sample which is also a good tool in avoiding any experimenter bias.

In view of the above assumptions, parametric statistics seems to be more reliable and authentic as compared to the non-parametric statistics. Such statistics is more powerful to establish the statistical significance of effects and difference among variables. It is more appropriate and reliable to use parametric statistics in case of large samples as it promises more accuracy of results. The data to be analysed under parametric statistics are usually from the interval scale.

However, along with many advantages, some disadvantages have also been noted in the parametric statistics. It is bound to follow the rigid assumption of normal distribution, which further narrows the scope of its usage. In case of small samples, normal distribution cannot be attained, and thus, parametric statistics cannot be used. Further, computation in parametric statistics is lengthy and complex because of large samples and numerical calculations. T-test, f-test and r-test are some of the major parametric statistics used for data analysis.

Non-parametric Statistics

Non-parametric statistics are not based on the assumption of normal distribution of population. Therefore, these are also known as distribution-

Introduction to Statistics

free statistics. They are not bound to be used with interval scale data or normally distributed data. The data with non-continuity are to be tackled with such statistics. In the samples, where it is difficult to maintain the assumption of normal distribution, non-parametric statistics are used for analysis. The samples with small number of items are treated with non-parametric statistics because of the absence of normal distribution. These can be used even for nominal data along with the ordinal data. Some of the usual non-parametric statistics include chi-square, Spearman's rank difference method of correlation, Kendall's rank difference method and Mann- Whitney U-test.

Assumptions of Non-parametric Statistics are as follows:

(1) We face many situations, where we cannot meet the assumptions and conditions, and thus, cannot use parametric statistical procedures. In such situation, we are bound to apply non-parametric statistics.

(2) If our sample is in the form of nominal or ordinal scale, and the distribution of sample is not normally distributed, and also the sample size is very small; it is always advisable to make use of the non-parametric tests for comparing samples and to make inferences or test the significance or trustworthiness of the computed statistics. In other words, the use of non-parametric tests is recommended in the following situations:

   (i) Where sample size is quite small. If the size of the sample is as small as N=5 or N=6, the only alternative is to make use of non-parametric tests.

   (ii) When assumption like normality of the distribution of scores in the population are doubtful, we use non-parametric tests.

   (iii) When the measurement of data is available either in the form of ordinal or nominal scales or when the data can be expressed in the form of ranks or in the shape of + signs or – signs and classification like "good-bad", etc. we use non-parametric statistics.

   (iv) The nature of the population from which samples are drawn is not known to be normal.

   (v) The variables are expressed in nominal form.

   (vi) The data are measures, which are ranked or expressed in numerical scores, having the strength of ranks.

Q2. What are the advantages and disadvantages of non-parametric statistics?

Ans. Advantages: Few advantages of using non-parametric statistics are as follows:

- Non-parametric methods can be used to analyse categorical (nominal scaling) data, rank (ordinal scaling) data and interval (ratio scaling) data.

- Non-parametric methods are generally easy to apply and quick to compute when sample size is small.
- Non-parametric methods require few assumptions but are very useful when the scale of measurement is weaker than required for parametric methods. Hence, these methods are widely used and yield a more general broad-based conclusion.
- Non-parametric methods provide an approximate solution to an exact problem whereas parametric methods provide an exact solution to an approximate problem.
- Non-parametric methods provide solution to problems that do not require to make the assumption that a population is distributed normally or any specific shape.

Limitations: Few major limitations of non-parametric statistic are follows:
- Non-parametric methods should not be used when all the assumptions of the parametric methods can be met. However, they are equally powerful when assumptions are met, when assumptions are not met these may be more powerful.
- Non-parametric methods require more manual computational time when sample size gets larger.
- Table values for non-parametric statistics are not as readily available as of parametric methods.
- Non-parametric tests are usually not as widely used and not well known as parametric tests.

Q3. Write a short note on Central Limit Theorem.

Ans. The Central Limit Theorem, first introduced by De Moivre during the early-eighteenth century, happens to be the most important theorem in statistics. According to this theorem, if we select a large number of simple random samples, say, from any population and determine the mean of each sample, the distribution of these samples means will tend to be described by the normal probability distribution with a mean μ and variance σ^2/n. This is true even if the population itself is not normal or in other words, we can say that the sampling distribution of sample means approaches to a normal distribution, irrespective of the distribution of population from where sample is taken and approximation to the normal distribution becomes increasingly close with increase in sample size. Symbolically, the theorem can be explained as follows:

When given n independent random variables, $X_1, X_2, X_3, \ldots X_n$, which have the same distribution (no matter what the distribution), then:

$$X = X_1 + X_2 + X_3 + \ldots X_n$$

is a normal variate. The mean μ and variance σ^2 of X are:

$$\mu = \mu_1 + \mu_2 + \mu_3 + \ldots + \mu_n = n\mu_1$$

$$\sigma^2 = \sigma_1^2 + \sigma_2^2 + \sigma_3^2 + \ldots + \sigma_n^2 = n\sigma_i^2$$

where μ_i and σ_i^2 are the mean and variance of X_i.

Q4. Discuss the procedure of testing the significance of the difference between the means and correlations of the samples.

Ans. The procedure of testing the significance of the difference between the means and correlations of the samples are as follows:

(1) Significance of the Difference between the Means of Two Independent Large Samples

Means are said to be independent or uncorrelated when computed from samples drawn at random from totally different and unrelated groups.

The frequency distribution of large sample means, drawn from the same population, fall into a normal distribution around the population mean (M_{pop}) as their measure of central tendency. It is reasonable to expect that the frequency distribution of the difference between the means computed from the samples drawn from two different populations will also tend to be normal with a mean of zero and standard deviation, which is called the standard error of the difference of means.

The standard error is denoted by σ_{dM} which is estimated from the standard errors of the two sample means, σ_{M_1} and σ_{M_2}. The formula is:

$$\sigma_{dM} = \sqrt{\frac{(\sigma_{M_1})^2}{N_1} + \frac{(\sigma_{M_2})^2}{N_2}}$$

in which

σ_{M_1} = SE of the mean of the first sample

σ_{M_2} = SE of the mean of the second sample

N_1 = Number of cases in first sample

N_2 = Number of cases in second sample

(2) Significance of the Differences between the Means of Two Dependent Samples

Means are said to be dependent or correlated when obtained from the scores of the same test administered to the same sample upon two occasions, or when the same test is administered to equivalent samples in which the members of the group have been matched person for person, by one or more attributes.

$$t = \frac{M_1 - M_2}{\sqrt{\sigma^2 M_1 + \sigma^2 M_2 - 2r_{12} \sigma M_1 \sigma M_2}}$$

in which

M_1 and M_2 = Means of the scores of the initial and final testing.

σM_1 = Standard error of the initial test mean.

σM_2 = Standard error of the final test mean.

r_{12} = Correlation between the scores on initial and final testing.

(3) Significance of the Difference between the Means of Three or More Samples

We compute CR and t-values to determine whether there is any significant difference between the means of two random samples. Suppose we have N(N>2) random samples and we want to determine whether there are any significant differences among their means. For this, we have to compute F-value, i.e. analysis of variance.

Analysis of variance has the following basic assumptions underlying it which should be fulfilled in the use of this technique:

- The population distribution should be normal. This assumption, however, is not especially important.
- Eden and Yates showed that even with a population departing considerably from normality, the effectiveness of the normal distribution still held.
- All the groups of certain criterion or of the combination of more than one criterion should be randomly chosen from the sub-population having the same criterion or having the same combination of more than one criterion. For instance, if we wish to select two groups in a population of MA Psychology Student trainees enrolled with IGNOU, say one of them are males and the other are females, we must choose randomly from the respective sub-populations. The assumption of randomness is the key stone of the analysis of variance technique. There is no substitute for randomisation.
- The sub-groups under investigation should have the same variability. This assumption is tested by applying F_{max} test.

    F_{max} = Largest Variance/Smallest Variance

    In analysis of variance, we have usually three or more groups, i.e. there will be three or more variances.

    Unless the computed value of F_{max} equals or exceeds the appropriate F critical value at .05 level, it is assumed that the variances are homogeneous and the difference is not significant.

Q5. Describe the most frequently used non-parametric tests for drawing statistical inference in case of unrelated or independent samples.

Or

Discuss the various non-parametric tests, which are used in the case of independent sample.

Ans. The most frequently non-parametric tests, which are used in drawing statistical inference in the case of independent or unrelated samples are as follows:

Chi-square test

In situations where the members of a random sample are classified into mutually exclusive categories, we wish to know whether the observed frequencies (i.e. number of subjects in different categories on the basis of our observation) in these categories are consistent with some hypothesis concerning the relative frequencies. This can further be explained with the following example:

Suppose we have taken a very limited opinion in a small sample of 90 students of class X regarding their plan for opting Arts, Science or Commerce at a later stage. The opinion of students and their frequencies are as follows:

Arts	Science	Commerce
35	28	27

As the three streams are equally popular among the students, we now assume that the difference in frequencies of these three exclusive categories is only due to chance. Presently, the chi-square test is the most suitable measure to test the agreement between these observed and expected results. Chi-square is denoted as χ^2 and is defined by the following equation:

$$\chi^2 = \sum \frac{(O-E)^2}{E}$$

where O is the observed or experimentally determined frequency and E is the expected frequency of occurrence based on some hypothesis.

When the square of the difference between observed and expected frequencies is divided by the expected frequency, in each case, the sum of these quotients is chi-square.

The Median Test

The Median test is used for testing whether two independent samples differ in central tendencies. It gives information as to whether it is likely that two independent samples have been drawn from populations with the same median. It is particularly useful whenever the measurements for the two samples are expressed in an ordinal scale.

In using the median test, we first calculate the combined median for all scores in both samples. Then both sets of scores at the combined median are dichotomised and the data are cast in a 2 × 2 table.

Table 1.1: 2 × 2 Table for Use of Median Test

	Sample I	Sample II	Total
No. of scores above combined median	A	B	A + B
No. of scores below combined median	C	D	C + D
Total	A + C	B + D	

Under the null hypotheses, we except about the half of each group's scores to be above the combined median and about half to be below, i.e. we would expect frequencies A and C to be about equal, and frequencies B and D to be about equal. In order to test this null hypothesis, we calculate χ^2 using the following formula:

$$\chi^2 = \frac{N(|AD-BC|-N/2)^2}{(A+B)(C+D)(A+C)(B+D)}$$

The Mann-Whitney U-Test

The Mann-Whitney U-test is more powerful than median test. It is a most useful alternative to the parametric t-test when the parametric assumptions cannot be met and when the measurements are expressed in ordinal scale values.

Suppose n_1 is the number of individuals in one of the two independent groups and n_2 the number of the individuals in the other. To apply the U test, we first combine the observations or scores from both groups, and rank these in order of increasing size. In this ranking, we have to consider the algebraic sign, that is, the lowest ranks are assigned to the largest negative numbers, if any. Then the ranks of each sample group are summed individually and represented as ΣR_1 and ΣR_2.

Next, we calculate two Us using the formulae:

$$U_1 = N_1 N_2 + \frac{N_1(N_1+1)}{2} - \Sigma R_1$$

and $U_2 = N_1 N_2 + \frac{N_2(N_2+1)}{2} - \Sigma R_2$

where,

N_1 = Number of individuals in first group

N_2 = Number of individuals in second group

ΣR_1 = Sum of ranks in first group

ΣR_2 = Sum of ranks in second group

The two Us are also related by the equation:

$U_1 = N_1 N_2 - U_2$

The only one U needs to be calculated, for the other can be easily determined by this equation.

The Z-value of U can be computed by the following formula:

$$Z = \frac{U - \frac{N_1 N_2}{2}}{\sqrt{\frac{(N_1)(N_2)(N_1+N_2+1)}{12}}}$$

It does not matter which U (larger or smaller) is used in the computation of Z. The sign of Z will depend on which U is used, but the numerical value will be identical.

Q6. Discuss the various non-parametric tests, which are used in the case of dependent sample.

Ans. A number of non-parametric tests are used in drawing inference in respect of dependent or related samples. These are:

Introduction to Statistics

(1) Sign Test: The sign test is the simplest type of all the non-parametric tests. Its name comes from the fact that it is based on the direction or the plus or minus signs of observations in a sample and not on their numerical magnitudes. The sign test can be of two types:

(i) **One-sample Sign Test:** In one-sample sign test, we set up the null hypothesis that + and − signs are the values of a random variable having the binominal distribution with $p = \frac{1}{2}$, i.e.

$$H_0 : p = \frac{1}{2} \text{ or that } \mu = \mu_0$$

Procedure: This test involves the following steps:

(a) Find the + and − sign for the given distribution. Put a plus (+) sign for a value greater than the mean value (μ_0), a minus (−) sign for a value smaller than the mean value and a zero (0) for a value equal to the mean value.

(b) Denote the total number of signs (ignoring zeros) by n and the number of less frequent signs by 'S'.

(c) Obtain the critical value (K) of less frequent signs (S) preferably at 5 per cent level of significance by using the following formula:

$$K = \frac{n-1}{2} - 0.98\sqrt{n}$$

(d) Compare the value of 'S' with the critical value (K). If the value of S is greater than the value of K (i.e. S > K) then the null hypothesis is accepted. If $S \leq K$, the null hypothesis is rejected.

Alter: The problem related to one sample test can also be solved by using Binomial Probability Distribution. When the sample size is fairly small (i.e., $n \leq 25$), we find probability of the less frequent signs p(S) by the sum of the probability of S of fewer S using the binominal distribution formula, $^nC_x q^{n-x} p^x$ with $p = \frac{1}{2}$. Then, we compare the above calculated value of probability with the expected value at 5 per cent level of significance, i.e. at $\alpha = 0.05$ for one tailed/two tailed tests. If the calculated probability P(S) is ≤ 0.05, null hypothesis is rejected and if P(S) > 0.05, the null hypothesis is accepted.

(ii) **Paired Sample Sign Test:** The sign test has very important applications in problems involving paired data such as data relating to the collection of an account receivable before and after a new collection policy; responses of mother and daughter towards ideal family size, etc. In such problems, each pair of sample values is replaced with a plus sign, if the first value is greater than the second; a minus sign, if the first value is smaller than the second; or a zero, if the two values are equal. Then we proceed in the same manner as in one-sample test.

When the sample size is fairly large (i.e. n>25), we use the normal approximation to the binomial distribution to carry out the sign test. The value of 'z' can be computed as:

$$Z = \frac{S - np}{\sqrt{np(1-p)}}$$

Then we get the critical value of Z at the desired level of significance.

If the calculated value of Z happens to be less than the critical value, then we accept the null hypothesis. If the case is reverse then we reject the null hypothesis.

(2) Wilcoxon's Signed-Rank Test: This is another non-parametric test, which has been developed by Sir Wilcoxon. This test is based on the ranking of the sample of observations. Like sign test, Wilcoxon's signed-rank test can be of two types:

(i) **Wilcoxon's One-Sample Signed-Rank Test:** In a one sample signed-rank test, we test the null hypothesis that $\mu = \mu_o$ against an appropriate alternative hypothesis at a desired level of significance.

Procedure: This test involves the following steps:

(a) Calculate the difference $d = x - \mu$ with algebraic signs.

(b) Assign ranks (ignoring the signs) to the difference in the increasing order of magnitude (i.e. from low to high) ignoring zero differences. In case of ties (i.e. when two or more values are the same), assign ranks to such pairs by averaging their rank positions.

(c) Put all the ranks against the +ve differences rank column (R^+) and all the ranks against the –ve rank column $(R-)$

(d) Get the total number of ranks, n

(e) If $n \leq 25$, then calculate the value of the test statistic given by $T = \Sigma R^+$ or ΣR^- ranks whichever is less.

(f) Then find the critical value of T from the Wilcoxon's T-table given in the appendix.

(g) If the calculated value of T is less than or equal to its critical value, then reject the null hypothesis. In the reverse case, accept the null hypothesis.

(ii) **Two Sample Signed Rank Test (or Paired-Sample Signed Rank Test):** The Wilcoxon's signed rank test has important applications in problem involving paired data. Such a test is widely used by the research scholars in their study of two related samples or matches pairs of ordinary data, viz. outputs of two similar machines, responses gathered before and after a treatment, etc. where we can find both the direction and magnitude of difference between the matched values. In these problems, we find the difference between each pair of values with algebraic signs. Then we proceed in the same manner as in the case of one sample signed rank test.

When N is larger than 25, the sum of the ranks is approximately normally distributed. The sum of ranks of the smaller of like signed ranks is designated as T.

The value of Z is determined by the formula:

$$Z = \frac{T - \frac{N(N+1)}{4}}{\sqrt{\frac{N(N+1)(2N+1)}{24}}}$$

in which
N = Number of pairs ranked
T = Sum of ranks of the smaller of like signed ranks

Q7. What is descriptive statistics? Discuss its advantages and disadvantages.

Ans. Descriptive statistics is a branch of statistics, which deals with descriptions of obtained data. On the basis of these descriptions, a particular group of population is defined for corresponding characteristics. The descriptive statistics include classification, tabulation, diagrammatic and graphical presentation of data, measures of central tendency and variability. These measures enable the researchers to know about the tendency of data or the scores, which further enhance the ease in description of the phenomena. Such single estimate of the series of data which summarises the distribution are known as parameters of the distribution. These parameters define the distribution completely. Basically descriptive statistics involves two operations:

(1) Organisation of data, and
(2) Summarisation of data.

Advantages: The advantages of descriptive statistics are as follows:
- It is essential for arranging and displaying data.
- It forms the basis of rigorous data analysis.
- It is easier to work with, interpret and discuss than raw data.
- It helps in examining the tendencies, variability and normality of a data set.
- It can be rendered both graphically and numerically.
- It forms the basis for more advanced statistical methods.

Disadvantages: The disadvantages of descriptive statistics are as follows:
- It can be misused, misinterpreted and incomplete.
- It can be of limited use when samples and populations are small.
- It offers little information about causes and effects.
- It can be dangerous if not analysed completely.
- There is a risk of distorting the original data or losing important detail.

Q8. What do you mean by classification of data?

Ans. Classification stands for the entire process of sorting out things 'similar' from amongst a group of things of different characteristics. In other words, a diverse heterogeneous data is classified into separate homogeneous classes according to the identity of characteristics that exist amongst the different individuals or quantities constituting the data. The process of arranging the data in groups and classes according to resemblance and similarities is technically called classification.

According to Corner, "Classification is the process of arranging things (either actually or notionally) in groups or classes according to their resemblances and affinities and gives expression to the unity of attributes that may subsist amongst a diversity of individuals."

Secrist had defined classification as, "It is the process of arranging data into sequences and groups according to their common characteristics or separating them into different related parts."

According to Tuttle A.M., "A classification is a scheme for breaking a category into a set of parts called classes according to some precisely defined differing characteristics possessed by all the elements of the category."

In classification of data, units having common characteristics are placed in a class and in this fashion; the whole data are divided into a number of classes.

A classification is a summary of the frequency of individual scores or ranges of scores for a variable. Once data are collected, it should be arranged in a format from which they would be able to draw some conclusions. Thus, by classifying data, the investigators move a step ahead in regard to making a decision. The classification of statistical data serves the following purposes:

(1) It condenses the raw data into a form suitable for statistical analysis.
(2) It removes complexities and highlights the features of the data.
(3) It facilitates comparisons and drawing inferences from the data. For example, if university students in a particular course are divided according to sex, their results can be compared.
(4) It provides information about the mutual relationships among elements of a data set. For example, based on literacy and criminal tendency of a group of people, it can be established whether literacy has any impact or not on criminal tendency.
(5) It helps in statistical analysis by separating elements of the data set into homogeneous groups, and hence, brings out the points of similarity and dissimilarity.

Q9. What do you mean by frequency distribution? Define various frequency distributions.

Ans. Generally, data are collected in the form of individual observations, and thus, they are known as raw or unorganised data. The statistician works with large amount of data. Before any conclusion can be drawn from such data, it must be condensed and arranged in a usable form. Hence, an effort is made to arrange the data into classes or categories and to determine the number of individuals' belongings to each class, which is called class frequency. This arrangement is known as frequency distribution.

According to Murray R. Spiegel, "A tabular arrangement of data by class, together with the corresponding class frequencies is called a frequency distribution or frequency table."

Types of Frequency Distribution: There are various types of frequency distribution:

(1) Ungrouped Frequency Distribution

Ungrouped frequency distribution is used when the data is of a qualitative nature, or when the variable under consideration is discrete.

(i) Frequency Distribution of a Qualitative Character

First of all, we consider an example:

A botanist obtained a variety of linseed by cross-breeding of two pure varieties. She observed the colour of flowers of plants grown through inbreeding of the new mixed type (called plants of F_2 generation). On the basis of these observations, she prepared the following table.

Table 1.2: Classification of Flowers in F_2 Population of Linseed by Colour

Colour	Number of Flowers (frequency)	Relative Frequency
Blue	169	0.538
Lilac	61	0.194
White	62	0.197
Pink	22	0.070
Total	314	0.999

- **Frequency:** Frequency indicates how frequently the corresponding form of the character under study occurs in the collected data. The figures in the second column of Table 1.2 are called frequencies of the four classes (or the four colours).
- **Total Frequency:** The sum of frequencies is called total frequency. For example, in Table 1.2, 314 is the total frequency.
- **Frequency Table:** The first two columns of Table 1.2 constitute a frequency table.
- **Relative Frequencies:** The ratio of frequency of the class and the total frequency is called relative frequency of the class. That is

$$\text{Relative frequency of a class} = \frac{\text{Frequency of the class}}{\text{Total frequency}}$$

$$\text{Relative frequency of a class} = \frac{\text{Frequency of the class}}{\text{Total frequency}}$$

For example, from Table 1.2, frequency distribution can also be written in terms of the proportions of blue, lilac, white and pink flowers in the group.

- **Dichotomy:** The simplest type of classification of a group of individuals by a qualitative character is called dichotomy.

(ii) **Ungrouped Frequency Distribution of a Discrete Variable**

Consider the data collected by a social scientist on household size for households in an urban locality, given in Table 1.3.

Table 1.3: Data on Household size for 80 Households in an Urban Locality

8	4	4	3	7	8	5	6
3	2	4	9	6	1	6	7
5	3	5	4	5	7	3	2
5	2	4	4	5	4	5	4
3	4	5	5	6	5	4	1
4	4	2	4	5	2	3	3
4	3	5	5	6	6	7	5
5	3	7	2	7	6	2	6
8	1	6	5	6	6	8	7
7	9	5	4	5	5	6	3

Introduction to Statistics

As in the case of a qualitative character, it would be necessary to count the number of times 1 appears, the number of times 2 appears and so on. We can count more easily if we follow a tallying system.

Thus, we take nine classes defined by the nine distinct values 1, 2,...., 9, noting that 9 was the largest household size recorded in the data. The second column in table 1.4 shows the tallies against each of these values. After counting the tallies, we write the frequencies in the third column. In the fourth column, we write the relative frequencies.

Table 1.4: Frequency Table for size of 80 Households

Household size	Tallies	Frequency	Relative frequency
1	|||	3	0.0375
2	⊢⊢⊢⊢ ||	7	0.0875
3	⊢⊢⊢⊢ ⊢⊢⊢⊢		11	0.1375
4	⊢⊢⊢⊢ ⊢⊢⊢⊢ ||||	14	0.1750
5	⊢⊢⊢⊢ ⊢⊢⊢⊢ ⊢⊢⊢⊢ ||||	19	0.2375
6	⊢⊢⊢⊢ ⊢⊢⊢⊢ ||	12	0.1500
7	⊢⊢⊢⊢ |||	8	0.1000
8	||||	4	0.0500
9	||	2	0.0250
Total		80	1.0000

Cumulative Frequencies: From Table 1.4, we can see that the number of households of size k or less is 3 for k=1, 3+7=10 for k=2, 10+11=21 for k=3, and so on. We obtained these figures by taking cumulative totals of the frequencies in Table 1.4, starting from the lowest observed value of the variable and going successively to the higher values. These are called cumulative frequencies of the less than type. Similarly, to get the number of households having size k or more, we take the cumulative total of the frequencies in Table 1.4, starting from the highest observed value of the variable and moving successively to the lower values. The figures obtained in this manner are called cumulative frequencies of the more than type. Cumulative frequencies of the more than type provide one mode of representation of the frequency distribution of a variable; those of the less than type provide another.

Table 1.5: Cumulative frequency table of "less than" type for size of 80 household

Household Size	Cumulative Frequencies
≤ 1	3
≤ 2	10
≤ 3	21
≤ 4	35
≤ 5	54
≤ 6	66
≤ 7	74
≤ 8	78
≤ 9	80

Table 1.6: Cumulative frequency table of "more than" type for size of 80 households

Household Size	Cumulative Frequencies
≥ 1	80
≥ 2	77
≥ 3	70
≥ 4	59
≥ 5	45
≥ 6	26
≥ 7	14
≥ 8	6
≥ 9	2
any value greater than 9	0

(2) Grouped Frequency Distributions

Grouped frequency distributions are just like simple frequency distributions except that they have groups (or sets) of scores in the left column instead of single scores. The categories in the left column contain groups or intervals of scores. When creating a grouped frequency distribution, scores in the raw data are tallied into score intervals rather than into single score categories.

Consider the data collected by a botanist.

Table 1.7: Petiole Length (in cm) of 198 Leaves of a four-year old Pipal Tree

4.5	5.4	5.3	6.3	5.7	5.5	4.1	2.9	2.7	6.0	5.9	1.8	3.7	4.1	5.6
2.6	3.0	6.0	7.8	4.5	5.7	4.5	8.0	5.5	7.5	3.1	3.1	5.2	6.8	9.2
5.5	4.5	5.5	7.0	4.5	4.0	5.9	3.8	6.0	5.2	5.6	7.0	6.3	5.1	6.0
6.3	4.5	5.0	5.3	5.6	6.3	3.4	5.1	6.7	6.2	7.2	6.2	5.0	6.1	6.3
4.7	4.1	6.1	5.6	5.5	4.4	6.0	5.0	3.4	5.0	2.5	5.7	5.2	6.1	6.5
5.5	5.5	4.5	5.5	7.7	7.0	7.3	6.5	6.7	6.1	6.7	4.7	8.5	4.7	6.7
6.5	8.2	6.9	3.9	7.2	4.2	6.1	1.6	7.2	6.5	3.6	5.9	5.3	6.6	5.0
6.2	1.9	2.2	5.2	6.6	4.9	5.9	5.4	6.5	6.6	6.8	4.1	4.7	5.7	4.1
5.7	5.0	5.7	5.2	2.8	4.3	4.6	4.9	6.0	5.9	4.5	3.7	5.7	3.8	5.6
5.2	3.9	6.5	5.0	5.2	6.0	2.3	5.2	3.2	5.5	7.1	7.0	3.2	7.2	5.9
5.3	1.6	6.9	6.1	6.3	6.7	2.4	6.3	4.8	4.6	6.7	1.5	6.8	5.9	5.3
7.0	4.3	6.7	5.4	4.7	5.1	5.2	7.4	4.5	6.4	5.0	2.0	5.7	4.6	4.9
5.2	6.0	4.5	6.1	3.5	5.9	5.0	6.8	5.0	1.0	5.5	4.9	5.9	5.2	6.1
0.8	5.3	5.9												

Here, the values are recorded correct to one decimal place. The lowest observation in the set is 0.8 and the highest is 9.2. If we take our classes as 0.6-1.3, 1.4-2.1, 2.2-2.9,....., 8.6-9.3, then the total number of classes will be 11. To get the frequencies for these classes, we go in for the tallying system.

Introduction to Statistics

Table 1.8: Frequency Table for the data of Table 1.7 on Petiole Length of Leaves of Pipal Tree

Petiole length (cm)	Tallies	Frequency
0.6 – 1.3	||	2
1.4 – 2.1	⊪		6
2.2 – 2.9	⊪ |||	8
3.0 – 3.7	⊪ ⊪	10
3.8 – 4.5	⊪ ⊪ ⊪ ⊪ ||||	24
4.6 – 5.3	⊪ ⊪ ⊪ ⊪ ⊪ ⊪ ⊪ ⊪ |||	43
5.4 – 6.1	⊪ ⊪ ⊪ ⊪ ⊪ ⊪ ⊪ ⊪ ⊪ ⊪ ||	52
6.2 – 6.9	⊪ ⊪ ⊪ ⊪ ⊪ ⊪ |||	33
7.0 – 7.7	⊪ ⊪ ⊪	15
7.8 – 8.5	||||	4
8.6 – 9.3			1
Total		**198**

But here the classes need to be redefined. The reason is that the value recorded as, say, 4.6 actually stands for some value between 4.55 and 4.65. Similarly, the values 5.7 stands for some value between 5.65 and 5.75. Thus, the class taken as 4.6–5.7 in Table 1.8, in fact, begins at 4.55 and ends at 5.75. The other classes have to be viewed in the same way.

Class Boundaries: The two end points of a class interval are called class boundaries (the lower and the upper).

Class Mark: The mid-point of the lower and upper class is called class mark.

Class Width: The difference between the upper class boundary and the lower class boundary is called class width or class interval.

Class-limits: The boundary values (end values) of class are called the class limits. The smaller of the two limits is known as the lower limit and the greater value is known as the upper limit. In the class 20–40, 20 is the lower limit and 40 is the upper limit.

Frequency Density: Frequency density of a class is the frequency per unit of width in the class, i.e.

$$\text{Frequency Density of a Class} = \frac{\text{Class Frequency}}{\text{Class Width}}$$

Q10. Discuss the three methods of describing the class limits for different classes. Also, explain the steps in the construction of a frequency distribution.

Ans. The three methods for describing the class limits for different classes are as follows:

(1) Exclusive Method

In exclusive method of class formation, classes are so formed that the upper limit of one class is the lower of the next class, and therefore, this method of classification ensures continuity between two successive classes which is essential for most of statistical calculations. Exclusive classes so obtained are given in Table 1.9.

Table 1.9: Different Types of Classes

Exclusive classes	Inclusive classes	True or Actual class limits or class boundaries
20-30	20-29	19.5-29.5
30-40	30-39	29.5-39.5
40-50	40-49	39.5-49.5
50-60	50-59	49.5-59.5
60-70	60-69	59.5-69.5
70-80	70-79	69.5-79.5
80-90	80-89	79.5-89.5

However, it is presumed that the score or observation equal to the upper limit of the class is exclusive, e.g. a score of 30 will be included in the class 30-40 and not in 20-30.

(2) Inclusive Method

Unlike exclusive classes, inclusive classes include scores or observations which are equal to upper limit of the class. In the formation of such classes, we start with the lower limit 20 of the scores for the first class and then the lowest class is formed as (20-29) so as to include 10 marks (10 being the class interval). These 10 marks are 20, 21, 22, ..., 28, 29. The remaining six classes are obtained by adding the class interval to each class limit of previous class until we get the highest class as (80-89). Inclusive classes so obtained are also given in Table 1.9.

From the preceding discussion, it should be clear that exclusive method should be used when data are of continuous nature or have been measured in fraction or unit. Inclusive way of forming classes may be preferred when measurements on the variable are given in whole numbers.

(3) True or Actual Class or Limits or Class Boundaries

In inclusive method of class formation, it was observed that the upper class limit is not equal to lower class limit of next class and so there is no continuity between classes. However, for most of statistical calculations, it is desirable that classes should be continuous. For overcoming this difficulty, we assume that an observation does not just represent a point on a continuous scale, but an interval of unit length of which the given observations is the middle point. For example, a score of 20 in an examination represent the interval 19.5 to 20.5 on a continuum. Similarly, a score of 29, then, is representable by the interval 28.5 to 29.5. Thus, the mathematical meaning of an observation is an interval, which extends from 0.5 unit below to 0.5 unit above the face value of an observation on a continuum. These class limits of an observation are termed as true or actual class limits. Thus, the true class limits for the class 20-29 becomes 19.5-29.5. The true limits for other inclusive classes are also shown in table 1.9.

After forming the classes, finally we count the number of observation falling in each class and record the appropriate number in frequency (denoted by f) column. The number of observations failing in each class is termed as class frequency. To facilitate counting these frequencies, we also prepare a tally chart with 'tally bar' column as shown in table 1.10.

Table 1.10: Grouped a frequency table (Exclusive Method)

Marks classes	'Tally bar'	Frequency (f)
20-30	||||	4
30-40	卌 |	6
40-50	卌 |||	8
50-60	卌 卌 ||	12
60-70	卌 ||||	9
70-80	卌 ||	7
80-90	||||	4
Total		N= 50

In table 1.10, four tally bars are marked for four marks, i.e. 21, 25, 25 and 29, which lie within the class (20-30), similarly six bars are marked for six scores lying in the class (30-40) and so on. In this way, the data are arranged in the form of a frequency distribution showing classes and the corresponding class frequencies. The total of all the frequencies is denoted by N. Similarly, the data can be grouped by using inclusive and true class limits. Such a frequency table is given in Table 1.11.

Table 1.11: Grouped a frequency table (Inclusive Method)

Marks classes	True class limits	Class Mid Points	Frequency (f)
20-29	19.5-29.5	24.5	4
30-39	29.5-39.5	34.5	6
40-49	39.5-49.5	44.5	8
50-59	49.5-59.5	54.5	12
60-69	59.5-69.5	64.5	9
70-79	69.5-79.5	74.5	7
80-89	79.5-89.5	84.5	4
Total			N= 50

In the process of forming a frequency distribution, we observe that individual observation lose their identity when grouped into classes. We need, therefore, a point to make some assumption about the location of all the observations included in a class. On the assumption that grouped observations are more or less uniformly distributed between class limits, a point mid-way between class limits can be chosen as representative of all the observation in that class. This point is called the mid-point of the class and can be obtained by averaging the lower and upper class limits as follows:

$$\text{Mid - point of the class} = \frac{\text{Lower class limit} + \text{Upper class limit}}{2}$$

Thus, the mid-point of the class 20-29 will be $\frac{20+29}{2} = 24.5$. The mid-points of the remaining classes are shown in Table 1.11.

Now, we are in a position to list the steps in grouping a large set of data into a frequency distribution.

Steps in the Construction of a Frequency Distribution
(1) Find the smallest and the largest observation in the raw data and find the range R.
(2) Decide on the number of classes.
(3) Divide range by the number of classes to estimate approximate size of the interval.
(4) Find the lower class limit of the lowest class and add to it the class interval to get the upper class limit.
(5) Obtain class-limits for the remaining classes by adding the class interval to the limits of the previous class.
(6) Count number of frequencies in each class and check against the total number of observations.

Q11. Discuss the concept of tabulation.
Or
List the various parts of a table and show them in a sample table.

Ans. Tabulation is the process of summarising classified or grouped data in the form of a table so that it is easily understood and an investigator is quickly able to locate the desired information. A table is a systematic arrangement of classified data in columns and rows. Thus, a statistical table makes it possible for the investigator to present a huge mass of data in a detailed and orderly form. It facilitates comparison and often reveals certain patterns in data which are otherwise not obvious. Classification and tabulation as a matter of fact, are not two distinct processes. Actually, they go together. Before tabulation, data are classified and then displaced under different columns and rows of a table. Example of data in tabular form is as follows:

Table 1.12

Monthly Income ( )	Tally Sheet	No. of Families (Frequency)
500-550	𝖭𝖭	5
550-600	𝖭𝖭 I	6
600-650	𝖭𝖭 𝖭𝖭	10
650-700	𝖭𝖭 𝖭𝖭 II	12
700-750	𝖭𝖭 IIII	9
750-800	𝖭𝖭	5
800-850	III	3
Total		50

In general, a statistical table consists of the following eight parts which are as follows:

(1) **Table Number:** Each table must be given a number. Table number helps in distinguishing one table from other tables. Usually tables are numbered according to the order of their appearance in a chapter. For example, the first table in the first chapter of a book should be given number 1.1 and second table of the same chapter be given 1.2. Table number is always mentioned in the centre on the top.

(2) **Title of the Table:** Title of the table gives the indication of the type of information contained in the body of the table. It is said that the title to the table is the same as heading to an essay. Next to the table number, we mention the title of the table. Its purpose is to answer the questions like:
- What is in the table?
- Where is it in the table?
- When did a particular information occur?
- How has a particular information been arranged?

Do's and Don'ts of the Title

Don't opt for long sentences. Title should be brief and to the point. Present the title in bold letters and/or in capital letters. Expressions used should not convey more than one meaning. Avoid the expressions like 'Table Presents.......' or 'A Detailed Comparison of Data Relating to........', etc. It should be like a telegraphic message.

(3) **Head Note:** Head note, also called prefatory note, is written just below the title. It shows contents and unit of measurement like (rupees crore) or (lakh tones) or (thousand bales). It should be written in brackets and should appear on the top of the right side just below the title. However, every table does not need a head note, like number of students in each class.

(4) **Stubs:** Stubs are used to designate rows. They appear on the left hand column of the table. Stubs consist of two parts:
- Stub head describes the nature of stub entry.
- Stub entry is the description of the row entries.

(5) **Caption:** Captions, also called box heads, designate the data presented in the columns of the table. It may contain more than one column heads, and each column head may be sub-divided in more than one sub-head. For example, we can divide the students of a college into hostlers and non-hostlers and then again into males and females. This will help us to know the number of male hostlers in, say, first year, second year and third year.

(6) **Body:** This is the most important part of a table. It contains a number of cells. Cells are formed due to the intersection of rows and columns. Data are entered in these cells.

(7) Footnote: A footnote is given at the bottom of a table. It helps in clarifying the point which is not clear in the table. A footnote may be keyed to the title or to any column or to any row heading. It is identified by symbols such as *, +, @, £, etc.

(8) Source Note: This may be the last part of a table, yet it is important. It speaks about the authenticity of the data quoted. It also offers opportunity to the reader to check the data if (s) he so desires and get more of it.

Table No.
(——————— TITLE ———————)
(in Crore of Rupees)

Stub Head	——————— Caption ———————			
	Column Head I		Column Head II	
	Sub-head	Sub-head	Sub-head	Sub-head
Stub Entries	MAIN	BODY OF	THE	TABLE
Total				

Footnote(s) :
Source   :

Fig. 1.1: Sample Table

Q12. Explain the various methods of graphical presentation of data.
Or
State the various forms of graphical presentation of Data.
[Dec-2014, Q.No.-4]

Ans. Besides formal tables, statistical data can also be presented in the form of various types of graphs. Graphs are a useful way of conveying information very quick and in brief. With the same ease and efficiency, they help in comparing data over time and space. They are visual aids and have a powerful impact on the people.

It is often said, "A picture is worth a thousand words." They attract a reader's attention to what they are supposed to convey about the data.

The graphical methods of presentation for the table 1.12 are as follows:

(1) Histogram, Frequency Polygon and Frequency Curve
Histogram is a very common type of graph for displaying classified data. It is a set of rectangle erected vertically. It has the following features:
  (i) It is a rectangular diagram;
  (ii) Since the rectangles are drawn with specified width and height, histogram is a two dimensional diagram. The width of a rectangle equals the class interval and height

$$= \frac{\text{Class frequency} \times \text{Width of the shortest class interval in the data}}{\text{Width of the class interval}}$$

  (iii) The area of each rectangle is proportional to frequency of the respective class.

Construction of Histogram

Step 1: On a graph paper, draw two perpendicular lines and call them as horizontal and vertical axis.

Step 2: Along the horizontal axis, we take classes (marks) 500-550, 550-600, ... (Here each is of equal width 50).

Step 3: Choose a suitable scale on the vertical axis to represent the frequencies (monthly income) of classes.

Step 4: Draw the histogram.

The histogram is shown in Fig. 1.2.

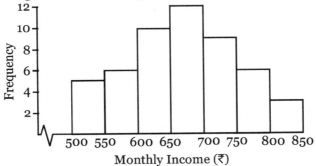

Fig. 1.2: Histogram

Advantages of Histogram

- The width of various rectangles shows the nature of classes in the distribution, i.e., whether of equal width or not.
- Area of a rectangle shows the proportion of the class frequency in the total.

Frequency Polygon

Frequency polygon has been derived from the word "polygon" which means many sides. In statistics, it means a graph of a frequency distribution. A frequency polygon is obtained from a histogram by joining the mid-points of the top of various rectangles with the help of straight lines, as shown in Fig. 1.3. In order that total area under the polygon remains equal to the area under histogram, two arbitrary classes, each with zero frequency, are added on both ends, as shown below:

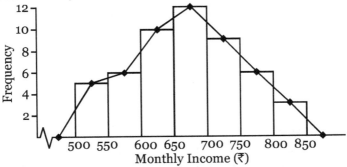

Fig. 1.3: Frequency Polygon

Frequency Curve

If the points, obtained in the case of frequency polygon are joined with the help of a smooth curve, we get a frequency curve as shown in Fig. 1.4.

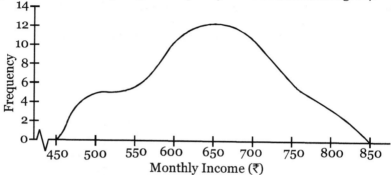

Fig. 1.4: Frequency Curve

(2) Cumulative Frequency Curve

Cumulative frequency curve, also known as ogive, is the graphical representation of cumulative frequency distribution. An ogive or cumulative frequency curve is the curve, which is constructed by plotting the cumulative frequencies in the form of a smooth curve. From such curves, we come to know about the frequencies corresponding to certain lower limits or upper limits in the distribution of data. For example, such curves would indicate how many students in class secured more than 40 marks or how many students secured less than 35 marks in an examination. There are two methods of constructing an ogive, which are as follows:

Less than Method

In this method, we start with the upper limits of the classes and go on adding the frequencies. When these frequencies are plotted, we get a rising curve. The resultant curve is called 'Less than' ogive.

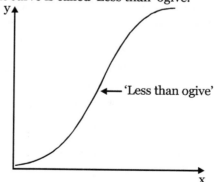

Fig. 1.5: Less than ogive

More than Method

In this method, we start with the lower limits of the classes and add frequencies from the bottom. When these frequencies are plotted, we get a declining curve. The resultant curve is called a 'More than' ogive.

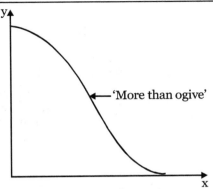

Fig. 1.6: More than ogive

Q13. What is diagram? Describe the various types of diagrams.

Ans. Diagram is an ideal method of presenting statistical data in visual form. By diagram we mean the pictorial representation of the quantitative information with a view to make them easily and readily understandable. There are various forms of diagrams which are as follows:

(1) Bar Diagrams

(i) **Simple Bar Diagram:** Like line diagrams, these figures are also used where only single dimension. Procedure is almost the same, only one thickness of lines is measured. These can also be drawn either vertically or horizontally. Breadth of these lines or bars should be equal. Similarly, distance between these bars should be equal. The breadth and distance between them should be taken according to space available on the paper.

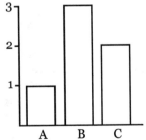

Fig. 1.7: Simple Bar Diagram

(ii) **Multiple Bar Diagram:** The diagram is used, when we have to make comparison between more than two variables. The number of variables may be 2, 3, 4 or more. In case of 2 variables, pair of bars is drawn. Similarly, in case of 3 variables, we draw triple bars. The bars are drawn on the same proportionate basis as in case of simple bars. The same shade is given to the same item. Distance between pairs is kept constant.

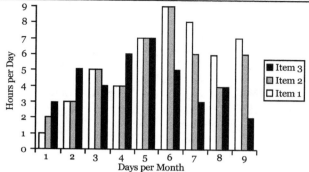

Fig. 1.8: Multiple Bar Diagram

(iii) **Sub-divided Bar Diagram:** The data which is presented by multiple bar diagram can be presented by this diagram. In this case, we add different variables for a period and draw it on a single bar as shown in the following examples. The components must be kept in same order in each bar. This diagram is more efficient if number of components is less, i.e. 3 to 5.

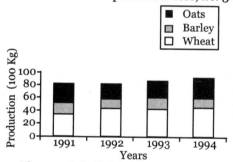

Fig. 1.9: Sub-divided Bar Diagram

(iv) **Percentage Bar Diagram:** Like sub-divide bar diagram, in this case, also data of one particular period or variable is put on single bar, but in terms of percentages. Components are kept in the same order in each bar for easy comparison.

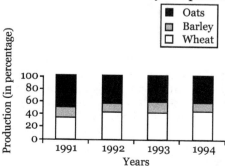

Fig. 1.10: Percentage Bar Diagram

(2) Pie Diagram

The pie diagram is a circle. Within each circle, there is a section that represents a percentage of a whole number. These sections are displayed like sections of a pie, which is where the graph's name originates. The pie graph can have as many pieces as necessary to represent the data. In constructing a pie diagram, the first step is to convert the various values of components of the variable into percentages and then the percentages transposed into corresponding degrees. The total percentage of the various components, i.e. 100 is taken as 360° (degrees around the centre of a circle) and the degree of various components are calculated in proportion to the percentage values of different components. It is expressed as:

$$\frac{360°}{100} \times \text{Component's Percentage}$$

It should be noted that in case the data comprises of more than one variable, to show the two-dimensional effect for making comparison among the variables, we have to obtain the square root of the total of each variable. These square roots would represent the radius of the circles and then they will be subdivided. A pie diagram helps us in emphasising the area and in ascertaining the relationship between the various components as well as among the variables. However, compared to a bar diagram, a pie diagram is less effective for accurate interpretation when the components are in large numbers.

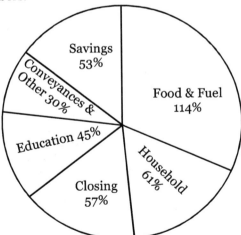

Fig. 1.11: A Pie diagram showing the expenditure on different items of a family

Q14. Explain the various measures of central tendency.

Or

Describe the measures of central tendency with hypothetical data. [June-2015, Q.No.-5]

Ans. Measures of central tendency are measures of the location of middle or center of a distribution. The definition of "middle" or "center" is

purposely left somewhat vague so that the term "central tendency" can refer to a wide variety of measures. Measures of central tendency are the best way to reduce a set of data and still retain part of the information. In other words, it is a way to summarise the set with a single value. An ideal measure of central tendency should have the following properties:
- simple to compute and easy to interpret;
- based on all observations;
- should not be influenced much by a few observations;
- should be capable of further algebraic treatment; and
- should be capable of being defined unambiguously.

Main measures of central tendency are:

(1) Mean

The arithmetic mean of a group of numbers is found by dividing their sum by the number of members in the group, e.g. the sum of the seven numbers 4, 5, 6, 9, 13, 14 and 19 is 70 so their mean is 70 divided by 7 or 10. Less often used is the geometric mean (for two quantities, the square root of their product; for n quantities, the nth root of their product).

(2) Median

In probability theory and statistics, a median is described as the numeric value separating the higher half of a sample, a population or a probability distribution, from the lower half. The median of a finite list of numbers can be found by arranging all the observations from the lowest value to the highest value and picking the middle one. If there is an even number of observations, then there is no single middle value; the median is then defined to be the mean of the two middle values.

(3) Mode

In statistics, the mode is the value that occurs the most frequently in a data set or a probability distribution. In some fields, notably education, sample data are often called scores, and the sample mode is known as the modal score. Like the statistical mean and the median, the mode is a way of capturing important information about a random variable or a population in a single quantity. The mode is, in general, different from the mean and median, and may be very different for strongly skewed distributions. The mode is not necessarily unique, since the same maximum frequency may be attained at different values. The most ambiguous case occurs in uniform distributions, wherein all values are equally likely. Thus,

$$\text{Mode} = L + \frac{f_1 - f_0}{2f_1 - f_0 - f_2} \times i$$

where,
- L = Lower limit of class
- f_1 = Frequency of model class
- f_0 = Frequency of preceding class
- f_2 = Frequency of succeeding class
- i = Class interval

For example,
Calculate mean, median and mode for the following data:

Classes	Frequency
50 - 60	8
60 - 70	10
70 - 80	16
80 - 90	14
90 - 100	10
100 - 110	5
110 - 120	2

Classes	Frequency (f)	Cummulative Frequency (CF)	x	fx
50 - 60	8	8	55	440
60 - 70	10	18	65	650
70 - 80	16	34	75	1200
80 - 90	14	48	85	1190
90 - 100	10	58	95	950
100 - 110	5	63	105	525
110 - 120	2	65	115	230
Total	65	–		$\Sigma fx = 5185$

For Mean:

$$\overline{X} = \frac{\Sigma fx}{N}$$

$$= \frac{5185}{65} = 79.76$$

For Median $= \left(\frac{N+1}{2}\right)^{th}$ observation $= \left(\frac{65+1}{2}\right)^{th}$ observation

$= 33^{th}$ observation

Now, 33th item lies in the 70 - 80 class.

$$\text{Median} = L + \frac{\frac{N+1}{2} - CF}{F} \times i$$

$$= 70 + \frac{33 - 18}{16} \times (80 - 70)$$

$$= 70 + \frac{15}{16} \times 10$$

$$= 70 + 9.375$$

$$= 79.375$$

For Mode:

Here, the greatest frequency 16 lies in class 70-80. Hence, this is the modal class and 70 is the lower limit of the modal class. Thus,
l = 70, f = 16, f_0 = 10, f_1 = 14, i = 10

$$\text{Mode} = L + \frac{f_1 - f_0}{2f_1 - f_0 - f_1} \times 10$$

$$= 70 + \frac{16 - 10}{32 - 10 - 14} \times 10$$

$$= 70 + \frac{6}{8} \times 10$$

$$= 77.5$$

Q15. What is dispersion? What are the common measures of dispersion?

Ans. The term dispersion is generally used in two senses: (a) firstly, dispersion refers to the variations of the items among themselves. If the value of all the items of the series is the same, there will be no variation among the various items and dispersion will be zero. On the other hand, the greater the variation among the different items in a series, the more will be the dispersion. (b) Secondly, dispersion refers to the variation of the items around an average. If the difference between the value of items and average is large, the dispersion will be high and on the other hand, if the difference between the value of the items and average is small, the dispersion will be low. Thus, dispersion is defined as scatterness or spreadness of the individual items in a given series.

Measures of Dispersion: A numerical measure that can be used to throw some light on the scatter or the homogeneity of data is called a measure of dispersion. It is of two types:

Absolute Measure: A measure variation or dispersion expressed in terms of original units is referred to absolute measure. This method is executed through the following methods:
    (a)   Range (R)
    (b)   Average of Mean Deviation (M.D.)
    (c)   Quartile Deviation or Semi-Inter-quartile Range (Q.D.)
    (d)   Standard Deviation (S.D.)

Relative Measure: A measure of variation or dispersion expressed in terms of a ratio or percentage is referred to a relative measure of variation or dispersion. This method is executed through the following methods:
    (a)   Coefficient of Range
    (b)   Coefficient of Quartile Deviation
    (c)   Coefficient of Mean or Average Deviation
    (d)   Coefficient of Standard Deviation

Measures of dispersion may be either absolute or relative. Measures of absolute variation are expressed in terms of the original data. In case the two sets of data are expressed in different units of measurement, then the absolute measures of variation are not comparable. In such cases, measures of relative variation should be used. The other type of comparison for which measures of

Introduction to Statistics

relative variation are used involves the comparison between two sets of data having the same unit of measurement but with different means. We shall consider in turn each of the four measures of variation.

Range

The range is defined as the difference between the highest (numerically largest) value and the lowest (numerically smallest) value in a set of data. Among the various measures of dispersion, the range is the simplest one. This measure can be applied where a researcher requires a quick result. Range is easy to calculate and simple to understand and this is its merit. It can be safely used when variations are not much, but it may give a misleading result if there are one or two abnormal items. Also, the demerits of the range are that it has no further algebraic properties and cannot be applied for open end distribution.

In symbols, this may be indicated as:

$R = H - L$,

Where,

R = Range; H = Highest Value; L = Lowest Value

For grouped data, the range may be approximated as the difference between the upper limit of the largest class and the lower limit of the smallest class.

The relative measure corresponding to range, called the coefficient of range, and is obtained by applying the following formula:

$$\text{Coefficient of Range} = \frac{H-L}{H+L}$$

Mean Deviation

The mean deviation is the arithmetic mean of absolute difference between the items in a distribution and the average of that distribution. Theoretically, mean deviation can be computed from the mean or the median or the mode. However, in actual practice, the mean is frequently used in computing the mean deviation. Under this method, algebraic signs (+, −) are ignored while taking the deviations from average.

For un-grouped data, the formula is:

$$\text{M.D. from mean} = \frac{\sum |X - \bar{X}|}{N} \quad \text{or M.D. from median} = \frac{\sum |X - \text{Med.}|}{N}$$

For grouped data, the formula is:

$$\text{M.D. from mean} = \frac{\sum f|X - \bar{X}|}{N} \quad \text{or M.D. from median} = \frac{\sum f|X - \text{Med.}|}{N}$$

Where, the two bars indicated that the sign of the difference within the two bars is taken as positive.

The formula for finding the co-efficient of mean deviation for un-grouped and grouped data, is:

$$\text{Coefficient of M.D.} = \frac{M.D}{\bar{X} \text{ or Med.}}$$

Quartile Deviation

Quartile Deviation is another measure of variation, also termed as semi-inter quartile range. Quartiles are the factors which divide the distribution into four equal parts, i.e. Q_1 (first quartile) gives the value of the 4th item and Q_3 (third quartile) gives the value of $3/4^{th}$ item. The difference between the Q_3 and Q_1 is termed as inter quartile range, when it is divided by two is termed as quartile deviation. It includes the middle 50 per cent of the distribution. It can be useful because it is not influenced by extremely high or extremely low scores. Quartile deviation is an ordinal statistic and is most often used in conjunction with the median. In case of symmetrical distribution, Q_1 and Q_3 are equidistant from the median. In asymmetrical distribution, Q_1 and Q_3 are not equidistant from median. Symbolically, the absolute measure of quartile deviation may be presented as:

$$Q.D. = \frac{Q_3 - Q_1}{2}$$

The relative measure of Q.D., called coefficient of quartile deviation, is calculated as:

$$\text{Coefficient of Q.D.} = \frac{Q_3 - Q_1}{Q_3 + Q_1}$$

Standard Deviation

It is the most familiar, important and widely used measure of variation. It is a significant measure for making comparison of variability between two or more sets of data in terms of their distance from the mean. Standard deviation may be defined as the square root of the arithmetic mean of the squares of deviations from arithmetic mean of given distribution. This measure is also known as root mean square deviation. If the values in a given data are dispersed more widely from the mean, then the standard deviation becomes greater. It is usually denoted by σ. The square of the standard deviation (σ^2) is called variance.

Standard deviation is calculated by using the following formula:
For ungrouped data:

$$\sigma = \sqrt{\frac{\sum(X-\overline{X})^2}{N}}$$

where,

σ = Standard deviation;
X = Observations;
$\overline{X}$ = Arithmetic mean;
$\sum(X-\overline{X})^2$ = the sum of the squares of deviations; and
N = Number of observations.

Introduction to Statistics

For grouped data:

$$\sigma = \sqrt{\frac{\sum f(X - \overline{X})^2}{N}}$$

where,

N is the sum of frequencies.

If the collected data are very large, then considering the assumed mean is more convenient to compute standard deviation. In such case, the formula is slightly modified as:

$$\sigma = \sqrt{\frac{\sum fdx^2}{N} - \left(\frac{\sum fdx}{N}\right)^2} \times c$$

where, c = common factor, $dx = \dfrac{m - A}{c}$

The relative measure of standard deviation is the coefficient of variation, denoted by C.V.

$$\text{C.V.} = \frac{\sigma}{\overline{X}} \times 100$$

Q16. Write short notes on the following:
(i) Skewness   [Dec-2014, Q.No.-10(b)]

Ans. The term 'Skewness' means lack of symmetry, i.e. if the distribution of data is not symmetrical, it is called a skewed distribution.

Any measure of skewness indicates the difference between the manner in which item are distributed in a particular distribution compared with a symmetrical (or normal) distribution. If skewness is positive, the frequencies in the distribution are spread out over a greater range of value on the high-value end of the curve (the right-hand side) than they are on the low-value end. If the curve is normal, the spread will be the same on both sides of the center point and the mean, median and mode will have the same value.

A simple method of finding the direction of skewness is to consider the tails of a frequency polygon. The concept of skewness will be clear from the following three figures showing symmetrical, positively skewed and negatively skewed distributions.

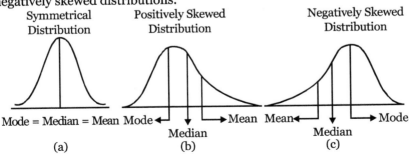

Fig. 1.12: Forms of Skewness

It is clear from figure (a) that the data are symmetrical when the spread of the frequencies is the same on both sides of the middle point of the frequency polygon. In this case, the values of mean, median and mode coincide, i.e. Mean = Median = Mode.

When the distribution is not symmetrical, it is said to be a skewed distribution. Such a distribution could be either positively skewed or negatively skewed. In figure (b), when there is a longer tail towards the right hand side of the center of distribution, the skewness is said to be "Positively Skewed". In such a situation, Mean > Median > Mode.

In figure (c), when there is a longer tail towards the left hand side of the center, then the skewness is said to be 'Negatively Skewed'. In such a case, Mean < Median < Mode.

In positively skewed distribution, dispersal of individual observations is greater towards the right of the central value. On the other hand, a greater dispersal of individual observations is towards the left of the central value. We can say, therefore, the concept of skewness not only refers to lack of symmetry in a distribution but also indicates the magnitude as well as the direction of skewness in a distribution. The relationship of mean, median and mode in measuring the degree of skewness is that, for a moderately symmetrical distribution the interval between the mean and the median is approximately $\frac{1}{3}$ rd of the interval between the mean and mode.

For, a moderately asymmetrical frequency distribution, the empirical relationship between mean, median and mode is given by Karl Pearson and is defined as:

Mode = 3(Median) − 2(Mean)

(ii) Kurtosis

Ans. Kurtosis is the measure of the shape of a frequency curve. It is a Greek word, which means bulginess. While skewness signifies the extent of asymmetry, kurtosis measures the degree of peakedness of a frequency distribution.

Karl Pearson classified curves into three types on the basis of the shape of their peaks. These are mesokurtic, leptokurtic and platykurtic. These three types of curves are shown in Fig. 1.13.

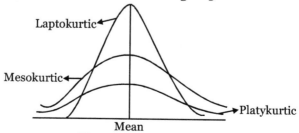

Fig. 1.13: Types of Curves

If a distribution is more peaked than normal it is said to be leptokurtic. This kind of peakedness implies a thin distribution. On the other hand, if a distribution is more flat than the normal distribution it is known as platykurtic distribution. A normal curve is known as mesokurtic.

Q17. Discuss the concept of statistical inference.

Or

What do you mean by inferential statistics?

Or

Write a short note on "Point estimation and Interval estimation". [June-2014, Q.No.-10(a)]

Or

Write short notes on the following:
(i) Estimation
(ii) Point estimation
(iii) Interval estimation

Ans. Statistical inference is that branch of statistics, which is concerned with using probability concept to deal with uncertainty in decision-making. The field of statistical inference has had a fruitful development since the latter half of the 19th century.

It refers to the process of selecting and using a sample statistic to draw inference about a population parameter based on a subset of it, i.e. the sample drawn from the population. Statistical inference treats two different classes of problems:

- Hypothesis testing, i.e. to test some hypothesis about parent population from which the sample is drawn.
- Estimation, i.e. to use the 'statistics' obtained from the sample as estimate of the unknown 'parameter' of the population from which the sample is drawn.

In both these cases, the particular problem at hand is structured in such a way that inferences about relevant population values can be made from sample data.

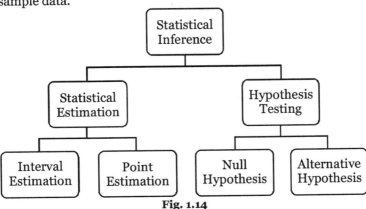

Fig. 1.14

When data are collected by sampling from a population, the most important objective of statistical analysis is to draw inferences or generalisations about that population from the information embodied in the sample. Statistical estimation, or briefly estimation, is concerned with the methods by which population characteristics are estimated from sample information. It may be pointed out that the true value of a parameter is an unknown constant that can be correctly ascertained only by an exhaustive study of the population. However, it is ordinarily too expensive or it is infeasible to enumerate complete population to obtain the required information. In case of finite population, the cost of complete censuses may be prohibitive and in case of infinite population, complete enumerations are impossible. A realistic objective may be to obtain a guess of estimate of the unknown true value or an interval of plausible values from the sample data and also to determine the accuracy of the procedure. Statistical estimation procedures provide us with the means of obtaining estimates of population parameters with desired degrees of precision.

Characteristics of Estimators: The basic characteristics of estimators are as follows:

- **Unbiasedness and Minimum Variance:** A statistic T is defined to be unbiased for a parameter θ if expectation of T is θ, i.e. $E(T) = \theta$. On the other hand, if, $E(T) = \theta + a(\theta)$, then the difference $a(\theta) = E(T) - \theta$ is known as **bias**. The bias is known to be positive if $a(\theta) > 0$ and negative if $a(\theta) < 0$. Our first priority would be to select an unbiased estimator of θ. However, there may be many unbiased estimator of θ. If $x_1, x_2, \ldots x_n$ denote n sample observations from a population with an unknown parameter θ, then any of the n observations or any linear function of them would be an unbiased estimator of θ.

- **Consistency:** If T is an estimator of θ, then it is obvious that T should be in the neighbourhood of θ. T is known to be consistent for θ, if the difference between T and θ can be made as small as we please by increasing the sample size n sufficiently.

- **Efficiency:** A statistic T is called as an efficient estimator of θ if it has the minimum standard error among all the estimators of θ for a fixed sample size n. Both the sample mean and sample median are consistent estimators for μ. But standard error of sample mean is less than that of sample median. Hence, sample median is only a consistent estimator of μ, whereas sample mean is both consistent and efficient estimator of μ.

- **Sufficiency:** A statistic T is known to be a sufficient estimator of θ if T contains sufficient information about θ so that we do not have to look for any other estimator of θ. Sample mean $(\bar{x})$ is a sufficient estimator of μ.

With respect to estimating a parameter, the following two types of estimates are possible:

(1) Point Estimates

A point estimate is a single number computed from the sample values $x_1, x_2, \ldots x_n$ which is used as an estimate of the unknown population parameter. The procedure in point estimation is to select a random sample of n observations, $x_1, x_2, \ldots x_n$ from a population $f(x, \theta^*)$ and then to use some preconceived method to arrive from these observations at a number say $\hat{\theta}$ (read theta hat) which we accept as an estimator of θ. The estimator θ is a single point on the real number scale, and thus, the name point estimation. $\hat{\theta}$ depends on the random variable that generate the sample, and hence, it too is a random variable with its own sampling distribution.

(2) Interval Estimates

As distinguished from a point estimate, which provides one single value of the parameter, an interval estimate of a population parameter is a statement of two values between which it is estimated that the parameter lies. An interval estimate would always be specified by two values, i.e. the lower one and the upper one. *In more technical terms, interval estimation refers to the estimation of a parameter by a random interval, called the confidence interval,* whose end points L and U with L<U are function of the observed random variables such that the probability that the inequality $L < \theta < U$ is satisfied in terms of pre-determined number, $1-\alpha$. L and U are called the confidence limits and are the random end points of interval estimate. Since in an interval estimate, we determine an interval of plausible values, hence the name interval estimation. Thus, on the basis of sample study, if we estimate the average income of the people living in a village as ₹875, it will be a point estimate. On the other hand, if we say that the average income could lie between ₹800 and ₹950, it will be an interval estimate.

On comparing these two methods of estimation, we find that point estimation has an advantage as much as it provides an exact value for the parameter under investigation. This merit, however, is also the defect of a point estimate. Being a single point on the real number scale, a point estimate does not tell us how close the estimator is to the parameter being estimated. Moreover, in scientific investigation, it is usually not necessary to know exact value of a parameter—rather it is desirable to have some degree of the confidence that the value obtained is within a certain range. The interval estimate does provide such confidence, and hence, interval estimate should generally be employed in practice.

Q18. What is hypothesis testing? Discuss the corelogic of hypothesis testing.

Ans. Hypothesis testing has a vital role in psychological measurements. By hypothesis, we mean the tentative answer to any question. Hypothesis testing is a systematic procedure for deciding whether the results of a research study, which examines a sample, support a particular theory or practical innovation, which applies to a population. Hypothesis testing is the central theme in most psychology research.

Hypothesis testing involves grasping ideas that make little sense. Real life psychology research involves samples of many individuals. At the same time, there are studies which involve a single individual.

The Corelogic of Hypothesis Testing

There is a standard kind of reasoning researchers use for any hypothesis testing problem. For example, ordinarily, among the population of babies that are not given the specially purified vitamin, the chance of a baby's starting to walk at age 8 months or earlier would be less than 2%. Thus, walking at 8 months or earlier is highly unlikely among such babies. But what if the randomly selected sample of one baby in our study does start walking by 8 months? If the specially purified vitamin had no effect on this particular baby's walking age (which means that the baby's walking age should be similar to that of babies that were not given the vitamin), it is highly unlikely (less than a 2% chance) that the particular baby we selected at random would start walking by 8 months. So, if the baby in our study does in fact start walking by 8 months, that allows us to reject the idea that the specially purified vitamin has no effect. And if we reject the idea that the specially purified vitamin has no effect, then we must also accept the idea that the specially purified vitamin does have an effect. Using the same reasoning, if the baby starts walking by 8 months, we can reject the idea that this baby comes from a population of babies with a mean walking age of 14 months. We, therefore, conclude that babies given the specially purified vitamin will start to walk before 14 months. Our explanation for the baby's early-walking age in the study is that the specially purified vitamin speeded up the baby's development.

The researchers first spelled out what would have to happen for them to conclude that the special purification procedure makes a difference. Having laid this out in advance, the researchers could then go on to carry out their study. In this example, carrying out the study means giving the specially purified vitamin to a randomly selected baby and watching to see how early that baby walks. Suppose the result of the study is that the baby starts walking before 8 months. The researchers would then conclude that it is unlikely the specially purified vitamin makes no difference, and thus, also conclude that it does make a difference.

This kind of testing the opposite-of-what-you-predict, roundabout reasoning is at the heart of inferential statistics in psychology. It is something like a double negative. One reason for this approach is that we have the information to figure the probability of getting a particular experimental result if the situation of there being no difference is true. In the purified vitamin example, the researchers know what the probabilities are of babies walking at different ages if the specially purified vitamin does not have any effect. It is the probability of babies walking at various ages that is already known from studies of babies in general – that is, babies who have not received the specially purified vitamin. (Suppose the specially purified vitamin has no effect. In that situation, the age at which babies start walking is the same whether or not they receive the specially purified vitamin.)

Without such a tortuous way of going at the problem, in most cases, we could just not do hypothesis testing at all. In almost all psychology research, we base our conclusions on this question: What is the probability of getting our research results. If the opposite of what we are predicting were true? That is, we are usually predicting an effect of some kind. However, we decide on whether there is such an effect by seeing if it is unlikely that there is not such an effect. If it is highly unlikely that we would get our research results if the opposite of what we are predicting were true, that allows us to reject that opposite prediction. If we reject that opposite prediction, we are able to accept our prediction. However, if it is likely that we would get our research results if the opposite of what we are predicting were true, we are not able to reject that opposite prediction. If we are not able to reject that opposite prediction, we are not able to accept our prediction.

Q19. Discuss the steps of testing a hypothesis.

Ans. There are five steps involved in testing a hypothesis:

(1) **Formulate a Hypothesis:** The first step is to set up two hypotheses instead of one in such a way that if one hypothesis is true, the other is false. Alternatively, if one hypothesis is false or rejected, then the other is true or accepted.

(2) **Set up a Suitable Significance Level:** Having formulated the hypothesis, the next step is to test its validity at a certain level of significance. The confidence with which a null hypothesis is rejected or accepted depends upon the significance level used for the purpose. A significance level of, say 5 per cent, means that in the long-run, the risk of making the wrong decision is about 5 per cent. In other words, one is likely to be wrong in accepting a false hypothesis or in rejecting a true hypothesis on 5 out of 100 occasions. A significance level of, say, 1 per cent implies that there is a risk of being wrong in accepting or rejecting the hypothesis on 1 out of every 100 occasions. Thus, a 1 per cent significance level provides greater confidence to the decision than a 5 per cent significance level.

(3) **Select Test Criterion:** The next step in hypothesis testing is the selection of an appropriate statistical technique as a test criterion. There are many techniques from which one is to be chosen. For example, when the hypothesis pertains to a large sample of more than 30, the Z-test implying normal distribution is used. When a sample is small (less than 30), the t-test will be more suitable. The test criteria that are frequently used in hypothesis testing are Z, t, F and χ^2.

(4) **Compute:** After having selected the statistical technique to test the hypothesis, the next step involves various computations necessary for the application of the particular test. These computations include the testing statistic as also its standard error.

(5) Make Decision: The final step in hypothesis testing is to draw a statistical decision, involving the acceptance or rejection of the null hypothesis. This will depend on whether the computed value of the test criterion falls in the region of acceptance or in the region of rejection at a given level of significance. It may be noted that the statement rejecting the hypothesis is much stronger than the statement accepting it. It is much easier to prove something false than to prove it true. Thus, when we say that the null hypothesis is not rejected, we do not categorically say that it is true.

Q20. What do you mean by one tailed and two tailed tests?

Or

Write a short note on "one-tail and two-tail test."

[Dec-2014, Q.No.-10(e)]

Ans. Suppose we have a null hypothesis H_0 and an alternative hypothesis H_1. We consider the distribution given by the null hypothesis and perform a test to determine whether or not the null hypothesis should be rejected in favour of the alternative hypothesis.

For testing this, there are two different types of tests that can be performed. A **one-tailed** test looks for an increase or decrease in the parameter, whereas a **two-tailed** test looks for any change in the parameter (which can be either increase or decrease).

We can perform the test at any level (usually 1%, 5% or 10%). For example, performing the test at a 5% level means that there is a 5% chance of wrongly rejecting H_0.

If we perform the test at the 5% level and decide to reject the null hypothesis, we say, "There is significant evidence at the 5% level to suggest the hypothesis is false".

One-Tailed Test

First, we choose a critical region. In a one-tailed test, the critical region will have just one part (the shaded portion in Fig. 1.15). If our sample value lies in this region, we reject the null hypothesis in favour of the alternative.

Suppose we are looking for a definite decrease. Then, the critical region will be to the left. Note, however, that in the one-tailed test, the value of the parameter can be as high as we like.

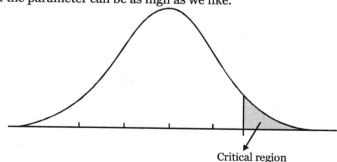

Critical region

Fig. 1.15: One-Tailed Test

For Example: Past records show that the mean marks of students taking statistics are 60 with standard deviation of 15 marks. A new method of teaching is adopted and a random sample of 64 students is chosen. After using the new method, the sample gives the mean marks of 65. Is the new method better?

Here, we are interested in knowing whether the marks increased on using the new teaching method.

Therefore, we use the one-tailed method.

The null hypothesis is: $H_0 : \mu = 60$

The alternative hypothesis is: $H_1 : \mu > 60$

Given, $\bar{x} = 65, \mu = 60, \sigma = 15$ and $n = 64$

Then,

$$Z = \frac{\bar{x} - \mu}{\sigma/\sqrt{n}} = \frac{65 - 60}{15/\sqrt{64}} = 2.66$$

Now, suppose the researcher had pre-determined the level of significance, which is 0.01 or 1% for his decision. Then 2.66 > 2.33 (since z-score is 2.33 for 0.01 level on the upper-tail of distribution).

Therefore, the observed value is highly significant. That is H_0 is rejected and H_1 is accepted.

This means the new teaching method is better.

Two-Tailed Test

In a two-tailed test, we are looking for either an increase or a decrease. Therefore, for example, H_0 might be that the mean is equal to 60 (as before). This time, however, H_1 would be that the mean is not equal to 60. In this case, therefore, the critical region has two parts:

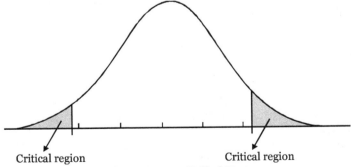

Critical region   Critical region
Fig. 1.16: Two-Tailed Test

For Example: Let test the parameter p of a Binomial distribution at the 10% level. Suppose a coin is tossed 10 times and we get 7 heads. So we want to test whether or not the coin is fair. If the coin is fair, p = 0.5.

Put this as the null hypothesis:

$H_0 : p = 0.5$

$H_1 : p =$ (does not equal) 0.5

Now, because the test is two-tailed, the critical region has two parts. Half of the critical region is to the right and half is to the left. Therefore, the critical region contains both the top 5% of the distribution and the bottom 5% of the distribution (since we are testing at the 10% level).

If H_0 is true, $X \sim \text{Bin}(10, 0.5)$.

If the null hypothesis is true, the probability $P(X \geq 7) = 1 - P(X < 7) = 1 - P(X \leq 6) = 1 - 0.8281 = 0.1719$ (this has come from a Poisson table)

Since, it is not in the critical region because the probability that X is at least 7 is not less than 0.05 (5%),

Therefore, there is not significant evidence at the 10% level to reject the null hypothesis.

Q21. Discuss the implications of rejecting or failing to reject the null hypothesis.

Ans. We can make two conclusions from the hypothesis-testing process. First, suppose we reject the null hypothesis it means our result supports the research hypothesis however, we would still not say that the results prove the research hypothesis or that the results show that the research hypothesis is true. This would be too strong because the results of research studies are based on probabilities. Specifically, they are based on the probability being low of getting our result if the null hypothesis were true. Proven and true are okay in logic and mathematics, but to use these worlds in conclusions from scientific research is quite unprofessional.

Second, when a result is not extreme enough to reject the null hypothesis, we do not say that the result supports the null hypothesis. We simply say the result is not statistically significant.

A result that is not strong enough to reject the null hypothesis means the study was inconclusive. The results may not be extreme enough to reject the null hypothesis, but the null hypothesis might still be false (and the research hypothesis true). Suppose an example that the specially purified vitamin had only a slight but still real effect. In that case, we would not expect to find a baby given the purified vitamin to be walking a lot earlier than babies in general. Thus, we would not be able to reject the null hypothesis, even though it is false.

Showing the null hypothesis to be true would mean showing that there is absolutely no difference between the populations it is always possible that there is a difference between the populations, but that the difference is much smaller than what the particular study was able to detect. Therefore, when a result is not extreme enough to reject the null hypothesis, the results are inconclusive. Sometimes, however, if studies have been done using large samples and accurate measuring procedures, evidence may build up in support of something close to the null hypothesis – that there is at most very little difference between the populations.

Q22. What are the Type I and Type II errors?

Or

Write a short note on "Type I Error".

[Dec-2013, Q.No.-9(a)]

Or

Write a short note on "Type I and Type II errors.
[June-2014, Q.No.-10(b)] [June-2015, Q.No.-10]

Ans. When a statistical hypothesis is tested, there are four possible results:
(1) The hypothesis is true but out test rejects it.
(2) The hypothesis is false but our test accepts it.
(3) The hypothesis is true and our test accepts it.
(4) The hypothesis is false and our test rejects it.

Obviously, the first two possibilities lead to errors. If we reject a hypothesis when it should be accepted (possibility No. 1), we say that a Type I error has been made. On the other hand, if we accept a hypothesis when it should be rejected (possibility No. 2), we say that a Type II error has been made. In either case, a wrong decision or error in judgment has occurred. The sizes of Type-I error and Type-II error are denoted by α and β respectively. The usual practice in testing of hypothesis is to fix α, the size of Type-I error and they try to obtain a criterion which minimises β, the size of Type-II error.

Q23. What is hypothesis? Explain the concept of null and alternative hypothesis.

Or

Differentiate between null and alternative hypothesis.

Or

What is null hypothesis?

Or

Write a short note on "Importance of alternative hypothesis". [June-2013, Q.No.-9(b)]

Or

Write a short note on "Alternative hypothesis".
[Dec-2013, Q.No.-9(c)]

Ans. A hypothesis is tentative statement about a characteristic of a population. It can be an assertion or a claim also. It is simply a quantitative statement about a population.

Null Hypothesis

In tests of hypothesis, we always begin with an assumption or hypothesis (i.e. assumed value of a population parameter). This is called null hypothesis. The null hypothesis asserts that there is no (significant) difference between the sample statistic and the population parameter and whatever the observed difference is there, is merely due to fluctuations in sampling from the same population. Null hypothesis is usually denoted by the symbol H_0. R.A. Fisher defined null hypothesis as, "the hypothesis which is tested for possible rejection under the assumption that it is true". In other words, the hypothesis (regarding some characteristics of population) which is to be verified with the help of a random sample or the hypothesis which is under test is called null hypothesis. For example, if we want to test the hypothesis that the mean of the population to be taken as μ_0, then the null hypothesis (H_0) is $\mu = \mu_0$.

Alternative Hypothesis

Any hypothesis different from the null hypothesis (H_0) is called an alternative hypothesis and is denoted by the symbol H_1. The two hypothesis H_0 and H_1 are such that if one is accepted, the other is rejected and vice versa. For example, if we want to test whether the population mean μ has a specified value μ_0, then (i) Null Hypothesis is $H_0 : \mu = \mu_0$ and (ii) Alternative Hypothesis may be (a) $H_1 : \mu \neq \mu_0$ (i.e., $\mu > \mu_0$ or $\mu < \mu_0$), or (b) $H_1 : \mu > \mu_0$ or (c) $H_1 : \mu < \mu_0$. Thus, there can be more than one alternative hypothesis.

Q24. Write short notes on the following:
(i) Level of Significance [Dec-2013, Q.No.-9(b)]
Ans. The level of significance refers to the degree of significance with which we accept or reject a particular hypothesis. Since 100 per cent accuracy is not possible in taking a decision over the acceptance or rejection of a hypothesis, we have to take the decision at a particular level of confidence which would speak of the probability of one being correct or wrong in accepting or rejecting a hypothesis. In most of the cases of hypothesis testing, such a confidence is fixed at 5 per cent level, which implies that our decisions would be correct to the extent of 95 per cent. For a greater precise, however, such a confidence may be fixed at 1 per cent level which would imply that the decision would be correct to the extent of 99 per cent. This level is usually denoted by the symbol, α (alpha) which represents the probability of committing the type I error (i.e. rejecting a null hypothesis which is true). The level of confidence (or significance), is always fixed in advance before applying the test procedures. It is important to note that if no level of significance is given, then we always take $\alpha = 0.05$.

(ii) Decision Errors
Ans. Decision errors make sense of statistical significance. These errors are possible in the hypothesis-testing process. This type of error we consider here is about how, in spite of doing all our figuring correctly, our conclusions from hypothesis-testing can still be incorrect. It is not about making mistakes in calculations or even about using the wrong procedures. Rather decision errors are situations in which the right procedures lead to the wrong decisions.

Decision errors are possible in hypothesis testing because we are making decisions about population based on information in samples. The whole hypothesis testing process is based on probabilities. The hypothesis-testing process is set up to make the probability of decision errors as small as possible. For example, we only decide to reject the null hypothesis if a sample's mean is so extreme that there is a very small probability (say, less than 5%) that we could have gotten such an extreme sample if the null hypothesis is true. But a very small probability is not the same as a zero probability! Thus, in spite of our best intentions, decision errors are always II errors.

Q25. What is the significance of size of sample in hypothesis testing?
Ans. The sampling distribution of the differences between means may look like a normal curve or t-distribution curve depending upon the size of the

Introduction to Statistics 45

samples drawn from the population. The t-distribution is a theoretical probability distribution. It is symmetrical, bell-shaped and similar to the standard normal curve. It differs from the standard normal curve, however, in that it has an additional parameter, called degrees of freedom, which changes its shape.

If the samples are large (N=30 or greater than 30), then the distribution of differences between means will be a normal one. If it is small (N is less than 30), then the distribution will take the form of a I distribution and the shape of the t-curve will vary with the number of degrees of freedom.

In this way, for large samples, statistics advocating normal distribution of the characteristics in the given population will be employed, while for small samples, the small sample statistics will be used.

Hence, in the case of large samples possessing a normal distribution of the differences of means, the value of standard error used to determine the significance of the difference between means will be in terms of standard sigma (z) scores. On the other hand, in the case of small samples possessing a t- distribution of differences between means, we will make use of t-values rather than z scores of the normal curve. From the normal curve table, we see that 95% and 99% cases lie at the distance of 1.96 and 2.58. Therefore, the sigma or z scores of 1.96 and 2.58 are taken as critical values for rejecting a null hypothesis.

If a computed z-value of the standard error of the differences between means approaches or exceeds the values 1.96 and 2.58, then we may safely reject a null hypothesis at the 0.05 and 0.01 levels.

To test the null hypothesis in the case of small sample means, we first compute the t ratio in the same manner as z scores in case of large samples. Then we enter the table of t-distribution (Table C in the Appendix) with $N_1 + N_2 - 2$ degrees of freedom and read the values of t given against the row of $N_1 + N_2 - 2$ degrees of freedom and columns headed by 0.05 and 0.01 levels of significance. If our computed t ratio approaches or exceeds the values of t read from the table, we will reject the established null hypothesis at the 0.05 and 0.01 levels of significance, respectively.

Q26. Elucidate the steps in setting up the level of significance.
Or
Delineate the steps in setting up the level of significance.
[June-2014, Q.No.-4]

Ans. The steps in setting up the level of significance are as follows:
(1) State the null hypothesis and the alternative hypothesis. (Note: The goal of inferential statistics is to make general statements about the population by using sample data. Therefore in testing hypothesis, we make our predictions about the population parameters).
(2) Set the criteria for a decision.
(3) Level of significance or alpha level for the hypothesis test: This is represented by μ which is the probability used to define the very unlikely sample outcomes, if the null hypothesis is true.

In hypothesis testing, the set of potential samples is divided into those that are likely to be obtained and those that are very unlikely if the hypothesis is true.

(4) **Critical Region:** This is the region which is composed of extreme sample values that are very unlikely outcomes if the null hypothesis is true. The boundaries for the critical region are determined by the alpha level. If sample data fall in the critical region, the null hypothesis is rejected. The cut off level that is set affects the outcome of the research.

(5) Collect data and compute sample statistics using the formula given below:

$$z = \frac{\bar{x} - \mu}{\sigma_x}$$

where, $\bar{x}$ = Sample mean,
μ = Hypothesised population mean, and
σ_x = Standard error between $\bar{x}$ and μ.

(6) Make a decision and write down the decision rule.
Z-Score is called a test statistics. The purpose of a test statistics is to determine whether the result of a research study (the obtained difference) is more than what would be expected by the chance alone.

$$z = \frac{\text{Obtained difference}}{\text{Difference due to chance}}$$

Now suppose, a manufacturer produces some type of articles of good quality. A purchaser by chance selects a sample randomly. It so happens that the sample contains many defective articles and it leads the purchaser to reject the whole product. Now, the manufacturer suffers a loss even though he has produced a good article of quality. Therefore, this Type-I error is called "producers risk".

On the other hand, if we accept the entire lot on the basis of a sample and the lot is not really good, the consumers are put to loss. Therefore, this Type-II error is called the "consumers risk".

Q27. Discuss the procedure for formulating hypothesis and stating conclusion with the help of examples.

Ans. The procedure for formulating hypothesis and stating conclusion are as follows:

(1) State the hypothesis as the alternative hypothesis H_1.

(2) The null hypothesis H_0 will be the opposite of H_1 and will contain an equality sign.

(3) If the sample evidence supports the alternative hypothesis, the null hypothesis will be rejected and the probability of having made an incorrect decision (when in fact H_0 is true) is α, a quantity that can be manipulated to be as small as the researcher wishes.

(4) If the sample does not provide sufficient evidence to support the alternative hypothesis, then conclude that the null hypothesis cannot be rejected on the basis of our sample. In this situation, we may wish to collect more information about the phenomenon under study.

This procedure can be explained with the help of example.

The logic used in hypothesis testing has often been likened to that used in the courtroom in which a defendant is on trial for committing a crime.

(a) Formulate appropriate null and alternative hypotheses for judging the guilt or innocence of the defendant.
(b) Interpret the Type-I and Type-II errors in this context.
(c) If we were the defendant, would we want α to be small or large? Explain.

Solution

(a) Under a judicial system, a defendant is "innocent until proven guilty". That is, the burden of proof is not on the defendant to prove his/her innocence; rather, the court must collect sufficient evidence to support the claim that the defendant is guilty. Thus, the null and alternative hypotheses would be:

H_0 : Defendant is innocent

H_1 : Defendant is guilty

(b) The four possible outcomes are shown in the table below. A Type-I error would be to conclude that the defendant is guilty, when in fact s/he is innocent; a Type-II error would be to conclude that the defendant is innocent, when in fact s/he is guilty.

Table 1.13: Conclusions and Consequences

		Decision of Court	
		Defendant is Innocent	Defendant is Guilty
True State of Nature	Defendant if Innocent	Correct decision	Type-II error
	Defendant is Guilty	Type-I error	Correct decision

(c) Most people would probably agree that the Type-I error in this situation is by far the more serious. Thus, we would want α, the probability of committing a Type-I error, to be very small indeed.

A convention that is generally observed when formulating the null and alternative hypotheses of any statistical test is to state H_0 so that the possible error of incorrectly rejecting H_0 (Type-I error) is considered more serious than the possible error of incorrectly failing to reject H_0 (Type-II error).

Q28. Explain the one-tailed and two-tailed test of significance.

Ans. The "tails" refer to the ends of the normal curve. When we test for statistical significance, we want to know whether the difference or relationship is so extreme, so far out in the tail of the distribution, that it is unlikely to have occurred by chance alone. When we hypothesise the direction of the difference or relationship, we state in which tail of the distribution we expect to find the difference or relationship.

Although there is controversy about this, the practice among many researchers is to use a one-tailed test of significance when a directional hypothesis is stated and a two-tailed test in all other situations. The advantage of using the one-tailed test is that it is more powerful, because the value yielded by the statistical test does not have to be so large to be significant at a given p level.

The normal curve is used to demonstrate the difference between one-tailed and two-tailed tests. From the discussion of the normal curve, we know that 95% of the distribution falls between ± 1.96 SD from the mean. Thus, only 5% falls beyond these two points: 2.5% of the distribution falls below a z-score of −1.96, and 2.5% falls above +1.96z. To be so "rare" as to occur only 5% of the time, a z-score would have to be −1.96z or less or +1.96z or greater. Note that we are using both tails of the distribution. Because 99% of the distribution falls between ±2.58 SD from the mean of the normal curve, a score would have to be −2.58 or less or +2.58 or more to be declared significant at the 0.01 level.

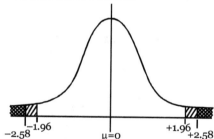

Fig. 1.17: Two-tailed test of significance using the normal curve

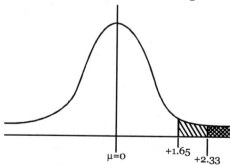

Fig. 1.18: One-tailed test of significance using the normal curve

Fig. 1.18 shows what occur when a directional hypothesis is stated. We examine only one tail of the distribution. In this example, we look at the positive side of the distribution. 50 per cent of the distribution falls below the mean and 45% falls between the mean and a z-score of +1.65.

Thus, 95% (50 + 45) of the distribution falls below +1.65z. To score in the upper 5% would require a score of +1.65 or greater. Given a one-tailed test of significance, we would need a score of +1.65z to be significant at the 0.05 level, whereas with a two-tailed test, we needed a score of ±1.96z. This is an example of the concept of power. With an a priori directional hypothesis, a lower z-score would be considered significant.

For the 0.01 level of significance and a one-tailed test, a z-score of +2.33 or greater is needed for significance. This is because 49% of the distribution falls between the mean and +2.33, and another 50% falls below the mean.

The main aim of GPH book is to provide knowledge as well as good marks in exam.

Gullybaba Publishing House Pvt. Ltd.

ISO 9001 & ISO 14001 Certified Co.

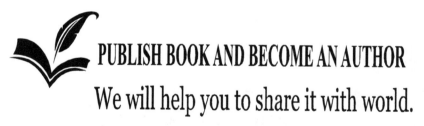

PUBLISH BOOK AND BECOME AN AUTHOR
We will help you to share it with world.

Gullybaba.com

Correlation and Regression

An Overview

We measure psychological attributes of people by using tests and scales in order to describe individuals. There are times when we realise that increment in one of the characteristics is associated with increments in other characteristics as well. For example, individual who are more optimistic about the future are more likely to be happy. On the other hand, those who are less optimistic about future are less likely to be happy. We would realise that as one variable is increasing, the other is also increasing and as the one is decreasing, the other is also decreasing. In the statistical language, it is referred to as correlation. It is description of "relationship" or "association" between two variables.

The term "regression" literally means, "stepping back towards the average". It was first used by a British biometrician, Sir Francis Galton, (1882-1911), in connection with the inheritance of stature. Galton found that the offspring of abnormally tall or short parents lend to "regress" or "step back" to the average population height. But the term "regression" as now used in statistics is only a convenient term without having any reference to biometry.

Q1. What is correlation? Give its interpretation. How would you test the significance of the correlation coefficient?

Or

How do we determine the strength of relationship between two variables?

Ans. In our day-to-day life, we find many examples when a mutual relationship exists between two variables, i.e. with fall or rise in the value of one variable, the fall or rise may take place in the value of other variable. For example, price of commodity rises as the demand for the commodity goes up. Upto a certain time-period, weight of a person increases with the increase in age. Similarly, the temperature rises with the rise in the sunlight. These facts indicate that there is certainly some mutual relationship that exists between the demand for commodity and its price, the age of a person and his weight, and the sunlight and temperature. The correlation refers to the statistical technique used in measuring the strength of the relationship between the variables.

Any curious reader will ask a question "how strong is the relationship between the two variables? For example, if we correlate intelligence with scores on reasoning and creativity, what kind of relationship will we expect?

Obviously, the relationship between intelligence and reasoning as well as the relationship between intelligence and creativity are positive. At the same time the correlation coefficient is higher for intelligence and reasoning than for intelligence and creativity, and therefore we realise that the relationship between intelligence and reasoning is stronger than relationship between intelligence and creativity. The strength of relationship between the two variables is an important information to interpret the relationship.

Correlation coefficient is said to be a measure of covariance between two series. It is denoted by r. The value of correlation coefficient always lie between or equal to –1 to 1.

The coefficient of correlation measures the degree of relationship between two sets of figures. As the reliability of estimates depends upon the closeness of relationship, it is imperative that utmost care be taken while interpreting the value of coefficient of correlation, otherwise fallacious conclusions can be drawn. The following general rules are given which would help in interpreting the value of r:

- When r = +1, it means there is perfect positive relationship between the variables.
- When r = –1, it means there is perfect negative relationship between the variables.
- When r = 0, it means that there is no relationship between the variables, i.e. the variables are uncorrelated.
- The closer r is to +1 or –1, the closer the relationship between the variables and the closer r is to 0, the less close the relationship.
- If we are to test the hypothesis that the correlation coefficient of the population is uncorrelated, we have to apply the following test:

$$t = \frac{r}{\sqrt{1-r^2}} \times \sqrt{n-2}$$

Here, t is based on (n − 2) degrees of freedom. If the calculated value of t exceeds $t_{0.05}$ for (n − 2), d.f., we say that the value of r is significant at 5% level. If $t < t_{0.05}$ the data are consistent with the hypothesis of an uncorrelated population.

Q2. Discuss the scatter diagram method of correlation.

Ans. Scatter diagram is a graphic method of finding out correlation between two variables. By this method, direction of correlation can be ascertained. For constructing a scatter diagram, X-variable is represented on X-axis and the Y-variable on Y-axis. Each pair of values of X and Y series is plotted in two-dimensional space of X–Y. Thus, we get a scatter diagram by plotting all the pair of values. Different points may be scattered in various ways in the scatter diagram whose analysis gives us an idea about the direction and magnitude of correlation in the following ways:

Perfect Positive Correlation (r = +1)

If all points are plotted in the shape of straight line, passing from lower corner of left side to the upper corner at right side, then both series X and Y have perfect positive correlation, as is clear from the Fig. 2.1:

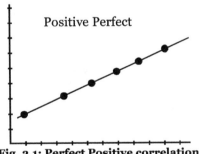

Fig. 2.1: Perfect Positive correlation

Perfect Negative Correlation (r = −1)

When all points lie on a straight line from up to down, then X and Y have perfect negative correlation, as it is clear from the Fig. 2.2 below:

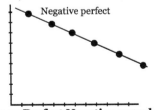

Fig. 2.2: Perfect Negative correlation

High Degree of Positive Correlation (0 < r < 1)

When concentration of points moves from left to right upward and the points are close to each other, then X and Y have high degree of positive correlation, as is clear from the Fig. 2.3:

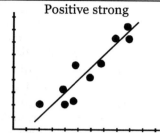

Fig. 2.3: High Degree of Positive Correlation

High Degree of Negative Correlation (r < 0)

When points are concentrated from left to right downward, and the points are close to each other, then X and Y have high degree of negative correlation, as is clear from the Fig. 2.4:

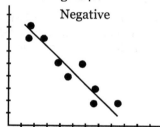

Fig. 2.4: High Degree of Negative Correlation

Zero Correlation (r = 0)

When all the points are scattered in four directions here and there and are lacking in any pattern, then there is absence of correlation as is clear from the Fig. 2.5:

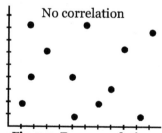

Fig. 2.5: Zero correlation

Q3. How to draw a scatter diagram?

Ans. The steps to draw a scatter diagram are as follows:

Step 1: Plotting the Axis

Draw the x and y-axis on the graph and plot one variable on x-axis and another on y-axis.

(Although, correlation analysis does not restrict us from plotting any variable on any axis, plot the causal variable on x-axis in case of implicitly assumed cause-effect relationship.)

Also, note that correlation does not necessarily imply causality.

Step 2: Range of Values

Decide the range of values depending on our data.
Begin from higher or lower value than zero.
Conventionally, the scatterplot is square.
So plot x and y values about the same length.

Step 3: Identify the pairs of values
Identify the pairs of values.
A pair of value is obtained from a data.
A pair of value is created by taking a one value on first variable and corresponding value on second variable.

Step 4: Plotting the graph
Now, locate these pairs in the graph.
Find an intersection point of x and y in the graph for each pair.
Mark it by a clear dot (or any symbol we like for example, star).
Then take second pair and so on as shown in Fig. 2.6:

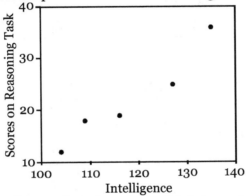

Fig. 2.6: Scatter diagram depicting relationship between intelligence and score on reasoning task

The graph shown above is scatterplot representing the relationship between intelligence and the scores on reasoning task. We have plotted intelligence on x-axis because it is a cause of the performance on the reasoning task. The scores on reasoning have started from 100 instead of zero simply because the smallest score on intelligence is 104 which is far away from zero. We have also started the range of reasoning scores from 10 since the lowest score on reasoning is 12. Then we have plotted the pair of scores. For example, subject A has score of 104 on intelligence and 12 on reasoning so we get x, y pair of 104, 12. We have plotted this pair on the point of intersection between these two scores in the graph by a dot. This is the lowest dot at the left side of the graph.

Q4. Describe the linear and non-linear relationship of correlation.
Or
Discuss linear and non-linear relationship between two variables.
Or
Describe linear and non-linear relationship with suitable examples. [June-2014, Q.No.-5]

Ans. The relationship between two variables can be of various types. Broadly, they can be classified as linear and non-linear relationships.

Linear Relationship

Linear relationship is one of the basic forms of relationship. It can be expressed as a relationship between two variables that can be plotted as a straight line. The linear relationship can be expressed in the following equation:

$$Y = \alpha + \beta X \qquad \text{...(i)}$$

In the equation (1),
- Y is a dependent variable (variable on y-axis);
- α (alpha) is a constant or Y intercept of straight line;
- β (beta) is slope of the line; and
- X is independent variable (variable on x-axis).

For example, there is data of five subject, A to E (Table 2.1) which is used to show the line which is best fit for the data.

Table 2.1

Subject	Intelligence	Scores on reasoning task
A	104	12
B	127	25
C	109	18
D	135	31
E	116	19

Fig. 2.7 shows that there is a linear relationship between two variables, intelligence and scores on reasoning task. The graph also shows the straight-line relationship indicating linear relation.

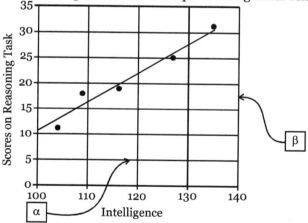

Fig. 2.7: Scatter showing linearity of the relationship between Intelligence and Scores on Reasoning Task

Non-linear Relationship

There are other forms of relationships as well. They are called as curvilinear or non-linear relationships. The Yerkes-Dodson Law, Steven's Power Law in Psychophysics, etc. are good examples of non-linear relationships. The relationship between stress and performance is popularly known as Yerkes-

Dodson Law. It suggests that the performance is poor when the stress is too little or too much. It improves when the stress is moderate. Fig. 2.8 shows this relationship. The non-linear relationships cannot be plotted as a straight line.

The performance is poor at extremes and improves with moderate stress. This is one type of curvilinear relationship.

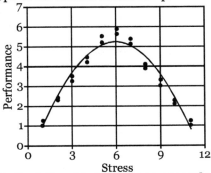

Fig. 2.8: Typical relationship between stress and performance

Q5. Explain the concept of direction of correlation.

Ans. The direction of the relationship is an important aspect of the description of relationship. If the two variables are correlated then the relationship is either positive or negative. The absence of relationship indicates "zero correlation".

Positive Correlation

The positive correlation indicates that as the value of one variable increases, the value of other variable also increases. Consequently, as the value of one variable decreases, the value of other variable also decreases. This means that both the variables move in the same direction. For example,

- As the intelligence (IQ) increases the marks obtained also increases.
- As income increases, the expenditure also increases.

The Fig. 2.9 shows scatterplot of the positive relationship.

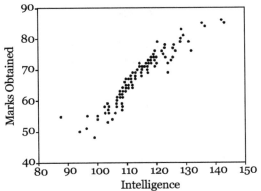

Fig. 2.9: Positive correlation: Scatter showing the positive correlation between intelligence and marks obtained

Negative Correlation

The Negative correlation indicates that as the value of one variable increases, the value of the other variable decreases. Consequently, as the value of one variable decreases, the value of the other variable increases. This means that the two variables move in the opposite direction. For example,
- As the intelligence (IQ) increases the errors on reasoning task decreases.
- As hope increases, depression decreases.

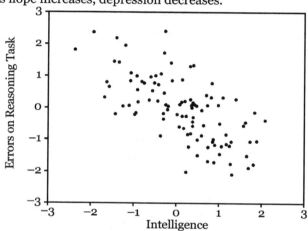

Fig. 2.10: Negative correlation: Scatter showing the negative correlation between intelligence and errors on reasoning task

No Relationship

Apart from positive and negative correlations, it is also possible that there is no relationship between x and y. That is the two variables do not share any relationship. If they do not share any relationship (that is, technically the correlation coefficient is zero), then, obviously, the direction of the correlation is neither positive nor negative. It is often called as zero correlation or no correlation. For example, guess the relationship between shoe size and intelligence.

This sounds an erratic question because there is no reason for any relationship between them. Therefore, there is no relationship between these two variables.

The data of one hundred individuals is plotted in Fig. 2.11. It shows the scatterplot for no relationship.

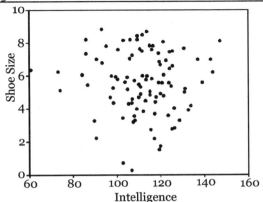

Fig. 2.11: Scatter between shoe size and intelligence

Q6. Write a short note on 'variance and covariance: building blocks of correlations'. [Dec-2014, Q.No.-10(c)]

Ans. Understanding product moment correlation coefficient requires understanding of mean, variance and covariance. These three concepts are as follows:

Mean

Mean of variable X (symbolised as $\overline{X}$) is sum of scores $\left(\sum_{i=1}^{n} X_i\right)$ divided by number of observations (n). The mean is calculated in the following way:

$$\overline{X} = \frac{\sum_{i=1}^{n} X_i}{n}$$

We can use this as a basic element to compute correlation.

Variance

The variance of a variable X (symbolised as S_X^2) is the sum of squares of the deviations of each X score from the mean of X $\left(\sum(X-\overline{X})^2\right)$ divided by number of observations (n), i.e.

$$S_X^2 = \frac{\sum(X-\overline{X})^2}{n}$$

Covariance

The covariance between X and Y (Cov_{XY} or S_{XY}) can be stated as:

$$Cov_{XY} = \frac{\sum(X-\overline{X})(Y-\overline{Y})}{n}$$

Covariance is a number that indicates the association between two variables. To compute covariance, deviation of each score on X from its mean ($\overline{x}$) and deviation of each score on Y from its mean ($\overline{y}$) is initially calculated. Then products of these deviations are obtained. Then, these products are summated. This sum gives us the numerator for covariance. Divide this sum by number of observations (n). The resulting number is covariance.

Q7. Discuss the Karl Pearson's coefficient of correlation.

Ans. Of the several mathematical methods of measuring correlation, the Karl Pearson's method, popularly known as Pearson's coefficient of correlation, is most widely used in practice. It is also known as product moment coefficient of correlation. It is denoted by the symbol r. It is one of the very few symbols that are used universally for describing the degree of correlation between two series. The formula for computing Pearsonian r is:

$$r = \frac{\sum xy}{N\sigma_x \sigma_y} \qquad \ldots(i)$$

Here $x = (X - \bar{X})$; $y = (Y - \bar{Y})$

σ_x = Standard deviation of series X

σ_y = Standard deviation of series Y

N = Number of pairs of observations
r = Correlation co-efficient

This method is to be applied only where deviations of items are taken from actual mean and not from assumed mean.

The above formula for computing Pearson's coefficient of correlation can be transformed to the following form, which is easier to apply:

$$r = \frac{\sum xy}{\sqrt{\sum x^2 \times \sum y^2}} \qquad \ldots(ii)$$

where $x = (X - \bar{X})$ and $y = (Y - \bar{Y})$

It is obvious that while applying this formula, we have not to calculate separately the standard deviation of X and Y series as is required by formula (i). This simplifies greatly the task of calculating correlation coefficient.

Steps
(1) Take the deviation of X series from the mean of X and denote these deviations by x.
(2) Square these deviations and obtain the total, i.e. $\sum x^2$.
(3) Take the deviations of Y series from the mean of Y and denote these deviations by y.
(4) Square these deviations and obtain the total, i.e. $\sum y^2$.
(5) Multiply the deviations of X and Y series and obtain the total, i.e. $\sum xy$.

Substitute the values of $\sum xy$, $\sum x^2$ and $\sum y^2$ in formula (ii).

When Deviations are taken from an Assumed Mean

When actual mean is in fraction, say the actual mean of X and Y series are 20.167 and 29.23, the calculation of correlation by the actual mean method would involve too many calculations and would take a lot of time. In such a case, we make use of the assumed mean method for finding out correlation.

Correlation and Regression

When deviations are taken from an assumed mean, the following formula is applicable:

$$r = \frac{N\sum dxdy - \sum dx \times \sum dy}{\sqrt{N\sum dx^2 - (\sum dx)^2}\sqrt{N\sum dy^2 - (\sum dy)^2}}$$

where dx = Deviations of X series from an assumed mean, i.e. $(X - \bar{X})$.

dy = Deviations of Y series from an assumed mean, i.e. $(Y - \bar{Y})$.

$\sum dx$ = Sum of the deviations of X series from an assumed mean.

$\sum dy$ = Sum of the deviations of Y series from an assumed mean.

$\sum dxdy$ = Sum of the product of the deviations of X and Y series from their assumed means

$\sum d_x^2$ = Sum of the squares of the deviations of X series from an assumed mean

$\sum d_y^2$ = Sum of the squares of the deviations of Y series from an assumed mean

Direct Method of Finding out Correlation Coefficient

Correlation coefficient can also be calculated without taking deviations of items either from actual mean or assumed mean, i.e. actual X and Y values. The formula in such a case is:

$$r = \frac{N\sum XY - (\sum X)(\sum Y)}{\sqrt{N\sum X^2 - (\sum X)^2}\sqrt{N\sum Y^2 - (\sum Y)^2}}$$

This formula would give the same answer as we get when deviations of items are taken from actual mean or assumed mean.

Q8. What are the properties of the coefficient of correlation?

Ans. The following are the important properties of the correlation coefficient, r:

- The coefficient of correlation lies between −1 and +1. Symbolically, $-1 \leq r \leq +1$.
- The coefficient of correlation is independent of change of scale and origin of the variables X and Y.
- The coefficient of correlation is the geometric mean of two regression coefficients. Symbolically, $r = \sqrt{b_{xy} \times b_{yx}}$
- The degree of relationship between the two variables is symmetric as shown below:

$$r_{xy} = \frac{\sum xy}{N\sigma_x\sigma_y} = \frac{\sum yx}{N\sigma_y\sigma_x} = r_{yx}.$$

Q9. Discuss in brief about the concept of unreliability of measurement.

Ans. One of the psychometric property psychological instruments should possess is reliability. Reliability refers to consistency of a measurement. If the instrument is consistent, then the test has high reliability. But at times one of the variable or both the variables may have lower reliability. In this case, the correlation between two less reliable variable reduces. Generally, while interpreting the correlation, the reliability is assumed to be high. The general interpretations of correlations are not valid if the reliability is low. This reduction in the correlation can be adjusted for the reliability of the psychological test. More advanced procedures are available in the books of psychological testing and statistics. They involve calculating disattenuated correlations. Correlation between two variables that have less than perfect reliability is adjusted for unreliability. This is called as disattenuated correlation. If both variables were perfectly reliable then correlation between them is disattenuated correlation.

Outliers

Outliers are extreme score on one of the variables or both the variables. The presence of outliers has deterring impact on the correlation value. The strength and degree of the correlation are affected by the presence of outlier. Suppose we want to compute correlation between height and weight. They are known to correlate positively. Look at the figure below. One of the scores has low score on weight and high score on height (probably, some anorexia patient).

Fig. 2.12 shows the impact of an outlier observation on correlation. Without the outlier, the correlation is 0.95. The presence of an outlier has drastically reduced a correlation coefficient to 0.45.

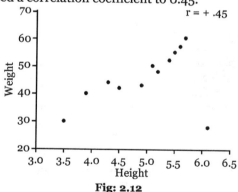

Fig: 2.12

Curvilinearity

The Pearson's product moment correlation is appropriate if the relationship between two variables is linear. The relationships are curvilinear then other techniques need to be used. If the degree of Curvilinearity is not very high, high score on both the variables go together, low scores go together, but the pattern is not linear then the useful option is Spearman's rho.

Q10. Explain point biserial correlation.

Ans. Point Biserial Correlation is a specialised form of the product moment correlation. It is used as a measure of linear correlation between a continuous measurement variable and a genuine dichotomous nominal

Correlation and Regression

variable. The point biserial correlation is especially useful in the analysis of the item of a test, i.e. in item-test correlations.

Point Biserial Correlation (r_{pb}) is Pearson's Product moment correlation between one truly dichotomous variable and other continuous variable. Algebraically, the r_{pb}=r. So we can calculate r_{pb} in a similar way.

Calculation of r_{pb}

As an example of the calculation of the Point Biserial Correlation (r_{pb}), we will use the date in Table 2.2. These are the cases of male (Sex=0) weights and the female (Sex=1) weights. We have chosen unequal numbers of males and females just to show that it is possible to do so.

Table 2.2: Calculation of point biserial correlation for weights of males and females

Sex	Weight	Sex	Weight
0	150	1	130
0	140	1	138
0	180	1	121
0	190	1	125
0	145	1	116
0	150	1	145
0	164	1	150
0	140	1	150
0	142	1	125
0	136	1	130
0	123	1	120
0	155	1	130
1	140	1	131
1	120		

$Mean_{male} = 151.25$ $Mean_{female} = 131.4$
$S_{male} = 18.869$ $S_{female} = 10.979$
$Mean_{weight} = 140.222$ $Mean_{sex} = 0.556$
$S_{weight} = 17.792$ $S_{sex} = 0.506$
$Cov_{XY} = -5.090$

$$r = \frac{Cov_{XY}}{S_X S_Y} = \frac{-5.090}{0.506 \times 17.792} = -0.565$$

The Pearson's correlation (point biserial correlation) between sex and marks obtained is −0.565. The sign is positive. The sign is arbitrary and need to be interpreted depending on the coding of the dichotomous group. The mean of the group coded 1 is less than the mean of the croup coded 0. The strength of correlation coefficient is calculated in a similar way. The correlation is −0.565, so the percentage of variance shared by both the variables is r^2 for Pearson's correlation. Same would hold true for point biserial correlation. The $(r_{pb})^2$ is $(-0.565)^2 = 0.319$. This means that 32% of the variability in weight can be accounted for by gender.

Relationship between r_{pb} and t

The relationship between r_{pb} and t is very important. It can be shown as

$$r_{pb}^2 = \frac{t^2}{t^2 + df}$$

where t is obtained from the t-test of the difference of means (for example, between the mean weights of males and females) and df = the degrees of freedom for t, namely $N_1 + N_2 - 2$. For example, if we were to run a t-test on the difference in mean weight between male and female subjects, using a t for two independent groups with unequal sample sizes,

$$s_p^2 = \frac{(N_1 - 1)s_1^2 + (N_2 - 1)s_2^2}{N_1 + N_2 - 2}$$

$$= \frac{11(18.869^2) + 14(10.979^2)}{12 + 15 - 2} = 224.159$$

$$t = \frac{\overline{X}_1 - \overline{X}_2}{\sqrt{\frac{s_p^2}{N_1} + \frac{s_p^2}{N_2}}} = \frac{151.25 - 131.4}{\sqrt{\frac{224.159}{12} + \frac{224.159}{15}}} = \frac{19.85}{5.799} = 3.42$$

With 25 df, the difference between the two groups is significant. We now calculate

$$r_{pb}^2 = \frac{t^2}{t^2 + df} = \frac{3.42^2}{3.42^2 + 25} = .319$$

$$r_{pb} = \sqrt{.319} = .565$$

which, with the exception of the arbitrary sign of the coefficient, agrees with the more direct calculation.

Significance Testing of r_{pb}

A test of r_{pb} against the null hypothesis $H_o : \rho = 0$ is simple to construct. Because r_{pb} is a Pearson product-moment coefficient, it can be tested in the same way as any r. Namely,

$$t = \frac{r_{pb}\sqrt{n-2}}{\sqrt{1-r_{pb}^2}}$$

on n − 2 df. Furthermore, because this equation can be derived directly from the definition of r_{pb}^2, the t = 3.42 obtained here is the same (except possible for the sign) as a t-test between the two levels of the dichotomous variable. This makes sense when we realise that a statement that males and females differ in weight is the same as the statement that weight varies with sex.

Q11. Discuss the concept of phi coefficient.

Ans. The phi (ϕ) coefficient is used when both variables are genuine dichotomies scored 1 or 0. For example, phi would be used to describe the relationship between the gender of high school students and whether they are counseled to take college preparatory courses or not. Gender is dichotomised as male = 0, female = 1. Being counseled to take college preparatory courses is scored 1, and not being so counseled is scored 0. It is possible to enter the pairs of dichotomous scores (1's and 0's) into a programme that computers Pearson r's and arrive at the phi-coefficient.

If we find the phi coefficient in school A is –0.15, which indicates that there is a slight tendency to counsel more boys than girls to take college preparatory courses. If in school B the phi coefficient is –0.51, it indicates a strong tendency in the same direction. As with the other correlations, the phi coefficient indicates both direction and strength or relationships.

Significance Testing of Phi (ϕ)

The significance can be tested by using the Chi-Square (χ^2) distribution.

- The ϕ can be converted into the χ^2 by obtaining a product of n and ϕ^2.
- The chi-square of $n\phi^2$ will have df = 1.
- The null and alternative hypothesis are as follows:

$H_o : \rho = 0$

$H_A : \rho > 0$

$\chi^2 = n\phi^2$

If the obtained value of the chi-square is less than the tabled value, we accept the null hypothesis.

One needs to know that this is primarily because of the small sample size. If we take a larger sample, then the values would be significant. The relationship between χ^2 and ϕ are:

$$\phi = \sqrt{\frac{\chi^2}{n}}$$

So one can compute the chi-square and then calculate the phi-coefficient.

Q12. Describe and explain the concept of Biserial and Tetrachoric correlation.

Ans. Biserial Correlation

The biserial correlation coefficient (r_b) is a measure of correlation. It is like the point-biserial correlation. But point-biserial correlation is computed while one of the variables is dichotomous and do not have any underlying continuity. If a variable has underlying continuity but measured dichotomously, then the biserial correlation can be calculated.

Suppose we measure hope with BHS and measure mood by classifying those who have clinically low vs. normal mood. Actually, it is fair to assume that mood is a normally distributed variable.

But this variable is measured discretely and takes only two values, low mood (0) and normal mood (1).

Let's call continuous variable as Y and dichotomised variable as X. The values taken by X are 0 and 1.

So biserial correlation is a correlation coefficient between two continuous variables (X and Y), out of which one is measured dichotomously (X). The formula is very similar to the point-biserial but yet different:

$$r_b = \left[\frac{\overline{Y}_1 - \overline{Y}_0}{S_Y}\right]\left[\frac{P_0 P_1}{h}\right]$$

Where

$\overline{Y}_0$ and $\overline{Y}_1$ = Y score means for data pairs with an X score of 0 and 1, respectively;

P_0 and P_1 = Proportions of data pairs with X scores of 0 and 1, respectively;

S_Y = Standard deviation for the Y data; and

h = ordinate or the height of the standard normal distribution at the point which divides the proportions of P_0 and P_1.

The relationship between the point-biserial and the biserial correlation is as follows:

$$r_b = \frac{r_{pb}\sqrt{P_0 P_1}}{h}$$

Tetrachoric Correlation (r_{TET})

Tetrachoric correlation is a correlation between two dichotomous variables that have underlying continuous distribution. If the two variables are measured in a more refined way, then the continuous distribution will result. For example, attitude to females and attitude towards liberalisation are two variables to be correlated. Now, we simply measure them as having positive or negative attitude. So we have 0 (negative attitude) and 1 (positive attitude) scores available on both the variables. Then the correlation between these two variables can be computed using Tetrachoric correlation (r_{tet}).

The correlation can be expressed as:
r = cosθ

where, θ is angle between the vector X and Y. Using this logic, r_{tet} can also be calculated.

$$r_{tet} = \cos\left[\frac{180°}{1+\sqrt{\frac{ad}{bc}}}\right]$$

For example, look at the following data summarised in Table 2.3.

Table 2.3: Data for Tetrachoric correlation

		X variable : Attitude towards women		
		0 (Negative attitude)	1 (Positive attitude)	Sum of row
Attitude towards Liberalisation	0 (Negative attitude)	68 (a)	32 (b)	100
	1 (Positive attitude)	30 (c)	70 (d)	100
	Sum of columns	98	102	total = 200

The table values are self-explanatory. Out of 200 individuals, 68 have negative attitude towards both variables, 32 have negative attitude to liberalisation but positive attitude to women, and so on. The tetrachoric correlation can be computed as follows:

$$r_{tet} = \cos\left[\frac{180°}{1+\sqrt{\frac{ad}{bc}}}\right] = \cos\left[\frac{180°}{1+\sqrt{\frac{(68)(70)}{(30)(32)}}}\right] = \cos 55.784° = .562$$

Therefore, the tetrachoric correlation between attitude towards liberalisation and attitude towards women is positive.

Q13. Discuss the rank correlation method.

Ans. Rank correlation coefficient method of finding out co-variability or the lack of it between two variables was developed by the British Psychologist Charles Edward Spearman in 1904. This measure is especially useful when quantitative measures for certain factors (such as in the evaluation of leadership ability or the judgement of female beauty) cannot be fixed, but the individual in the group can be arranged in order thereby obtaining for each individual a number indicating his/her rank in the group. Spearman's rank correlation is defined as:

$$R = 1 - \frac{6\sum D^2}{N(N^2 - 1)}$$

where R= Rank coefficient of correlation;
   D= Difference of Rank between paired items in two series; and
   N=No. of observations.

Features of Spearman's Correlation Coefficient
- The sum of the differences of ranks between two variables shall be zero. Symbolically, $\sum d = 0$.

- Spearman's correlation coefficient is distribution-free or non-parametric because no strict assumptions are made about the form of population from which sample observations are drawn.
- The Spearman's correlation coefficient is nothing but Karl Pearson's correlation coefficient between the ranks. Hence, it can be interpreted in the same manner as Pearsonian correlation coefficient.

In rank correlation, there are two types of problems:

Where Ranks are Given:

Where actual ranks are given to us, the steps required for computing rank correlation are:

- Take the differences of the two ranks, i.e. $(R_1 - R_2)$ and denote these differences by D.
- Square these differences and obtain the total $\sum D^2$.
- Apply the formula $R = 1 - \dfrac{6 \sum D^2}{N^3 - N}$

Spearman's rho with Tied Ranks

The ranks are known as tied ranks when two or more subjects have the same score on a variable. In this situation, we cannot apply the Spearman's rho (r_s) formula. A correction is required in this formula in order to calculate correct value of Spearman's rho. The easier procedure of correction actually uses Pearson's formula on the ranks. The formula and the steps are as follows:

$$r = r_s = \dfrac{\sum XY - \dfrac{(\sum X)(\sum Y)}{n}}{\sqrt{\left[\sum X^2 - \dfrac{(\sum X)^2}{n}\right]\left[\sum Y^2 - \dfrac{(\sum Y)^2}{n}\right]}}$$

where,
   r_s = Spearman's rho;
   X = Ranks of variable X;
   Y = Rank on variable Y; and
   n = Number of pairs.

Steps for r_s with Tied Ranks

(1) If the data are not in ranks, then convert it into rank-order.
(2) Appropriately rank the ties (Cross-check the ranking by using sum of ranks check). This is the basic information for the Spearman's rho.
(3) Compute the square of rank of X and rank of Y for all the observations.
(4) Multiply the rank of X by rank of Y for each observation.
(5) Obtain sum of all the columns. Now all the basic data for the computation is available.
(6) Enter this data into the formula and calculate r_s.

Q14. Discuss Kendall's *tau*. Also, explain its significance testing.

Ans. Kendall's *tau* is another useful measure of correlation. It is as an alternative to Spearman's rho (r_s). This correlation procedure was developed by Kendall (1938). Kendall's *tau* is based on an analysis of two sets of ranks, X and Y. Kendall's *tau* is symbolised as τ, which is a lowercase Greek letter tau. The parameter (population value) is symbolised as τ and the statistics computed on the sample is symbolised as $\tilde{\tau}$. The range of *tau* is from − 1.00 to + 1.00. The interpretation of *tau* is based on the sign and the value of coefficient. The *tau* value closer to ±1.00 indicates stronger relationship. Positive value of *tau* indicates positive relationship and vice versa. It should be noted that Kendall's Concordance Coefficient is a different statistics and should not be confused with Kendall's *tau*.

Null and Alternative Hypothesis

When the Kendall's *tau* is computed as a descriptive statistics, statistical hypothesis testing is not required. If the sample statistic $\tilde{\tau}$ is computed to estimate population correlation τ, then null and alternative hypothesis are required.

The null hypothesis states that:

$H_o : \tau = 0$

It stated that the value of Kendall's *tau* between X and Y is zero in the population represented by sample.

The alternative hypothesis states that:

$H_A : \tau \neq 0$

It states that the value of Kendall's *tau* between X and Y is not zero in the population represented by sample. This alternative hypothesis requires a two-tailed test.

Depending on the theory, the other alternatives could be written. They are either:

- $H_A : \tau < 0$ or
- $H_A : \tau > 0$.

The first H_A denotes that the population value of Kendall's *tau* is smaller than zero.

The second H_A denotes that the population value of Kendall's *tau* is greater than zero. Remember, only one of them has to be tested and not both. One-tailed test is required for these hypotheses.

Logic of Tau and Computation

The *tau* is based on concordance and discordance between two sets of ranks. For example, table 2.4 shows ranks of four subjects on variables X and Y as RX and RY. In order to obtain concordant and discordant pairs, we need to order one of the variables according to the ranks, from lowest to highest (we have ordered X in this fashion).

Take a pair of ranks for two subjects A (1,1) and B (2,3) on X and Y.

Now, if sign or the direction of $R_X - R_X$ for subject A and B is similar to the sign or direction of $R_Y - R_Y$ for subject A and B, then the pair of ranks is said to be concordant (i.e., in agreement).

In case of subject A and B, the $R_X - R_X$ is $(1 - 2 = -1)$ and $R_Y - R_Y$ is also $(1 - 3 = -2)$. The sign or direction of A and B pair is in agreement. So pair A and B is called as concordant pair.

In second example of B and C pair, the $R_X - R_X$ is $(2 - 3 = -1)$ and $R_Y - R_Y$ is also $(3 - 2 = +1)$. The sign or the direction of B and C pair is not in agreement. This pair is called as discordant pair.

Table 2.4

Subject	R_x	R_y
A	1	1
B	2	2
C	3	3
D	4	4

Now, we illustrate a method to obtain the number of concordant (n_C) and discordant (n_D) pairs of this small data in the table 4.4 above.

Steps for computing Kendall's *Tau* are as follows:

Step 1: First, Ranks of X are placed in second row in the ascending order.
Step 2: Accordingly, ranks of Y are arranged in the third row.
Step 3: Then the ranks of Y are entered diagonally.
Step 4: Start with the first element in the diagonal, which is 1 (row 4).
Step 5: Now move across the row.
Step 6: Compare it (1) with each column element of Y. If it is smaller then enter C in the intersection. If it is larger, then enter D in the intersection. For example, 1 is smaller than 3 (column 3) so C is entered.
Step 7: In the next row (row 5), 3 is in the diagonal which is greater than 2 (column 4) of Y, so D is entered in the intersection.
Step 8: Then "C and D" are computed for each row.
Step 9: The n_C is obtained from $\sum\sum C$ (i.e. 5) and
Step 10: n_D is obtained from $\sum\sum D$ (i.e. 1).
Step 11: These values are entered in the equation:

$$\tilde{\tau} = \frac{n_C - n_D}{\left[\dfrac{n(n-1)}{2}\right]}$$

where,

$\tilde{\tau}$ = value of τ obtained on sample;
n_C = number of concordant pairs;
n_D = number of discordant pairs; and
n = number of subjects.

Table 2.5

Correlation and Regression

Subject	A	B	C	D	ΣC	ΣD
Rank of X	1	2	3	4		
Rank of Y	1	3	2	4		
		1	C	C	3	0
		3	D	C	1	1
			2	C	1	0
				4	0	0
					ΣΣC = 5	ΣΣD = 1

$$\tilde{\tau} = \frac{n_C - n_D}{\left[\frac{n(n-1)}{2}\right]} = \frac{5-1}{\left[\frac{4(4-1)}{2}\right]} = \frac{4}{6} = 0.667$$

Significance Testing of tau (τ)

The statistical significance testing of Kendall's *tau* is carried out by using z transformation. The z can be calculated as:

$$z = \frac{\tilde{\tau}}{\sqrt{\frac{2(2n+5)}{9n(n-1)}}}$$

Q15. Explain the concept of partial correlation.

Ans. A partial correlation between two variables is one that partials out or nullifies the effects of a third variable (or a number of other variables) upon both the variables being correlated. Two variables, A and B, are closely related. The correlation between them is partialled out, or controlled for the influence of one or more variables is known as partial correlation. Therefore, when it is assumed that some other variable is influencing the correlation between A and B, then the influence of this variable(s) is partialled out for both A and B. Hence, it can be considered as a correlation between two sets of residuals. Suppose a simple case of correlation between A and B is partialled out for C. This can be represented as $r_{AB.C}$ which is read as correlation between A and B partialled out for C. The correlation between A and B can be partialled out for more variables as well.

For example, the researcher is interested in computing the correlation between anxiety and academic achievement controlled from intelligence. Then correlation between academic achievement (A) and anxiety (B) will be controlled for Intelligence (C). This can be represented as: $r_{\text{Academic Achievement(A) Anxiety (B). Intelligence (C)}}$. To calculate the partial correlation (r_p); we will need a data on all three variables. The computational formula is as follows:

$$r_p = r_{AB.C} = \frac{r_{AB} - r_{AC} r_{BC}}{\sqrt{(1 - r_{AC}^2)(1 - r_{BC}^2)}}$$

The data of academic achievement, anxiety and intelligence is given below in Table 2.6. Here, the academic achievement test, the anxiety scale and intelligence test is administered on ten students.

Table 2.6: Data of academic achievement, anxiety and intelligence for 10 students

Student	Academic Achievement	Anxiety	intelligence
1	15	6	25
2	18	3	29
3	13	8	27
4	14	6	24
5	19	2	30
6	11	3	21
7	17	4	26
8	20	4	31
9	10	5	20
10	16	7	25

In order to compute the partial correlation between the academic achievement and anxiety partialled out for Intelligence, we first need to compute the Pearson's Product moment correlation coefficient between all three variables.

The correlation between anxiety (B) and academic achievement (A) is – 0.369.

The correlation between intelligence (C) and academic achievement (A) is 0.918.

The correlation between anxiety (B) and intelligence (C) is – 0.245.

Now, we can calculate the partial correlation as:

$$r_{AB.C} = \frac{r_{AB} - r_{AC}r_{BC}}{\sqrt{(1-r_{AC}^2)(1-r_{BC}^2)}} = \frac{-0.369 - (0.918 \times -0.245)}{\sqrt{(1-0.918^2)(1-(-0.245^2))}} = \frac{-.1441}{0.385} = -0.375$$

The partial correlation between the two variables, academic achievement and anxiety controlled for intelligence, is –0.375. We will realise that the correlation between academic achievement and anxiety is –0.369. Whereas, after partialling out for the effect of intelligence, the correlation between them has almost remained unchanged. While computing this correlation, the effect of intelligence on both the variables, academic achievement and anxiety, was removed.

The following figure explains the relationship between them:

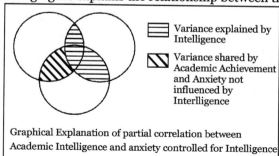

Graphical Explanation of partial correlation between Academic Intelligence and anxiety controlled for Intelligence

Fig. 2.13: Venn diagram explaining the partial correlation

Correlation and Regression

Significance Testing of the Partial Correlation

We can test the significance of the partial correlation for the null hypothesis

$$H_o : \rho_p = 0$$

and the alternative hypothesis

$$H_o : \rho_p = 0$$

where, the ρ_p denotes the population partial correlation coefficient. The t-distribution is used for this purpose. Following formula is used to calculate the t-value.

$$t = \frac{r_p \sqrt{n-v}}{\sqrt{1-r_p^2}}$$

where,

r_p = partial correlation computed on sample, $r_{AB.C}$
n = sample size,
v = total number of variables employed in the analysis.

The significance of the r_p is tested at the df = n – v.

In the present example, we can employ significance testing as follows:

$$t = \frac{r_p\sqrt{n-v}}{\sqrt{1-r_p^2}} = \frac{-.375\sqrt{10-3}}{\sqrt{1-(-.375^2)}} = \frac{-0.992}{0.927} = -1.07$$

We test the significance of this value at the df = 7 in the t- distribution table [Appendix table C]. We will realise that at the df = 7, the table provides the critical value of 2.36 at 0.05 level of significance. The obtained value of –1.07 is smaller than this value. Therefore, we accept the null hypothesis stating that $H_o : \rho_p = 0$.

Large sample example:

A counselling psychologist is interested in understanding the relationship between practice of study skills and marks obtained. But s/he is skeptical about the effectiveness of the study skills. S/he believes that they can be effective because they are good cognitive techniques or they can be effective simply because the students believe that the study skills are going to help them. The first is attribute of the skills while second is placebo effect. S/he wanted to test this hypothesis. So, along with measuring the hours spent in practicing the study skills and marks obtained, s/he also took measures on belief that study skill training is useful. S/he collected the data on 100 students. The obtained correlations are as follows.

The correlation between practice of study skills (A) and unit test marks (B) is 0.69

The correlation between practice of study skills (A) and belief about usefulness of study skills (C) is 0.46

The correlation between marks in unit test (B) and belief about usefulness of study skills (C) is 0.39

$$r_{AB.C} = \frac{r_{AB} - r_{AC}r_{BC}}{\sqrt{(1-r_{AC}^2)(1-r_{BC}^2)}} = \frac{0.69 - (0.46 \times 0.39)}{\sqrt{(1-0.46^2)(1-0.39^2)}} = \frac{.5106}{0.8175} = 0.625$$

The partial correlation between practice of study skills (A) and unit test marks (B) is 0.625. Let's test the null hypothesis about the partial correlation for a null hypothesis which states that $H_0 : \rho_p = 0$.

$$t = \frac{r_p \sqrt{n-v}}{\sqrt{1-r_p^2}} = \frac{0.625\sqrt{100-3}}{\sqrt{1-.625^2}} = \frac{6.15}{0.781} = 7.87$$

The t-value is significant at 0.05 level. So we reject the null hypothesis and accept that there is a partial correlation between A and B. This means that the partial correlation between practice of study skills (A) and unit test marks (B) is non-zero at population. We can conclude that the correlation between practice of study skills (A) and unit test marks (B) still exists even after controlled for the belief in the usefulness of the study skills. Thus, the skepticism of our researcher is unwarranted.

Q16. Explain the concept of linear regression.

Or

Write a short note on linear regression.

[June-2015, Q.No.-11]

Ans. Regression goes one-step beyond correlation in identifying the relationship between two variables. It creates an equation so that values can be predicted within the range framed by the data. That is if we know X, we can predict Y and if we know Y, we can predict X. This is done by an equation called regression equation.

When the correlation between X and Y are scattered in the graph and we can draw a straight line covering the entire data. This line is called the regression line.

Here is the line and the regression equation superimposed on the scatterplot:

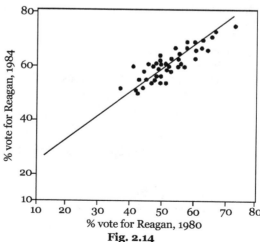

Fig. 2.14

From this line, we can predict X from Y that is % votes in 1984 if known, we can find out the % of votes in 1980. Similarly, if we know % of votes in 1980, we can know % of votes in 1984.

The regression line seen in the above diagram is close to the scatterplots. That is the predicted values need to be as close as possible to the data. Such a line is called the best fitting line or regression line. There are certain guidelines for regression lines:
 (1) Use regression lines when there is a significant correlation to predict values.
 (2) Do not use if there is not a significant correlation.
 (3) Stay within the range of the data. *For example*, if the data is from 10 to 60, do not predict a value for 400.
 (4) Do not make predictions for a population based on another population's regression line.

The y-variable is often termed as the criterion variable and the x-variable as the predictor variable. The slope is often called the regression coefficient and the intercept the regression constant. The slope can also be expressed compactly as $\beta_1 = r \times s_y / s_x$.

Normally, we then predict values for y based on values of x. This still does not mean that y is caused by x. It is still imperative for the researcher to understand the variables under study and the context they operate under before making such an interpretation. Of course, simple algebra also allows one to calculate x values for a given value of y.

The regression equation can also be written as

$$y = \beta_0 + \beta_1 x$$

where y, β_0, and β_1 represents population statistics. If a cap appears above the variable, then they probably represent sample statistics. Remember x is our independent variable for both the line and the data.

The y-intercept of the regression line is β_0 and the slope is β_1. The following formulas give the y-intercept and the slope of the equation.

$$\beta_0 = \frac{(\sum y)(\sum x^2) - (\sum x)(\sum xy)}{n(\sum x^2) - (\sum x)^2}$$

$$\beta_1 = \frac{n(\sum xy) - (\sum x)(\sum y)}{n(\sum x^2) - (\sum x)^2}$$

Q17. Briefly discuss about the part or semi-partial correlation.

Ans. The part correlation is also known as semi-partial correlation (r_{sp}). Semi-partial correlation or part correlation is correlation between two variables, one of which is partialled for a third variable.

In partial correlation $(r_p = r_{AB.C})$, the effect of the third variable (C) is partialled out from BOTH the variables (A and B).

In semi-partial correlations $\left(r_{sp} = r_{A(B.C)}\right)$, as the name suggests, the effect of third variable (C) was partialled out from only one variable (B) and NOT from both the variables.

In order to compute the semi-partial correlation coefficient, following formula can be used:

$$r_{SP} = r_{A(B.C)} = \frac{r_{AB} - r_{AC}r_{BC}}{\sqrt{1 - r_{BC}^2}}$$

where,

$r_{A(B.C)}$ is a semi-partial correlation of A with the B after linear relationship that C has with B is removed;

r_{AB} Pearson's product moment correlation between A and B;

r_{AC} Pearson's product moment correlation between A and C; and

r_{BC} Pearson's product moment correlation between B and C.

The significance of the semi-partial correlation can be tested by using t-distribution. The null hypothesis and the alternate hypothesis are as follows.

$H_0 : \rho_{SP} = 0$

$H_A : \rho_{SP} \neq 0$

Where, the ρ_{SP} is the semi-partial correlation in the population. We test the null hypothesis whether the semi-partial correlation in the population is zero. This can be done by using following formula:

$$t = \frac{r_{SP}\sqrt{n-v}}{\sqrt{1-r_{SP}^2}}$$

where,

t = students t-value;

r_{SP} = semi-partial correlation computed on sample;

n = sample size; and

v = number of variables used in the analysis.

The significance of this t-value is tested at the df = n−v, when three variables are involved then the df = n − 3.

Q18. Write a short note on multiple correlation coefficient (R).
Ans. The multiple correlation coefficient (R) denotes a correlation of one variable with multiple other variables. The multiple correlation coefficient is denoted as $R_{A.BCD...k}$ which denotes that A is correlated with B, C, D upto k variables.

For example, we want to compute multiple correlation between A with B and C then it is expressed as $R_{A.BC}$. In this case, we create a linear combination of the B and C which is correlated with A.

For example, academic achievement, anxiety and intelligence are three variables. The correlation between academic achievement with the linear combination of anxiety and intelligence is multiple correlation.

This denotes the proportion of variance in academic achievement explained by intelligence and anxiety. We denote this as:

$R_{(Academic\ Achievement.\ Intelligence,\ Anxiety)}$, which is a multiple correlation.

The Multiple R can be calculated for two predictor variables as follows:

$$R_{A.BC} = \sqrt{\frac{r_{AB}^2 + r_{AC}^2 - 2r_{AB}r_{AC}r_{BC}}{1 - r_{BC}^2}}$$

where,

$R_{A.BC}$ = Multiple correlation between A and linear combination of B and C;

r_{AB} = Correlation between A and B;

r_{AC} = Correlation between A and C; and

r_{BC} = Correlation between B and C.

Q19. What do you understand by the regression analysis? Explain its significance.

Or

Explain the concept of regression. Give formula of regression line.

Or

Write a short note on Regression. [Dec-2014, Q.No.-10(d)]

Ans. Regression is the study of nature of relationship between the variables, so that one may be able to predict the unknown value of one variable for a known value of another variable.

If two variables are significantly correlated, and if there is some theoretical basis for doing so, it is possible to predict values of one variable from the other. This observation leads to a very important concept known as 'Regression Analysis'.

Regression analysis, in general sense, means the estimation or prediction of the unknown value of one variable from the known value of the other variable. It is one of the most important statistical tools which is extensively used in almost all sciences like natural, social and physical. It is specially used in business and economics to study the relationship between two or more variables that are related causally and for the estimation of demand and supply graphs, cost functions, production and consumption functions and so on.

According to M. M. Blair, "Regression analysis is a mathematical measure of the average relationship between two or more variables in terms of the original units of the data."

The study of regression is very useful and important in statistical analysis, which is clear from the following points:

- **Nature of Relationship:** Regression analysis explains the nature of relationship between two variables.
- **Estimation of Relationship:** The mutual relationship between two or more variables can be easily measured by regression analysis.

- **Prediction:** By the regression analysis, the value of a dependent variable can be predicated on the basis of an independent variable. For example, if price of a commodity rises, what will be the probable fall in demand; this can be predicated by regression.
- **Useful in Economic and Business Research:** Regression analysis is very useful in business and economic research. With the help of regression, business and economic policy can be formulated.

Formula for Regression Lines

- Regression Equation of Y on X:

$$Y - \overline{Y} = b_{yx}(X - \overline{X})$$

Where,
(When we use actual values of X and Y)

$$b_{yx} = \frac{N.\Sigma XY - \Sigma X.\Sigma Y}{N.\Sigma X^2 - (\Sigma X)^2}$$

Or
(When deviations are taken from actual means of X and Y)

$$b_{yx} = \frac{\Sigma xy}{\Sigma x^2}$$

where, $x = X - \overline{X}; y = Y - \overline{Y}$

Or
(When deviations are taken from assumed means of X and Y)

$$b_{yx} = \frac{N.\Sigma dxdy - \Sigma dx.\Sigma dy}{N.\Sigma dx^2 - (\Sigma dx)^2}$$

where, $dx = X - A$, $dy = Y - A$

Or
(When we use r, σ_y and σ_x)

$$= r \times \frac{\sigma_y}{\sigma_x}$$

- Regression Equation of X on Y:

$$X - \overline{X} = b_{xy}(Y - \overline{Y})$$

Where,
(When we use actual values of X and Y)

$$b_{xy} = \frac{N.\Sigma XY - \Sigma X.\Sigma Y}{N.\Sigma Y^2 - (\Sigma Y)^2}$$

Or
(When deviations are taken from actual mean)

$$b_{xy} = \frac{\Sigma xy}{\Sigma y^2}$$

Or

(When deviations are taken from assumed mean)

$$b_{xy} = \frac{N.\Sigma dxdy - \Sigma dx.\Sigma dy}{N \times \Sigma dy^2 - (\Sigma dy)^2}$$

Or

(When we use r, σ_x and σ_y)

$$b_{xy} = r \times \frac{\sigma_x}{\sigma_y}$$

- In Grouped Frequency Distribution

$$b_{yx} = \frac{N.\Sigma fdxdy - \Sigma fdx \Sigma fdy}{N.\Sigma fdx^2 - (\Sigma fdx)^2} \times \frac{i_x}{i_y}$$

and $b_{xy} = \dfrac{N.\Sigma fdxdy - \Sigma fdx \Sigma fdy}{N.\Sigma fdy^2 - (\Sigma fdy)^2} \times \dfrac{i_x}{i_y}$

Where, $N = \Sigma f$, stands for the total frequency.

Q20. What do know about predicting one variable from another is done?

Ans. In making prediction from one variable to another, the variable being predicted is called the dependent variable and the variable predicting the dependent variable is called the independent variable. The dependent variable may also be referred to as the criterion or outcome while the independent variable may also be referred to as the predictor or regressor. One way of facilitating such predictions is to obtain a linear equation that somehow fits, or represents, the available data. This equation can then be used to predict the variable Y from the variable X.

If X is predicting Y, then typically it is said that 'X is regressed on Y'.

Some variables can be used in prediction in psychology, which are given in Table 2.7. Look at the following statements.

Table 2.7: Statements having Two Variables

- Stress leads to health deterioration.
- Openness increases creativity.
- Extraversion increases social acceptance.
- Social support influences coping with mental health problems.
- Stigma about mental illness decides the help seeking behaviour.
- Parental intelligence leads to child's intelligence.
- Attitude to job and attrition depends on affective commitment to the organisation.

Let's identify the X and Y in statements, which are given in the box above:

- In the first statement, Stress (X) led to the health (Y) deterioration.
- In the second statement, Openness (X) increases the creativity (Y).
- In the third statement, Extroversion (X) increases the social acceptance (Y).

- In fourth statement, Social support (X) influences the coping with mental health problems (Y).
- In the fifth statement, Stigma about mental illness (X) decided the help seeking behaviour (Y).
- In the sixth statement, Parental intelligence (X) leads to child's intelligence (Y).
- In the last statement, Attitude (Y) to job and attrition depends on affective commitment(X) to the organisation.

Q21. Explain the simple linear regression model.

Or

How can you identify linear relationship between a dependent variable and an independent variable? Explain by examining the scatter diagram.

Ans. Let us start with an example. When the floor of a house is plastered with cement, we know that one should not walk on it until it gets set. The setting time is an important characteristic of cement and it is mandatory that any cement manufacturing company should adhere to certain specification limits. Once the cement is produced, its setting time cannot be changed. Therefore, the manufacturers should be in a position to predict the setting time well before it is produced. Fortunately, it is possible to do this because the setting time depends, to a large extent, on the chemical composition of the raw materials used to produce cement.

In Table 2.8, we will find data on 25 samples of cement. For each sample, we have a pair of observations (x, y), where x is percentage of SO_3 a chemical, and y is the setting time in minutes. Our aim is to study how y depends on x. We will refer to y as the dependent variable or response, and x as independent variable or regressor. We know that it is often easy to understand data through a graph. So, let us plot the data on a scatter diagram. A scatter diagram is a sample two–dimensional graph in which the horizontal axis represents x and the vertical axis represents y. Each pair of points is plotted on the graph.

Table 2.8: Data on SO_3 and Setting Time

S.No. (i)	Percentage of SO_3(x)	Setting Time (in minutes) (y)
1	1.84	190
2	1.91	192
3	1.90	210
4	1.66	194
5	1.48	170
6	1.26	160
7	1.21	143
8	1.32	164
9	2.11	200
10	0.94	136

11	2.25	206
12	0.96	138
13	1.71	185
14	2.35	210
15	1.65	178
16	1.19	170
17	1.56	160
18	1.53	160
19	0.96	140
20	1.67	168
21	1.68	152
22	1.28	160
23	1.35	116
24	1.49	145
25	1.78	170
Total	39.04	4217
Sum of Squares	64.446	726539

From this figure, we see that y increases as SO_3 increases. Whenever we find this type of increasing (or decreasing) trend in a scatter diagram, it indicates that there is a linear relationship between x and y. We may observe that the relationship is not perfect in the sense that a straight line cannot be drawn through all the points in the scatter diagram.

Nevertheless, we may approximate it with some linear equations. Suppose we use the formula y = 90 + 50x to predict y based on x. To examine how good this formula is, we need to compare the actual values of y with the corresponding predicated values. When x = 0.96, the predicted y is equal to 138(= 90 + 50 × 0.96). Let (x_i, y_i) denote the values of (x,y) for the ith sample. From Table 2.6, notice that $x_{12} = x_{19} = 0.96$ whereas $y_{12} = 138$ and $y_{19} = 140$.

Let $\hat{y}_i = 90 + 50 x_i$. That is, $\hat{y}_i$ is the predicated value of y (using y = 90 + 50x) for the ith sample. Since, $x_{12} = x_{19} = 0.96$, both $\hat{y}_{12}$ and $\hat{y}_{19}$ are equal to 138. The difference $\hat{e}_i = y_i - \hat{y}_i$, the error in prediction, is called the residual. Observe that $\hat{e}_{12} = 0$ and $\hat{e}_{19} = 2$. The formula we have considered above, y = 90 + 50x, is called a simple linear regression equation.

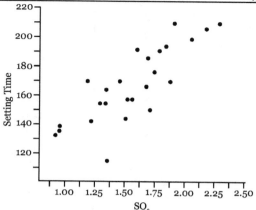

Fig. 2.15: Scatter Diagram of Setting Time vs SO_3

If we recall from our study of coordinate geometry, this equation is the equation of a straight line. We can easily see that $\hat{y}_i$ and $\hat{e}_i$ depend on the straight line we choose to predict y. That is, if we change the equation, let us say, from y = 90 + 50x to y = 100 + 45x, then the $\hat{y}_i$ and $\hat{e}_i$ will be different.

Q22. Write the procedure to get best linear regression formula.
Ans. The procedure to get best linear regression formula is as follows:

(1) Calculate a sum S_{xx} defined by

$$S_{xx} = \sum_{i=1}^{n} x_i^2 - n\bar{x}^2 \qquad \ldots(i)$$

where x_i's are the given values of the data and $\bar{x} = \dfrac{\sum x_i}{n}$ is the mean of the observed values and n is the sample size.

The sum S_{xx} is called the corrected sum of squares.

(2) Calculate a sum S_{xx} defined by

$$S_{xx} = \sum_{i=1}^{n} x_i^2 - n\bar{x}^2 \qquad \ldots(ii)$$

where x_i's are the given values of the data and $\bar{x} = \dfrac{\sum x_i}{n}$ is the mean of the observed values and n is the sample size.

The sum S_{xx} is called the corrected sum of squares.

(3) Calculate $\dfrac{S_{xy}}{S_{xx}} = b$ say. That is

$$b = \frac{S_{xy}}{S_{xx}} \qquad \ldots(iii)$$

(4) Find $\bar{y} - b\bar{x} = a$ say.

These measures define a and b which will give the best possible fit through the original X and Y points.

Alternatively, for fitting a regression equation of the type $\hat{Y} = a + bX$ to the given values of X and Y variables, we can find the values of the two constants, viz. a and b by using the following two normal equations:

$$\sum Y_i = na + b\sum X_i$$
$$\sum X_i Y_i = a\sum X_i + b\sum X_i^2$$

and then solving these equations for finding a and b values. Once these values are obtained and have been put in the equation, $\hat{Y} = a + bX$, we say that we have fitted the regression equation of Y on X to the given data. In a similar fashion, we can develop the regression equation of X and Y, viz. $\hat{X} = a + bX$, presuming Y as an independent variable and X as dependent variable.

Q23. Enumerate the assumptions of regression analysis.

Ans. Some of the important assumptions for doing the regression analysis are as follows:
- Independence among the pairs of score.
  This assumption implies that the scores of any two observations (subjects in case of most of the psychological data) are not influenced by each other. Each pair of observation is independent. This is assured when different subjects provide different pairs of observation.
- The variance of the error terms is constant for each value of X.
- The relationship between X and Y is linear.
- The error terms follow the normal distribution with a mean zero and variance one.
- Independence of Error Terms. The error terms are independent. They are uncorrelated.
- The population of X and the population of Y follow normal distribution and the population pair of scores of X and Y has a normal bivariate distribution.

The last assumption states that the population distribution of both the variables (X and Y) is normal. This also means that the pair of scores follows bivariate normal distribution. This assumption can be tested by using statistical tests for normality.

Q24. Discuss Multiple Linear Regression.

Ans. In multiple regression, we try to predict the value of one variable given the values of other variables. Let us consider the case of three variables y, x_1 and x_2. We assume there exists linear relationship between them. Thus, $y = a + bx_1 + cx_2$

where, a, b and c are constants.

We apply the same method of ordinary least square to obtain the estimates $\left(\hat{a}, \hat{b} \text{ and } \hat{c}\right)$ of a, b and c to minimise the sum of the square of errors.

Thus, our task is to $\underset{\hat{a},\hat{b},\hat{c}}{\text{Min}} E = \sum e_i^2 = \sum_{i=1}^{n} \left(y_i - \hat{a} - \hat{b}x_{1i} - \hat{c}.x_{2i}\right)^2$

Differentiating E with respect to $\hat{a}, \hat{b}$ and $\hat{c}$ we get following three normal equations:

$$\sum \left(y_i - \hat{a} - \hat{b}x_{1i} - \hat{c}.x_{2i}\right) = 0 \qquad \ldots(i)$$

$$\sum \left(y_i - \hat{a} - \hat{b}x_{1i} - \hat{c}.x_{2i}\right)x_{1i} = 0 \qquad \ldots(ii)$$

$$\sum \left(y_i - \hat{a} - \hat{b}x_{1i} - \hat{c}.x_{2i}\right)x_{2i} = 0 \qquad \ldots(iii)$$

Dividing (i) by n (total number of observations), we get:

$$\bar{y} = \hat{a} + \hat{b}\bar{x}_1 + \hat{c}.\bar{x}_2 \text{ or } \hat{a} = \left(\bar{y} - \hat{b}\bar{x}_1 - \hat{c}.\bar{x}_2\right)$$

Substituting $\hat{a} = \left(\bar{y} - \hat{b}\bar{x}_1 - \hat{c}.\bar{x}_2\right)$ in equation (ii) and (iii), we get:

$$\sum y_i x_{1i} = \left(\bar{y} - \hat{b}\bar{x}_1 - \hat{c}.\bar{x}_2\right)\sum x_{1i} + \hat{b}\sum x_{1i}^2 + \hat{c}\sum x_{2i}x_{1i} \qquad \ldots(iv)$$

$$\sum y_i x_{2i} = \left(\bar{y} - \hat{b}\bar{x}_1 - \hat{c}.\bar{x}_2\right)\sum x_{2i} + \hat{b}\sum x_{2i}x_{1i} + \hat{c}\sum x_{2i}^2 \qquad \ldots(v)$$

From (iv),

$$\sum y_i x_{1i} - x\bar{y}.\bar{x} = \hat{b}\left(\sum x_{1i}^2 - x\bar{x}_1^2 \hat{b}\sum x_{1i}^2\right) + \hat{c}\left(\sum x_{2i}.x_{1i} - x\bar{x}_1\bar{x}_2\right)$$

Dividing both sides by n, we get:

$$\text{cov}(y,x_1) = \sigma_{x_1}^2.\hat{b} + \text{cov}(x_1,x_2)\hat{c} \qquad \ldots(vi)$$

Similarly, from Equation (v), we get:

$$\text{cov}(y,x_2) = \text{cov}(x_1,x_2).\hat{b} + \sigma_{x_2}^2.\hat{c} \qquad \ldots(vii)$$

Solving (v) and (vi), we get:

$$\hat{b} = \frac{\text{cov}(y,x_1)\sigma_{x_2}^2 - \text{cov}(x_1,x_2).\text{cov}(y,x_2)}{\sigma_{x_1}^2 \sigma_{x_2}^2 - \text{cov}(x_1,x_2)^2}$$

$$= \frac{\sigma_{x_1}^2 \sigma_{x_2}^2 \left\{ \frac{\sigma_y}{\sigma_{x_1}} \frac{\text{cov}(y,x_1)}{\sigma_{x_1}\sigma_y} - \frac{\sigma_y}{\sigma_{x_2}} \frac{\text{cov}(x_1,x_2)}{\sigma_{x_1}\sigma_{x_2}} \frac{\text{cov}(y,x_2)}{\sigma_y \sigma_{x_2}} \right\}}{\sigma_{x_1}^2 \sigma_{x_2}^2 \left\{ 1 - \left(\frac{\text{cov}(x_1,x_2)}{\sigma_{x_1}\sigma_{x_2}} \right)^2 \right\}}$$

$$= \frac{\frac{\sigma_y}{\sigma_{x_1}}\left(\gamma_{yx_1} - \gamma_{x_1 x_2} \cdot \gamma_{yx_2} \right)}{1 - \gamma_{x_1 x_2}^2}$$

[γ_{xy} = correlation coefficient between variables x and y]

and $\hat{c} = \dfrac{\sigma_{x_1}^2 \cdot \text{cov}(y,x_2) - \text{cov}(x_1,x_2) \cdot \text{cov}(y,x_2)}{\sigma_{x_1}^2 \sigma_{x_2}^2 - \text{cov}(x_1,x_2)^2}$

which can be further simplified as $\hat{c} = \dfrac{\frac{\sigma_y}{\sigma_{x_2}}\left(\gamma_{yx_2} - \gamma_{yx_1} \cdot \gamma_{x_1 x_2} \right)}{1 - \left(\gamma_{x_1 x_2} \right)^2}$

Note: $\hat{b}$ and $\hat{c}$ give the effect of x_1 and x_2 on y respectively.

Since $\hat{b}$ is the per unit effect of x_1 on y after eliminating the effects of x_2, it gives the partial regression coefficient of y and x_1 eliminating the effects of x_2. It is often denoted by b_{123}. Similarly, $\hat{c}$ is often denoted by $b_{13.2}$.

The general multiple linear regression takes of the form:
$$Y_i = B_1 X_{1i} + B_2 X_{2i} + B_3 X_{3i} + \ldots + B_k X_{ki} + u_i \quad i = 1, 2, \ldots, n$$
where u_i is the error term.

Solved Practical Problems

Q1. Given the following pairs of values of the variable X and Y:

X:	10	20	30	40	50	60
Y:	25	50	75	100	125	150

(i) Make a Scatter Diagram.

Ans.

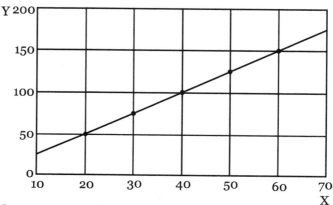

(ii) Is there any correlation between the variables X and Y?

Ans. By looking at the scatter diagram, we can say that there is perfect positive correlation between X and Y variables.

Q2. Find correlation coefficient between the sales and expenses from the data given below:

Firm:	1	2	3	4	5	6	7	8	9	10
Sales (₹ in Lakh):	50	50	55	60	65	65	65	60	60	50
Expenses (₹ in Lakh):	11	13	14	16	16	15	15	14	13	13

Ans. Calculation of Correlation Coefficient

Firm	Sales X	$x = (X-\bar{X})$	x^2	Expenses Y	$y = (Y-\bar{Y})$	y^2	xy
1	50	– 8	64	11	– 3	9	+ 24
2	50	– 8	64	13	– 1	1	+ 8
3	55	– 3	9	14	0	0	0
4	60	+ 2	4	16	+ 2	4	+4
5	65	+ 7	49	16	+ 2	4	+ 14
6	65	+ 7	49	15	+ 1	1	+ 7
7	65	+ 7	49	15	+ 1	1	+ 7
8	60	+ 2	4	14	0	0	0
9	60	+ 2	4	13	– 1	1	– 2
10	50	– 8	64	13	– 1	1	+ 8
N = 10	ΣX = 580	Σx = 0	Σx² = 360	ΣY = 140	Σy = 0	Σy² = 22	Σxy = 70

$$\bar{X} = \frac{\Sigma X}{N} = \frac{580}{10} = 58, \quad \bar{Y} = \frac{\Sigma Y}{N} = \frac{140}{10} = 14$$

$$r = \frac{\Sigma xy}{\sqrt{\Sigma x^2 \Sigma y^2}} = \frac{70}{\sqrt{360 \times 22}} = \frac{70}{88.994} = 0.787$$

Hence, there is a high degree of positive correlation between the two variables, i.e. as the value of sales goes up, the expenses also go up.

Q3. The following data relate to the age of 10 employees and the number of days on which they reported sick in a month:

Age:	20	30	32	35	40	46	52	55	58	62
Sick days:	1	2	5	3	4	6	5	7	8	9

Calculate Karl Pearson's coefficient of correlation and interpret its value.

Ans. Let age and sick days be represented by variables X and Y respectively.

Calculation of Correlation Coefficient

Age (X)	(X − 43) dx	dx²	Sick days (Y)	(Y − 5) dy	dy²	dxdy
20	−23	529	1	−4	16	+92
30	−13	169	2	−3	9	+39
32	−11	121	5	0	0	0
35	−8	64	3	−2	4	+16
40	−3	9	4	−1	1	+3
46	+3	9	6	+1	1	+3
52	+9	81	5	0	0	0
55	+12	144	7	+2	4	24
58	+15	225	8	+3	9	45
62	+19	361	9	+4	16	76
ΣX = 430	Σdx = 0	Σdx² = 1712	ΣY = 50	Σdy = 0	Σdy² = 60	Σdxdy = 298

$$r = \frac{N\Sigma dxdy - \Sigma dx \Sigma dy}{\sqrt{N\Sigma dx^2 - (\Sigma dx)^2} \sqrt{N\Sigma dy^2 - (\Sigma dy)^2}}$$

$$= \frac{10 \times 298 - (0)(0)}{\sqrt{10 \times 1712 - (0)^2} \times \sqrt{10 \times 60 - (0)^2}} = \frac{2980}{\sqrt{17120} \times \sqrt{600}} = \frac{2980}{130.84 \times 24.49}$$

= 0.930

Thus, there is a very high degree of positive correlation between age and sick days taken. Hence, we can conclude that as the age of an employee increases, he is liable to be sick more often than others.

Q4. Two managers are asked to rank a group of employees in order of potential for eventually becoming top managers. The rankings are as follows:

Employee	Ranking by Manager I	Ranking by Manager II
A	10	9
B	2	4
C	1	2
D	4	3
E	3	1
F	6	5
G	5	6
H	8	8
I	7	7
J	9	10

Compute the coefficient of rank correlation and comment on the value.

Ans.

Calculation of Rank Correlation Coefficient

Employee	Ranking by Manager I R_1	Ranking by Manager II R_2	$(R_1 - R_2)^2$ D^2
A	10	9	1
B	2	4	4
C	1	2	1
D	4	3	1
E	3	1	4
F	6	5	1
G	5	6	1
H	8	8	0
I	7	7	0
J	9	10	1
N = 10			$\sum D^2 = 14$

$$R = 1 - \frac{6\sum D^2}{N^3 - N} = 1 - \frac{6 \times 14}{990} = 1 - 0.085 = 0.915$$

Thus, we find that there is high degree of positive correlation in the ranks assigned by the two managers.

Q5. Calculate the coefficient of correlation between age group and rate of mortality from the following data:

Age Group	0 – 20	20 – 40	40 – 60	60 – 80	80 – 100
Rate of Mortality	350	280	540	760	900

Ans.

Age group	Rate of mortality	x	$dx = \frac{x-50}{20}$	dx^2	y	$dy = \frac{y-540}{10}$	dy^2	dxdy
0-20	350	10	−2	4	350	−19	361	38
20-40	280	30	−1	1	280	−26	676	26
40-60	540	50	0	0	540	-	-	0
60-80	760	70	1	1	760	22	484	22
80-100	900	90	2	4	900	36	1296	72
			0	10		13	2817	158

$$r = \frac{N\sum dxdy - \sum dx \sum dy}{\sqrt{N\sum dx^2 - (\sum dx)^2}\sqrt{N\sum dy^2 - (\sum dy)^2}}$$

$$= \frac{5 \times 158 - 0 \times 13}{\sqrt{5 \times 10 - (0)^2} \times \sqrt{5 \times 2817 - (13)^2}} = \frac{790}{\sqrt{50} \times \sqrt{13916}} = \frac{790}{834.04} = 0.95$$

Q6. Calculate the ranks correlation coefficient for the following data of marks of 2 tests given to candidates for a clerical job:

Preliminary Test:	92	89	87	86	83	77	71	63	53	50
Final Test:	86	83	91	77	68	85	52	82	37	57

Ans. Calculation of Rank Correlation Coefficient

Preliminary test X	R_1	Final test Y	R_2	$(R_1 - R_2)$ D^2
92	10	86	9	1
89	9	83	7	4
87	8	91	10	4
86	7	77	5	4
83	6	68	4	4
77	5	85	8	9
71	4	52	2	4
63	3	82	6	9
53	2	37	1	1
50	1	57	3	4
N = 10				$\sum D^2 = 44$

$$R = 1 - \frac{6\sum D^2}{N^3 - N} = 1 - \frac{6 \times 44}{990} = 1 - 0.267 = 0.733$$

Thus, there is a high degree of positive correlation between preliminary and final test.

Q7. Preference prices and debenture prices of a certain company are given below:

Preference Prices (x)	Debenture Prices (y)
73.2	97.8
85.8	99.2
78.9	98.8
75.8	98.3
77.2	98.5
81.2	96.7
83.8	97.1

Use the method of Rank Correlation to determine the relationship between preference prices and debenture prices.

Ans.

Reference price (x)	Debenture price (y)	R_1	R_2	$D = R_1 - R_2$	D^2
73.2	97.8	7	5	2	4
85.8	99.2	1	1	0	0
78.9	98.8	4	2	2	4
75.8	98.3	6	4	2	4
77.2	98.5	5	3	2	4
81.2	96.7	3	7	−4	16
83.8	97.1	2	6	−4	16
N = 7					$\Sigma D^2 = 48$

$$R = 1 - \frac{6\sum D^2}{N^3 - N} = 1 - \frac{6 \times 48}{343 - 7} = 1 - \frac{288}{336} = 1 - 0.86 = 0.14$$

Hence, preference prices and debenture prices are directly related, i.e. there is positive relationship.

Q8. From the following data, compute the coefficient of correlation between X and Y series.

	X-Series	Y-Series
Number of items:	15	15
Arithmetic mean:	25	18
Squares of deviations from mean:	136	138

Summation of product of deviations of X and Y series from their respective arithmetic means = 122.

Ans. Given, $N = 15, \overline{X} = 25, \overline{Y} = 18, \Sigma x^2 = 136, \Sigma y^2 = 138, \Sigma xy = 122$

Applying the formula,

$$r = \frac{\sum xy}{\sqrt{\sum x^2 \cdot \sum y^2}} = \frac{122}{\sqrt{136 \times 138}} = \frac{122}{\sqrt{18768}} = \frac{122}{136.996} = +0.89$$

Q9. Following results were obtained from an analysis of 12 pairs of observations:
$N = 12, \sum X = 30, \sum Y = 5, \sum X^2 = 670, \sum Y^2 = 285, \sum XY = 334$
Later on it was discovered that one pair of values (X = 11, Y = 4) were copied wrongly, the correct value of the pair was (X = 10, Y = 14). Find the correct value of correlation coefficient.

Ans. Corrected $\sum X = 30 - (11) + (10) = 29$

Corrected $\sum Y = 5 - (4) + (14) = 15$

Corrected $\sum X^2 = 670 - (11)^2 + (10)^2 = 649$

Corrected $\sum Y^2 = 285 - (4)^2 + (14)^2 = 465$

Corrected $\sum XY = 334 - 11 \times 4 + 10 \times 14 = 430$

The correct value of correlation coefficient is given by:

$$r = \frac{N\sum XY - \sum X \cdot \sum Y}{\sqrt{N \cdot \sum X^2 - (\sum X)^2} \sqrt{N \cdot \sum Y^2 - (\sum Y)^2}}$$

$$= \frac{12 \times 430 - (29)(15)}{\sqrt{12 \times 649 - (29)^2} \sqrt{12 \times 465 - (15)^2}}$$

$$= \frac{5160 - 435}{\sqrt{7788 - 841} \sqrt{5580 - 225}} = \frac{4725}{\sqrt{6947} \sqrt{5355}}$$

$$= \frac{4725}{83.35 \times 73.18} = \frac{4725}{6099.553} = 0.7746$$

Q10. Calculate "r" for the following data:

S. No.	Set X	Set Y
1	30	25
2	35	30
3	35	35
4	40	40
5	45	55
6	55	50
7	65	70
8	50	60
9	45	45
10	50	40
Total	450	450

Ans.

S.No.	X	Y	x = (X−X̄)	y = (Y−Ȳ)	x^2	y^2	xy
1	30	25	−15	−20	225	400	300
2	35	30	−10	−15	100	225	150
3	35	35	−10	−10	100	100	100
4	40	40	−5	−5	25	25	25
5	45	55	0	10	0	100	0
6	55	50	10	5	100	25	50
7	65	70	20	25	400	625	500
8	50	60	5	15	25	225	75
9	45	45	0	0	0	0	0
10	50	40	5	−5	25	25	−25
N = 10	Σx = 450	Σy = 450	Σx = 0	Σy = 0	Σx^2= 1000	Σy^2= 1750	Σxy = 1175

$$\overline{X} = \frac{\sum X}{N} = \frac{450}{10} = 45$$

$$\overline{Y} = \frac{\sum Y}{N} = \frac{450}{10} = 45$$

$$r = \frac{\sum xy}{\sqrt{\sum x^2 \sum y^2}} = \frac{1175}{\sqrt{1000 \times 1750}} = \frac{1175}{1322.8} = +0.888$$

Q11. Find out Rho (Spearman's rank correlation) for the following data:

S. No.	X	Y
1	7	8
2	11	16
3	16	14
4	9	12
5	6	8
6	17	16
7	7	9
8	11	12
9	5	7
10	14	15

Ans.

Correlation and Regression

S. No.	X	Y	Rank X	Rank Y	(Rank X)²	(Rank Y)²	(Rank X)(Rank Y)
1	7	8	3.5	2.5	12.25	6.25	8.75
2	11	16	6.5	9.5	42.25	90.25	61.75
3	16	14	9	7	81.00	49.00	63.00
4	9	12	5	5.5	25.00	30.25	27.50
5	6	8	2	2.5	4.00	6.25	5.00
6	17	16	10	9.5	100.00	90.25	95.00
7	7	9	3.5	4	12.25	16.00	14.00
8	11	12	6.5	5.5	42.25	30.25	35.75
9	5	7	1	1	1.00	1.00	1.00
10	14	15	8	8	64.00	64.00	64.00
			55	55	384.00	383.50	375.75

$$r_s = \frac{\sum XY - \frac{(\sum X)(\sum Y)}{n}}{\sqrt{\left[\sum X^2 - \frac{(\sum X)^2}{n}\right]\left[\sum Y^2 - \frac{(\sum Y)^2}{n}\right]}} = \frac{375.75 - \frac{(55)(55)}{10}}{\sqrt{\left[384 - \frac{55^2}{10}\right]\left[383.5 - \frac{55^2}{10}\right]}}$$

$$= \frac{73.25}{81.2496} = 0.902$$

Q12. Find Rank-Difference Coefficient of correlation from the following data: **[Dec-2013, Q.No.-3]**

Student	Score on Test I	Score on Test II
	X	Y
A	10	16
B	15	16
C	11	24
D	14	18
E	16	22
F	20	24
G	10	14
H	8	10
I	7	12
J	9	14
N = 10		

Ans.

Subject	X	Y	Rank x	Rank y	x^2	y^2	xy
A	10	16	4.5	5.5	20.25	30.25	24.75
B	15	16	8	5.5	64	30.25	44.00
C	11	24	6	9.5	36	90.25	57.00
D	14	18	7	7	49	49	49.00
E	16	22	9	8	81	64	72.00
F	20	24	10	9.5	100	90.25	95.00
G	10	14	4.5	3.5	20.25	12.25	15.75
H	8	10	2	1	4	1	2.00
I	7	12	1	2	1	4	2.00
J	9	14	3	3.5	9	12.25	10.50
			$\Sigma x = 55$	$\Sigma y = 55$	$\Sigma x^2 = 384.5$	$\Sigma y^2 = 383.5$	$\Sigma xy = 372$

$$r_s = \frac{\sum xy - \frac{(\sum x)(\sum y)}{n}}{\sqrt{\left[\sum x^2 - \frac{(\sum x)^2}{n}\right]\left[\sum y^2 - \frac{(\sum y)^2}{n}\right]}}$$

$$= \frac{372 - \frac{(55)(55)}{10}}{\sqrt{\left[384.5 - \frac{(55)^2}{10}\right]\left[383.5 - \frac{(55)^2}{10}\right]}}$$

$$= \frac{69.5}{\sqrt{(82)(81)}} = \frac{69.5}{81.4} = 0.853$$

Q13. Calculate the regression equation of X on Y and Y on X from the following data:

X	1	2	3	4	5
Y	2	5	3	8	7

Ans.

Calculation of Regression Equations

X	Y	X^2	Y^2	XY
1	2	1	4	2
2	5	4	25	10
3	3	9	9	9
4	8	16	64	32
5	7	25	49	35
$\Sigma X = 15$	$\Sigma Y = 25$	$\Sigma X^2 = 55$	$\Sigma Y^2 = 151$	$\Sigma XY = 88$

Regression equation of X on Y is given by,
X = a + bY

The normal equations are,
$\sum X = Na + b\sum Y$
$\sum XY = a\sum Y + \sum Y^2$
Substituting the value, we get,
15 = 5a + 25b ...(i)
88 = 25a + 151b ...(ii)
Solving (i) and (ii), we get,
a = 0.5 and b = 0.5
Hence, the required regression equation of X on Y is given by,
X = 0.5 + 0.5Y
Regression equation of Y on X is: Y = a + bX
Normal equation are:
$\sum Y = Na + b\sum X$
$\sum XY = a\sum X + b\sum X^2$
Substituting the values, we get
25 = 5a + 15b ...(iii)
88 = 15a + 55b ...(iv)
Solving (iii) and (iv), we get
a = 1.10 and b = 1.30
Hence, the required equation of Y on X is given by
Y = 1.10 + 1.30X

Q14. **The following table is showing the test scores made by salesmen on the intelligence test and their weekly sales:**

Salesmen:	1	2	3	4	6	7	8	9	10
Test Score:	40	70	50	60	50	90	40	60	60
Sale (₹ '000):	2.5	6.0	4.0	5.0	2.5	5.5	3.0	4.5	3.0

Calculate the regression line of sales on test scores and estimate the probable weekly sales volume if a salesman makes a score of 100.

Ans. Let sales be denoted by Y and test scores by X. We have to fit a regression equation of Y on X, i.e. $Y - \overline{Y} = b_{yx}(X - \overline{X})$.

Calculation of Regression Line

Salesmen	Test Score X	(X − X̄) x	x^2	Sales Y	(Y − Ȳ) y	y^2	xy
1	40	−20	400	2.5	−1.5	2.25	+30
2	70	+10	100	6.0	+2.0	4.00	+20
3	50	−10	100	4.0	0	0	+
4	60	0	0	5.0	1.0	1.00	+
5	80	+20	400	4.0	0	0	+
6	50	−10	100	2.5	−1.5	2.25	+15
7	90	+30	900	5.5	+1.5	2.25	+45
8	40	−20	400	3.0	−1.0	1.00	+20
9	60	0	0	4.5	+0.5	0.25	+
10	60	0	0	3.0	−1.0	1.00	+
N = 10	ΣX = 600	ΣX = 0	Σx^2 = 2400	ΣY = 40	Σy = 0	Σy^2 = 14	Σxy = 130

$$\bar{X} = \frac{\Sigma X}{N} = \frac{600}{10} = 60$$

$$\bar{Y} = \frac{\Sigma Y}{N} = \frac{40}{10} = 4$$

$$b_{yx} = \frac{\Sigma xy}{\Sigma x^2} = \frac{130}{2400} = 0.054$$

When we calculate regression line of Y on X, use formula:

$$Y - \bar{Y} = b_{xy}(X - \bar{X})$$

Putting value, we find:

Y − 4 = 0.054 × (X − 60)
Y = 0.76 + 0.054X

When X is 100, Y would be

Y = 0.76 + 0.054(100) = 6.16

Thus, the most probable weekly sales volume if salesman makes a score of 100 is 6.16 thousand rupees.

Q15. The following is the heights of fathers (X) and their sons (Y) in inches:

X	65	66	67	67	68	69	70	72
Y	67	68	65	68	73	73	70	72

Obtain the equation of the line of regression of X on Y. Also find estimate of X for Y = 70.

Ans.

Correlation and Regression

X	Y	dx = X − A_x	$(dx)^2$	dy = Y − A_y	$(dy)^2$	dxdy
65	67	−3	9	−2	4	6
66	68	−2	4	−1	1	2
67	65	−1	1	−4	16	4
67	68	−1	1	−1	1	1
68	73	0	0	4	16	0
69	73	1	1	4	16	4
70	70	2	4	1	1	2
72	72	4	16	3	9	12
		$\Sigma dx = 0$	$\Sigma dx^2 = 36$	$\Sigma dy = 4$	$\Sigma dy^2 = 64$	$\Sigma dxdy = 31$

N = 8 where A_x = 68 and A_y = 69 are assumed means from X and Y series respectively,

$$b_{xy} = \frac{N \times \Sigma dxdy - \Sigma dx \times \Sigma dy}{N \times \Sigma dy^2 - (\Sigma dy)^2} = \frac{31 \times 8 - 0 \times 4}{64 \times 8 - (4)^2} = \frac{248}{496}$$

$b_{xy} = 0.5$

$$\overline{X} = A_x + \frac{\Sigma dx}{N} = 68 + \frac{0}{8} = 68$$

$$\overline{Y} = A_y + \frac{\Sigma dy}{N} = 69 + \frac{4}{8} = 69.5$$

The equation of line of regression of X on Y is,

$X - \overline{X} = b_{xy}(Y - \overline{Y})$

(X − 68) = 0.5 (Y − 69.5)
X − 68 = 0.5Y − 34.75
X − 0.5Y = 68 − 34.75
X − 0.5Y = 33.25 required line of regression,

when, Y = 70
X − 0.5 × 70 = 33.25
X = 35 + 33.25
X = 68.25

Q16. The following table gives the age of cars of a certain make and actual maintenance costs. Obtain the regression equation for costs related to age. Also estimate the maintenance cost for ten year old car.

Age of car (years)	2	4	6	8
Maintenance cost (in Hundreds)	10	20	25	30

Ans. Let the given table is as,

(X) Age of car (years)	2	4	6	8
(Y) Maintenance cost (in Hundreds)	10	20	25	30

N = 4

We have to obtain regression line for cost related to age, i.e. regression line of Y on X. We shall also find out cost of maintenance for ten years, i.e. Y at X = 10.

The equation of Y on X is,
$$Y - \overline{Y} = b_{yx}(X - \overline{X}) \quad \ldots(i)$$

X	Y	dx = X − A_x	dy = Y − A_y	$(dx)^2$	$(dy)^2$	dxdy
2	10	−2	−10	4	100	20
④	㉠	0	0	0	0	0
6	25	2	5	4	25	10
8	30	4	10	16	100	40
		$\Sigma dx = 4$	$\Sigma dy = 5$	$\Sigma dx^2 = 24$	$\Sigma dy^2 = 225$	$\Sigma dxdy = 70$

$$b_{yx} = \frac{N\Sigma dxdy - \Sigma dx \Sigma dy}{N\Sigma dx^2 - (\Sigma dx)^2} = \frac{70 \times 4 - 4 \times 5}{24 \times 4 - (4)^2} = \frac{280 - 20}{96 - 16} = \frac{260}{80} = 3.25$$

$$\overline{X} = A_x + \frac{\Sigma dx}{N} = 4 + \frac{4}{4} = 4 + 1 = 5$$

$$\overline{Y} = A_y + \frac{\Sigma dy}{N} = 20 + \frac{5}{4} = 21.25$$

Putting all values in (i)
Y − 21.25 = 3.25 (X − 5)
Y − 21.25 = 3.25X − 16.25
Y = 3.25X + 5

Y = 3.25X + 5 is required line, i.e. regression equation for cost related to Age when,
X = 10
Y = 3.25 × 10 + 5 = 32.5 + 5 = 37.5
Y = 37.5

i.e. maintenance cost for 10 year old car is 37.5 (in hundreds).

Q17. A company wants to assess the impact of R&D expenditure on its annual profit. The following table presents the information for the last eight years:

Years:	2012	2011	2010	2009	2008	2007	2006	2005
R&D expenditure (₹'000):	9	7	5	10	4	5	3	2
Annual Profit (₹'000):	45	42	41	60	30	34	25	20

Estimate the regression equation and predict the annual profit for 2013 for an allocated sum of ₹10000 as R&D expenditure.

Ans. Let R&D expenditure be denoted by X and annual profit by Y.

Calculation of Regression Equation

Correlation and Regression

Year	X	(X – 6) dx	dx²	Y	(Y – 37) dy	dy²	dxdy
2005	2	–4	16	20	–17	289	+68
2006	3	–3	9	25	–12	144	+36
2007	5	–1	1	34	–3	9	+3
2008	4	–2	4	30	–7	49	+14
2009	10	+4	16	60	+23	529	+92
2010	5	–1	1	41	+4	16	–4
2011	7	+1	1	42	+5	25	+5
2012	9	+3	9	45	+8	64	+24
	$\Sigma X = 45$	$\Sigma dx = -3$	$\Sigma dx^2 = 57$	$\Sigma Y = 297$	$\Sigma dy = 1$	$\Sigma dy^2 = 1125$	$\Sigma dxdy = 238$

Fitting regression equation of Y on X, we get,

$$(Y - \overline{Y}) = b_{yx}(X - \overline{X})$$

$$\overline{Y} = \frac{\Sigma Y}{N} = \frac{297}{8} = 37.125;$$

$$\overline{X} = \frac{\Sigma X}{N} = \frac{45}{8} = 5.625$$

$$b_{yx} = \frac{N \Sigma dxdy - \Sigma dx \Sigma dy}{N \Sigma dx^2 - (\Sigma dx)^2} = \frac{8 \times 238 - (-3)(1)}{8 \times 57 - (-3)^2} = \frac{1904 + 3}{456 - 9}$$

$$= \frac{1907}{447} = 4.266$$

Y – 37.125 = 4.266(X – 5.625)
Y – 37.125 = 4.266X – 23.996
Y = 13.129 + 4.266X
When X is 10, Y shall be,
Y = 13.129 + 4.266(10) = 55.789

Thus, the likely expenditure on Research and Development for an allocation for ₹10,000 is ₹55,789.

Q18. Write the regression equations for the following:

Academic achievement	Anxiety
x	y
1	4
3	2
4	1
5	0
8	0

Ans.

x	y	x^2	y^2	xy
1	4	1	16	4
3	2	9	4	6
4	1	16	1	4
5	0	25	0	0
8	0	64	0	0
$\Sigma x = 21$	$\Sigma y = 7$	$\Sigma x^2 = 115$	$\Sigma y^2 = 21$	$\Sigma xy = 14$

Thus,

$$\beta_0 = \frac{\left(\sum y\right)\left(\sum x^2\right) - \left(\sum x\right)\left(\sum xy\right)}{n\left(\sum x^2\right) - \left(\sum x\right)^2}$$

$$= \frac{7 \times 115 - 21 \times 14}{5 \times 115 - (21)^2} = \frac{805 - 294}{575 - 441} = \frac{511}{134} = 3.81$$

$$\beta_1 = \frac{n\left(\sum xy\right) - \left(\sum x\right)\left(\sum y\right)}{n\left(\sum x^2\right) - \left(\sum x\right)^2}$$

$$= \frac{5 \times 14 - 21 \times 7}{5 \times 115 - (21)^2} = \frac{70 - 147}{575 - 441} = \frac{-77}{134} = -0.575$$

Thus, the regression equation is $y = \beta_0 + \beta_1 x$,

y= 3.81−0.575x

Best help books for IGNOU students—GPH books.

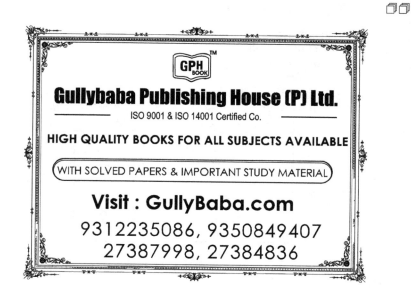

Normal Distribution

An Overview

So far we have confined ourselves to descriptive statistics, i.e. how to organise a distribution of scores and how to describe its shape, central value and variation. We have used histogram and frequency polygon to illustrate the shape of a frequency distribution, measures of central tendency to describe the central value and measures of variability to indicate its variation. All these descriptions have gone a long way in providing information about a set of scores, but we also need procedures to describe individual scores or cutting point scores to categorise the entire group of individuals on the basis of their ability or the nature of test paper, which a psychometrician or teacher has used to assess the outcomes of the individual on a certain ability test. For example, suppose a teacher has administered a test designed to appraise the level of achievement and a student has got some score on the test. What did that score mean? The obtained score has some meaning only with respect to other scores either the teacher may be interested to know how many students lie within the certain range of scores? Or how many students are above and below certain referenced score? Or how many students may be assign A, B, C, D, etc. grades according to their ability? To have an answer to such problems, the bell-shaped curve, which is known as normal curve, and the related distribution of scores, through which the bell-shaped curve is obtained, generally known as normal distribution.

The normal distribution is a very important concept in the behavioural sciences because many variables used in behavioural research are assumed to be normally distributed. In behavioural science, each variable has a specific mean and standard deviation; there is a family of normal distribution rather than just a single distribution. However, if we know the mean and standard deviation for any normal distribution, we can transform it into the standard normal distribution.

Q1. What is Normal Probability Curve? Discuss its theoretical base. Also explain the properties of Normal Probability Curve.

Or

Elucidate the properties of the Normal Probability Curve.

Or

Explain Normal Distribution and highlight its characteristics. [Dec-2012, Q.No.-7]

Or

Elucidate the concept of Normal curve and its properties. [Dec-2014, Q.No.-7]

Ans. The Normal Probability Curve is the ideal symmetrical frequency curve. It is supposed to be based on the data of a population. In it, the measures are concentrated closely around the centre and taper off from this central point or top to the left and right. There are very few measures at the low score end of the scale; an increasing number upto a maximum at the middle position; and a symmetrical falling-off towards the high score end of the scale. The curve exhibits almost perfect bilateral symmetry. It is symmetrical about central altitude. The altitude divides it into two parts, which will be similar in shape and equal in area. The curve, which is also called Normal Curve, is a bell-shaped figure. It is very useful in psychological and educational measurements. It is shown in Fig. 3.1:

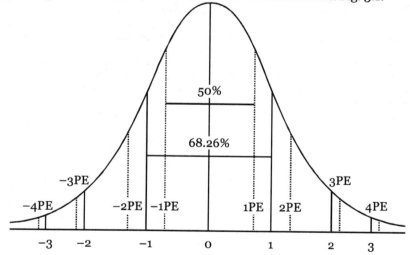

Fig. 3.1: Normal Probability Curve

Normal probability curve is the frequency polygon of any normal distribution.

Theoretical Base of the Normal Probability Curve: The Normal Probability Curve is based upon the law of probability (the various games of chance) discovered by French Mathematician Abraham Demoiver (1667-1754). In the eighteenth century, he developed its mathematical equation and graphical representation also.

The law of probability and the normal curve that illustrates it is based upon the law of chance or the probable occurrence of certain events. It can be represented by a bell-shaped curve with definite characteristics.

Characteristics or Properties of Normal Probability Curve (NPC): The characteristics of the normal probability curve are as follows:

(1) **The Normal Curve is Symmetrical:** The normal probability curve is symmetrical around its vertical axis called ordinate. The symmetry about the ordinate at the central point of the curve implies that the size, shape and slope of the curve on one side of the curve are identical to that of the other. In other words, the left and right halves to the middle central point are mirror images, as shown in the Fig. 3.2.

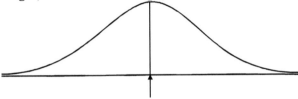

M = Md = Mo
Fig. 3.2: Normal Probability Curve

(2) **The Normal Curve is Unimodal:** Since there is only one maximum point in the curve, thus, the normal probability curve is unimodal, i.e. it has only one mode.

(3) **The Maximum Ordinate occurs at the Center:** The maximum height of the ordinate always occur at the central point of the curve, i.e. the mid-point. In the unit normal curve, it is equal to 0.3989.

(4) **The Normal Curve is Asymptotic to the X-Axis:** The normal probability curve approaches the horizontal axis asymptotically, i.e. the curve continuously decrease in height on both ends away from the middle point (the maximum ordinate point); but it never touches the horizontal axis. Therefore, its ends extend from minus infinity $(-\infty)$ to the plus infinity $(+\infty)$.

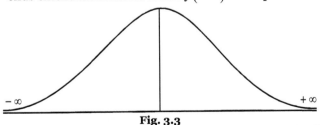

Fig. 3.3

(5) **The Height of the Curve declines Symmetrically:** In the normal probability curve, the height declines symmetrically in either direction from the maximum point.

(6) **The Points of Influx occur at point ±1 Standard Deviation (±1 σ):** The normal curve changes its direction from convex to concave at a point recognised as point of influx. If we draw the perpendiculars from these two points of influx of the curve to the horizontal x-axis, those touch at a distance one standard deviation unit from above and below the mean (the central point).

(7) **The Total Percentage of Area of the Normal Curve within Two Points of Influxation is fixed:** Approximately 68.26% area of the curve lies within the limits of ±1 standard deviation (±1 σ) unit from the mean.

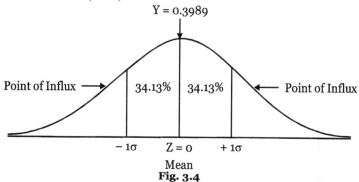

Fig. 3.4

(8) **The Total Area under Normal Curve may be also considered 100 Per cent Probability:** The total area under the normal curve may be considered to approach 100 per cent probability; interpreted in terms of standard deviations. The specified areas under each unit of standard deviation are shown in Fig. 3.5.

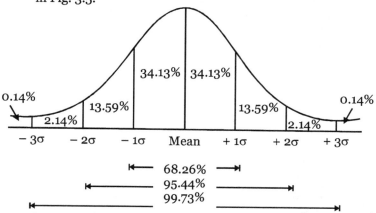

Fig. 3.5: The Percentage of the Cases Falling Between Successive Standard Deviation in Normal Distribution

(9) **The Normal Curve is Bilateral:** The 50% area of the curve lies to the left side of the maximum central ordinate and 50% of the area lies to the right side. Hence, the curve is bilateral.

(10) **The Normal Curve is a Mathematical Model in Behavioural Sciences Especially in Mental Measurement:** This curve is used as a measurement scale. The measurement unit of this scale is $\pm 1\sigma$.

Q2. What does normal curve/normal distribution indicate? Also, explain the applications/uses of normal distribution curve.

Ans. Normal curve has great significance in the mental measurement and educational evaluation. It gives important information about the trait being measured.

If the frequency polygon of observations or measurement of certain trait is a normal curve, it is an indication that:

(1) The measured trait is normally distributed in the universe.
(2) Most of the cases, i.e. individuals are average in the measured trait and their percentage in the total population is about 68.26%.
(3) Approximately 15.87% (50 to 34.13%) of cases are high in the trait measured.
(4) Similarly, 15.87% of the cases are low in the trait measured.
(5) The test which is used to measure the trait is good.
(6) The test which is used to measure the trait has good discrimination power as it differentiates between poor, average and high ability group individuals.
(7) The items of the test used are fairly distributed in terms of difficulty level.

Applications/Uses of Normal Distribution Curve: There are number of applications of normal curve in the field of psychology as well as educational measurement and evaluation. These are as follows:

(1) To determine the percentage of cases (in a normal distribution) within given limits or scores.
(2) To determine the percentage of cases those are above or below a given score or reference point.
(3) To determine the limits of scores which include a given percentage of cases to determine the percentile rank of an individual or a student in his own group.
(4) To find out the percentile value of an individual on the basis of his percentile rank.
(5) Dividing a group into sub-groups according to certain ability and assigning the grades.
(6) To compare the two distributions in terms of overlapping.
(7) To determine the relative difficulty of test items.

Q3. What is the importance of normal distribution?

Ans. The normal distribution, also called the normal probability distribution happens to be most useful theoretical distribution for continuous variables. It is approximation to binomial distribution.

Whether or not p is equal to q, the binomial distribution tends to the form of the continuous curve when n becomes large at least for the material part of the range. In fact, that corresponding between binomial and the normal curve is surprisingly close even for low values of n provided p and q are fairly near equality. The limiting frequency curve, obtained as n, becomes large and is called the normal frequency curve or simply the normal curve.

The normal curve is represented in several forms. The following is the basic form relating to the curve with mean and standard deviation.

The Normal Distribution

$$P(X) = \frac{1}{\sigma\sqrt{2\pi}} e^{-\frac{(x-\mu)^2}{2\sigma^2}}$$

X = Values of the continuous random variable;
μ = Mean of the normal random variable;
e = Mathematical constant approximated by 2.7183; and
π = Mathematical constant approximated by 3.1416.

$\left(\sqrt{2\pi} = 2.5066\right)$

When we say that curve has unit area, we mean total frequency N is equated to 1. To obtain ordinates for particular distribution, the ordinates given by the above formula are multiplied by N. The equation to a normal curve corresponding to a particular distribution is given by:

$$y = \frac{N}{\sigma\sqrt{2\pi}} e^{-x^2/2\sigma^2}$$

The quantity $\frac{N}{\sigma\sqrt{2\pi}}$ in the above formula is equal to the maximum ordinate (y_o) of the normal curve corresponding to distribution of stated total frequency N and stated standard deviation σ.

A random variable with any mean and standard deviation can be transformed to a standardised normal variable by subtracting the mean and dividing by the standard deviation. For a normal distribution with mean μ and standard deviation σ, the standardised variable z is obtained as:

$$z = \left(\frac{X-\mu}{\sigma}\right)$$

Characteristics of Normal Distribution

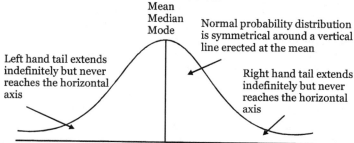

Fig. 3.6: Frequency curve for the Normal Probability Distribution

- The curve has a single peak, thus it is unimodal, i.e. it has only one mode and has a bell-shape.
- Because of the symmetry of the normal probability distribution (skewness = 0), the median and the mode of the distribution are also at the centre. Thus, for a normal curve, the mean, median and mode have the same value.
- The two tails of the normal probability distribution extend indefinitely but never touch the horizontal axis.

Q4. Discuss the types of divergence occur in the normality (the non-normal distribution). Also, explain the factors causing divergence in the normal distribution/normal curve.

Or

Describe with example, the divergence from Normality (The Non-Normal Distribution). [June-2014, Q.No.-8]

Or

Write a short note on Kurtosis. [June-2015, Q.No.-12]

Ans. There are two types of divergence occur in the normal curve. These are as follows:

(1) **Skewness:** A distribution is said to be "skewed" when the mean and median fall at different points in the distribution and the balance, i.e. the point of center of gravity is shifted to one side or the other to left or right. In a normal distribution the mean equals, the median exactly and the skewness is of course zero (SK = 0).

There are two types of skewness which appear in the normal curve.

(i) **Negative Skewness:** Distribution said to be skewed negatively or to the left when scores are massed at the high end of the scale, i.e. the right side of the curve are spread out more gradually towards the low end, i.e. the left side of the curve. In negatively skewed distribution, the value of median will be higher than that of the value of the mean.

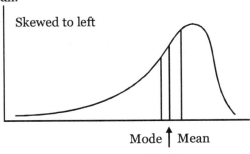

Fig. 3.7: Negative Skewness

(ii) **Positive Skewness:** Distributions are skewed positively or to the right, when scores are massed at the low, i.e. the left end of the scale, and are spread out gradually towards the high or right end as shown in Fig. 3.8.

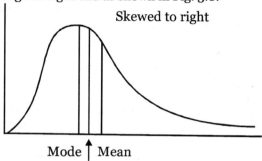

Fig. 3.8: Negative Skewness

(2) **Kurtosis:** The term kurtosis refers to (the divergence) in the height of the curve, especially in the peakness. There are two types of divergence in the peakness of the curve:

(i) **Leptokurtosis:** In a leptokurtic distribution, the frequency distribution curve is more peaked than to the normal distribution curve.

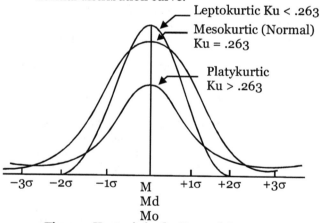

Fig. 3.9: Kurtosis in the Normal Curve

(ii) **Platykurtosis:** Platykurtosis refers to being flatter ("plat" "flat") than a normal distribution. In other words, a distribution of flatter peak then to the normal, is known as platykurtosis distribution.

When the distribution and related curve is normal, the vain of kurtosis is 0.263 (KU = 0.263). If the value of the KU is greater than 0.263, the distribution and related curve obtained will be platykurtic. When the value of KU is less than 0.263, the distribution and related curve obtained will be leptokurtic.

Factors causing divergence in the normal distribution/normal curve: The factors causing divergence in the normal distribution/normal curve are as follows:

(1) **Selection of the Sample:** Selection of the subjects (individuals) produces skewness and kurtosis in the distribution. If the sample size is small or sample is biased one, skewness is possible in the distribution of scores obtained on the basis of selected sample or group of individuals.

If the scores made by small and homogeneous groups are likely to yield narrow and leptokurtic distribution. Scores from small and highly heterogeneous groups yield platykurtic distribution.

(2) **Unsuitable or Poorly Made Tests:** If the measuring tool or test is inappropriate, or poorly made, the asymmetry is possible in the distribution of scores. If a test is too easy, scores will pile up at the high end of the scale, whereas the test is too hard, scores will pile up at the low end of the scale.

(3) **The Trait being measured is Non-Normal:** Skewness or Kurtosis or both will appear when there is a real lack of normality in the trait being measured, e.g. interest, attitude, suggestibility, deaths in old age or early-childhood due to certain degenerative diseases, etc.

(4) **Errors in the Construction and Administration of Tests:** The unstandardised with poor item-analysis test may cause asymmetry in the distribution of the scores. Similarly, while administrating the test, the unclear instructions, i.e. errors in timings, errors in the scoring, practice and motivation to complete the test — all these factors may cause skewness in the distribution.

Q5. Discuss the measuring of skewness and kurtosis.

Or

What is the formula to measure skewness in a distribution?

Or

What formula is used to calculate the value of kurtosis in distribution?

Ans. In psychology and education, the divergence in normal distribution/normal curve has a significant role in construction of the ability and mental tests and to test the representativeness of a sample taken from a large population. Further, the divergence in the distribution of scores or measurements obtained of a certain population reflects some important information about the trait of population measured. Thus, there is a need to measure the two divergence, i.e. skewness and kurtosis of the distribution of the scores.

Measuring Skewness: There are two methods to study the skewness in a distribution. These are as follows:

(1) **Observation Method:** There is a simple method of detecting the directions of skewness by the inspection of frequency polygon prepared on the basis of the scores obtained regarding a trait of the population or a sample drawn from a population.

Looking at the tails of the frequency polygon of the distribution obtained, if longer tail of the curve is towards the higher value or upper side or right side to the centre or mean, the skewness is positive. If the longer tail is towards the lower values or lower side or left to the mean, the skewness is negative.

(2) **Statistical Method:** To know the skewness in the distribution, we may also use the statistical method. For the purpose, we use measures of central tendency, specifically mean and median values and use the following formula.

$$S_K = \frac{3(\text{Mean} - \text{Median})}{\sigma}$$

Another measure of skewness based on percentile values, is as under:

$$S_K = \frac{(P_{90} - P_{10})}{2} - P_{50}$$

Here, it is to be kept in mind that the above two measures are not mathematically equivalent. A normal curve has the value of $S_k = 0$. Deviations from normality can be negative and positively direction leading to negatively skewed and positively skewed distributions respectively.

Measuring Kurtosis: For judging whether a distribution lacks normal symmetry or peakedness; it may detected by inspection of the frequency polygon obtained. If a peak of curve is thin and sides are narrow to the centre, the distribution is leptokurtic and if the peak of the frequency distribution is too flat and sides of the curve are deviating from the centre towards $\pm 4\sigma$ or $\pm 5\sigma$ then the distribution is platykurtic.

Kurtosis can be measured by following formula using percentile values.

$$K_U = \frac{Q}{P_{90} - P_{10}}$$

where Q = quartile deviation, i.e.

P_{10} = 10th percentile

P_{90} = 90th percentile

A normal distribution has $K_U = 0.263$. If the value of K_U is less than 0.263 $(K_U < 0.263)$, the distribution is leptokurtic and if K_U is greater than 0.263 $(K_U > 0.263)$, the distribution is platykurtic.

Q6. Define the following terms:
(i) Parameter
Ans. In a statistical inquiry, our interest lies in one or more characteristics of the population. A measure of such a characteristic is called a *parameter*. For example, we may be interested in the mean income of the people of some region for a particular year. We may also like to know the standard deviation of these incomes of the people. Here, both mean and standard deviation are parameters.

(ii) Statistic

Ans. Sometimes it is difficult to obtain information about the whole population. In other words, it may not be always possible to compute a population parameter. In such situations, we try to get some idea about the parameter from the information obtained from a sample drawn from the population. This sample information is summarised in the form of a *statistic*. For example, sample mean or sample median or sample mode is called a statistic. Thus, a statistic is calculated from the values of the units that are included in the sample. So, a *statistic can be defined as a function of the sample values.*

(iii) Estimator and Estimate

Ans. The basic purpose of a statistic is to estimate some population parameter. The procedure followed or the formula used to compute a statistic is called an *estimator* and the value of a statistic so computed is known as an *estimate*.

(iv) Sampling Error

Ans. Sampling error refers to the difference between the mean of the entire population and the mean obtained of the sample taken from the population.

Thus, sampling error = $M_{pop} \sim M$ or $\overline{M} - M$

As the difference is low, the mean obtained on the basis of sample is near to the population mean and sample mean is considered to be representing the population mean (or M_{pop}).

(v) Standard Error

Ans. The standard error refers to the intra differences in the sample measurements of number of samples taken from a single population.

As the intra differences in the number of sampling observation, i.e. the statistics of the same parent population is less and tending to zero, we may say the obtained sample statistics is quite reliable and can be considered as representative of the M_{pop} or $\overline{M}$.

Standard Error of sampling measurements on statistics is calculated by using the formula given below:

$$S.E.M \text{ or } \sigma_M = \frac{\overline{\sigma}}{\sqrt{N}}$$

Where, S.E.M = Standard error of sampling measurement;

$\overline{\sigma}$ = Standard deviation of the scores obtained from the population; and

N = Size of the sample or total number of units in a sample.

The standard error of any statistics depends mathematically upon two characteristics, i.e.
- the variability or spread of scores around the mean of the population and
- the number of units or cases in the sample taken from the population.

Q7. Analyse t-ratio distribution and its role in inferential statistics with the help of an example.

Ans. Suppose we have drawn 100 samples of equal size (say n = 500) from a parent population and we calculate the mean value of the scores of a trait of the population obtained from each sample. Thus, we have a distribution of 100 means.

Of course, all these samples means will not be alike. Some may have comparatively large values and some may have small. If we draw a frequency polygon of the mean values or the "statistics" obtained, the curve will be *bell-shaped,* i.e. the normal curve and having the same characteristics or properties as the normal probability curve has.

The distribution of statistics values or sample statistical measurements is known as the "sampling-distribution" of the statistics.

The corresponding standard score formula, i.e. $z = \dfrac{X-M}{\sigma}$, may now become as:

$$t = \dfrac{M - M_{pop}}{S.E._M} \text{ or } \dfrac{M - \overline{M}}{S.E.\overline{M}}$$

where

t = Standard score of the sample measures or statistics and termed as "t-ratio";

M = Mean of specific statistics or sample measure;

$\overline{M}$ or M_{pop} = Mean of the parameter value of the specific statistics or mean of the specific statistics of the population; and

$S.E._M$ = Standard Error of the statistics, i.e. the standard deviation of the sampling distribution of the statistics.

Actually, t is defined as we have defined the z. It is the ratio of deviation from the mean or other parameter, in a distribution of sample statistics, to the standard error of that distribution.

To distinguish z score of the sampling distribution of sample statistics, we use "t" which is also known as "student's t".

The t-ratio was discovered by an English statistician, W.S. Gossett in 1908 under the pen name "student". Therefore, the "t" ratio is also known as "student's t" and its distribution is known as "student's t-distribution".

As the t-ratio is the standard score (like z-score) with mean = 0 and standard deviation ± 1, therefore the t-ratio is a deviation of sample mean (M) from population mean $\left(\overline{M} \text{ or } M_{pop}\right)$.

If this deviation is large, the sample statistics mean is not reliable or trustworthy and if the deviation is small, the sample statistics mean is reliable and representative to the mean of its parent population $\left(\overline{M}\right)$.

Q8. Describe the standard error of large and small size sample means.

Or

Describe standard error of the mean for large and small sample. [Dec-2014, Q.No.-8]

Ans. The standard error of mean measures the degree to which the mean is affected by the errors of measurement as well as by the errors of sampling or sampling fluctuations from one random sample to the other. In other words, how dependable is the mean obtained from a sample to its parameter, i.e. population mean (M_{pop}).

Keeping in mind the sample size, there are two situations, i.e. large sample and small sample.

The Standard Error of Mean of Large Sample: The standard error of the mean gives us a clue as to how far such sample means may be expected to deviate from the population mean. If the mean of a particular sample may be taken as an estimate of the population mean, any deviation of such a sample mean from the population mean may be regarded as an error of estimation. The standard error of a mean tells us how large the errors of estimation are in any particular sampling situation.

The formula for the standard error of the mean in a large sample is:

$$SE_M \text{ or } \bar{\sigma}_M = \frac{\bar{\sigma}}{N}$$

in which
$\bar{\sigma}$ = The standard deviation of the population; and
N = The number of cases in the sample.

This formula requires the knowledge of the parameter (i.e. standard deviation of the population) in order to compute the standard error of the mean. Since the value of $\bar{\sigma}$ is not known, we have to make the estimate of this standard error.

When we have computed mean (M) and standard deviation (σ) of a large sample, the estimation of $\bar{\sigma}_M$ can be made by the following formula:

$$\sigma_M = \frac{\sigma}{\sqrt{N}}$$

in which
σ = Standard deviation of the sample; and
N = The number of cases in the sample.

The Standard Error of Means of Small Sample: The small sample means, when size of sample (N) is about 30 or less, is treated as small sample. The formula for the standard error of small sample mean score is as follows:

$$S.E._M \text{ or } S_M = \sigma/\sqrt{N-1}$$

As here $S.E._M$ = Standard error of mean of small sample
σ = Standard deviation of the population
N = Size of the sample, i.e. 30 or below

Q9. What do you understand by the degree of freedom? Explain with the help of an example.

Or

Write a short note on Degrees of freedom.

[June-2014, Q.No.-10(c)]

Ans. The number of degrees of freedom, usually denoted by the Greek Symbol— v (read as nu) can be interpreted as the number of useful items of information generated by a sample of given size with respect to the estimation of a given population parameter. Thus, a sample of size 1 generates one piece of useful information if one is estimating the population mean but none if one is estimating the population variance. In order to know about the variance, one need at least a sample of size $n \geq 2$. The number of degrees of freedom, in general, is the total number of observation minus the number of independent constraints imposed on the observations.

Suppose the expression $\sum X = X_1 + X_2 + X_3$ has four terms. We can arbitrarily assign values of any three of these four values (for example, $15 = X_1 + 2 + 8$) but the value of the fourth is automatically determined (for example, $X_1 = 5$).

In this example, there are 3 degrees of freedom. If n is the number of observations and k is the number of independent constants then $n - k$ is the number of degree of freedom.

If we consider sample of size n drawn from a normal population with mean (μ) and if for each sample we compute t, using the sample mean $\bar{x}$ and sample standard deviation s, the distribution for t can be obtained. The probability density function of the t-distribution is given by:

$$f(t) = \frac{Y_0}{\left(1 + \frac{t^2}{v}\right)^{(v+1)/2}} = -\infty < t < \infty$$

Y_0 is a constant depending on n such that the total area under the curve is one.

$v = n - 1$ is called the number of degrees of freedom.

Q10. **State the importance and application of standard error of mean.**

Or

Write a short note on "Importance of standard error of mean". [June-2013, Q.No.-9(c)]

Ans. The standard error of statistics has wide use in inferential statistics. It helps the experimenter or researcher in drawing concrete conclusions rather than abstract ones.

The various uses of standard error of the statistics are as under:
  (1) Various devices are used for determining the reliability of a sample taken from the large population. The reliability of the sample depends upon the reliability of the statistics, which is very easy to calculate.
  (2) The main focus of the standard error of statistics is to estimate the population parameters. No sampling device can ensure that the sample selected from a population may be representative. Thus, the formula of the standard error of statistics provides us

the limits of the parameters, which may remain in an interval of the prefixed confidence interval.

(3) The method of estimating the population parameters the research work feasible, where the population is unknown as impossible to measure. It makes the research work economical from the point of crew of time, energy and money.

(4) Another application of the standard error of the statistics is to determine the size of the sample for experimental study or a survey study.

(5) The last application of the standard error of statistics to determine the significance of difference of two groups to ascertained by eliminating the sampling or change by estimating the sampling or change errors.

Q11. Write those assumptions on which testing of the difference of two sample means is based.

Ans. The assumptions on which testing of the difference of two sample means is based are as follows:

(1) The variable or the trait being measured or studied is normally distributed in the universe.

(2) There is no difference in the Means of the two or more populations, i.e. My = Mz. If there is a violation or deviation in the above assumptions in testing the significant difference in the two means, we cannot use "CR" or t-test of significance. In such condition, there are other methods, which are used for the purpose.

(3) The samples are drawn from the population using random method of sample selection.

(4) The size of the sample drawn from the population is relatively large.

Q12. Explain the standard error of the difference of two means and critical ratio (CR).

Ans. Suppose we have two independent large populations, say A and B, and let us say that we have taken several numbers of samples (say two) from each population. Now if we compute the mean values of the scores of a trait of the two populations, we have 100 sample means obtained from the population A and 100 sample means obtained from the population B, and let us say that we find that there is a difference between the two sample means of population A and B. Thus, in this way, we have 100 differences of sample means. If we plot the frequency polygon of these hundred samples, certainly, we will have a normal curve, and the distribution of the sample mean differences will be known as Sampling Distribution of Mean Differences.

The standard error of the sample mean differences can be obtained by computing standard deviation of the sampling distribution of mean differences. This can be computed by using the formula:

$$S.E_M \text{ or } \Sigma_{DM} = \frac{\Sigma_1^2 + \Sigma_2^2}{N_1 + N_2}$$ (In case of two independent populations)

where

Σ_1 = Standard deviation of the scores of a trait of the sample-1

Σ_2 = Standard deviation of the scores of a trait of the sample-2
N_1 = Number of cases in sample-1
N_2 = Number of cases in sample-2

After having the standard error of the sample mean differences, the next step is to decide how far the particular sample mean difference is deviating from the two population mean differences $(M_1 \sim M_2)$ on the normal probability curve scale. For the purpose, we have to calculate Z-score of the particular two sample mean differences, using the formula:

$$Z = \frac{X - M}{\sigma_{DM}}$$

or

$$Z = \frac{(M_1 \sim M_2) - (M_1 \sim M_2)}{\sqrt{\frac{\Sigma_1^2 + \sigma^2}{N_1 + N_2}}}$$

To distinguish the Z score of the difference of two sample means, the symbol CR (Critical Ratio) is used. Therefore,

$$CR = \frac{(M_1 \sim M_2) - (M_1 \sim M_2)}{\Sigma_{DM}}$$

If the two independent populations are alike or same about a trait being measured, then
$M_1 \sim M_2 = 0$

$$\therefore CR = \frac{(M_1 \sim M_2) - 0}{\sigma_{DM}}$$

Or $$CR = \frac{(M_1 \sim M_2)}{\sigma_{DM}}$$

This is the general formula to decide the significance of the difference exists in the two sample means taken from the two independent populations.

The formula of CR clearly indicates that it is a simple ratio between difference of the two sample means and the standard error of the sample mean differences. Further, it is nothing but a Z-score, which indicates how far the two sample mean differences are deviating from the two parent population mean differences, which is zero.

Q13. What is meant by uncorrelated (independent) and correlated (dependant) sample means?

Ans. When we are interested to test whether two groups differ significantly on a trait or characteristics measured, the two situations arises with respect to differences between means:

  (1) Uncorrelated or Independent two sample means; and
  (2) Correlated or Dependant two sample means.

The two sample means are uncorrelated or independent when computed from different samples selected by using random method of sample selection from one population or from different populations or from uncorrelated tests administered to the same sample.

The two sample means are correlated when a single group of population is tested in two different situations by using the same test. In other words, when one test is used on a single group before the experiment and after the experiment or when the units of the group or the population from which two sample are drawn are not mutually exclusive.

In the latter situation, the modified formula for calculating the standard error of the difference of two sample means is applied.

Thus, to test the significance of sample means, there are always following four situations:
- (1) Two large independent samples, i.e. when N_1 and $N_2 > 30$;
- (2) Two small independent samples, i.e. when N_1 and $N_2 < 30$;
- (3) Two large correlated samples; and
- (4) Two small correlated samples.

Q14. What are the points to be remembered while testing the significance in two means?

Or

Write a short note "Points to remember while testing the significance of difference in two means".

[June-2014, Q.No.-10(e)]

Ans. The points to be kept in mind while testing the difference between two means are as follows:
- (1) Set up null hypothesis (H_0) and the alternative hypothesis (H_1), according to the requirements of the problem.
- (2) Decide about the level of significance for the test, usually in behavioural or social science, .05 and .01 levels are taken into consideration for acceptance or rejection of the null hypothesis.
- (3) Decide whether one-tailed or two-tailed test of significance for independent or the correlated means.
- (4) Decide whether the large or small samples are involved in the problem or in the experiment.
- (5) Calculate either CR value or t-ratio value as per nature and size of the samples.
- (6) Calculate degree of freedom (df). It should be $N_1 + N_2 - 2$ for independent t or uncorrelated samples. While in case of correlated samples, it should be $N - 1$.
- (7) Consult the t-distribution table with df keeping in mind the level of significance.
- (8) Compare the calculated value of "t" with the t-value given in the table [Appendix Table C] with respect to df and level of significance.
- (9) Interpret the Results:
  If null hypothesis (H_0) is rejected, there is a significant difference between the two means.

If null hypothesis is accepted, there is no significant difference in the two means. Whatever the difference exists, it has arisen due to sampling fluctuations or chance factors only.

Q15. What is meant by analysis of variance? Describe its assumptions.

Or

Explain some of the basic assumptions of analysis of variance.

Ans. We use z-test and t-test to determine whether there is any significant difference between the means of two random samples. Suppose we have 6 random samples and we want to determine whether there are any significant differences among their means.

For this, we would have to use $\frac{6(6-1)}{2} = 15$ t-tests to determine the significance of the difference between the six means by taking two means at a time. This procedure is cumbersome and time consuming. The technique of analysis of variance would make it possible to determine if any of the two of the means differ significantly from each other by a single test, called F-test, rather t-tests. The F-test enables us to determine whether the sample means differ from one another (between group variance) to a greater extent than the test scores differ from their own sample means (within groups variance) using the ratio:

$$F = \frac{\text{Variance between groups}}{\text{Variance within groups}}$$

The significance of F-ratio is determined from Table D of the Appendix. This table indicates the F-critical values necessary to reject the null hypothesis at selected levels of significance.

Analysis of variance has certain basic assumptions underlying it. Johnson (1961) presents certain assumptions, which should be fulfilled in the use of this technique:

(1) The population should be normal. This assumption, however, is not especially important. Eden Yates showed that even with a population departing considerably from normality, the effectiveness of the normal distribution still held. Besides the findings of Eden and Yates, the study of Norton cited by Guilford (1965, pp. 300-301) also points out that F is rather insensitive to variations in the shape of population distribution.

(2) All the groups of a certain criterion or of the combination of more than one criterion should be randomly chosen from the sub-population having the same criterion or having the same combination of more than one criterion. For instance, if we wish to select two groups in a school population, one of the third grade and the other of the fourth grade, we must choose randomly the respective sub-populations. This assumption is the keystone of the analysis of variance technique. Failure to fulfil this assumption gives biased results.

(3) The sub-groups under investigation should have the same variability. We should test this assumption before we run through the analysis of variance. Otherwise, a false interpretation of the results may follow. This assumption is tested either by applying Bartlett's test of homogeneity or by applying Hartley's test.

Q16. Define variance. State its characteristics. Differentiate between standard deviation and variance.

Or

Write a short note on "Characteristics of variance".

[June-2013, Q.No.-9(a)]

Or

Write a short note on Variance. [June-2014, Q.No.-10(d)]

Ans. In the terminology of statistics, the distance of scores from a central point, i.e. mean is called deviation and the index of variability is known as the mean deviations or standard deviation (σ).

In the study of sampling theory, some of the results may be somewhat more simply interpreted if the variance of a sample is defined as the sum of the squares of the deviation divided by its degree of freedom (N–1) rather than as the mean of the squares deviations.

The variance is the most important measure of variability of a group. It is simply the square of SD of the group, but its nature is quite different from standard deviation, though formula for computing variance is same as standard deviation (SD).

$$\therefore \text{Variance} = \text{S.D.}^2 \text{ or } \sigma^2 = \frac{\sum(X-M)^2}{N}$$

where

X = Raw scores of a group; and

M = Mean of the raw scores.

Thus, we can define variance as "the average of sum of squares of deviation from the mean of the scores of a distribution".

Characteristics of Variance: The following are the main features of variance:

(1) The variance is the measure of variability, which indicates among groups or between groups difference as well as within group difference.
(2) The variance is always in plus sign.
(3) The variance is like an area. While SD has direction like length and breadth has the direction.
(4) The scores on normal curve are shown in terms of units, but variance is an area, therefore either it should be in left side or right side of the normal curve.
(5) The variance remains the same by adding or subtracting a constant in a set of data.

Q17. Describe the procedure for analysis of variance with the help of an illustration.

Ans. In its simplest form, the analysis of variance can be used when two or more than two groups are compared on the basis of certain traits or characteristics or different treatments of simple independent variable is studied on a dependent variable and having two or more than two groups.

It is to be noted here that when we have taken a large group or a finite population, to represent its total units the symbol 'N' will be used.

When the large group is divided into two or more than two sub groups having equal number of units, the symbol 'n' will be used and for number of groups the symbol 'k' will be used.

Illustration: Suppose in an experimental study, three randomly selected groups having equal number of units say 'N' have been assigned randomly, three kinds of reinforcement, viz. verbal, kind and written were used. After a certain period, the achievement test was given to three groups and mean values of achievement scores were compared. The mean scores of three groups can then be compared by using ANOVA. Since there is only one factor, i.e. type of reinforcement is involved, the situation warrants a single classification or one way ANOVA, and can be arranged in the form of the following table.

Table 3.1

S.N.	Group - A Scores of Verbal Reinforcement		Group - B Scores of Kind Reinforcement		Group - C Scores of Written Reinforcement	
	X_a	X_a^2	X_b	X_b^2	X_c	X_c^2
	X_{a1}	(X_{a1}^2)	X_{b1}	(X_{b1}^2)	X_{c1}	(X_{c1}^2)
	X_{a2}	(X_{a2}^2)	X_{b2}	(X_{b2}^2)	X_{c2}	(X_{c2}^2)
	X_{a3}	(X_{a3}^2)	X_{b3}	(X_{b3}^2)	X_{c3}	(X_{c3}^2)
	X_{a4}	(X_{a4}^2)	X_{b4}	(X_{b4}^2)	X_{c4}	(X_{c4}^2)
	X_{a5}	(X_{a5}^2)	X_{b5}	(X_{b5}^2)	X_{c5}	(X_{c5}^2)
	.	.	.	.	.	.
	X_{an}	(X_{an}^2)	X_{bn}	(X_{bn}^2)	X_{cn}	(X_{cn}^2)
Sum	$\sum X_a$	$\sum X_a^2$	$\sum X_b$	$\sum X_b^2$	$\sum X_{c1}$	$\sum X_{c1}^2$
Mean	$\frac{\sum X_a}{n} = M_a$		$\frac{\sum X_b}{n} = M_b$		$\frac{\sum X_c}{n} = M_c$	

To test the difference in the means, i.e. M_a, M_b and M_c, the one-way analysis of variance is used. To apply one-way analysis of variance, the following steps are to be followed:

Step 1: Correction term $C_x = \dfrac{(\sum x)^2}{N} = \dfrac{(\sum x_a + \sum x_b + \sum x_x)^2}{n_1 + n_2 + n_3}$

Step 2: Sum of Squares of Total $SS_T = \sum x^2 - Cx$

$= \sum x^2 - \dfrac{(\sum x)^2}{N}$

$$= \left(\sum x_a^2 + \sum x_b^2 + \sum x_c^2\right) - \frac{\left(\sum x_3\right)}{N}$$

Step 3: Sum of Squares among the Groups $SS_A = \frac{\left(\sum x\right)^2}{N} - Cx$

$$= \frac{\left(\sum x_a\right)^2}{n_1} + \frac{\left(\sum x_b\right)^2}{n_2} + \frac{\left(\sum x_c\right)^2}{n_3} - \frac{\left(\sum x\right)^2}{N}$$

Step 4: Sum of Squares Within the Groups $SS_W = SS_T - SS_A$

Step 5: Mean Scores of Squares Among the Groups $MSS_A = \frac{SS_A}{k-1}$

Where k = number of groups.

Step 6: Mean Sum of Squares Within the Groups $MSS_W = \frac{SS_W}{n-k}$

Where N = Total number of units.

Step 7: F-ratio, i.e. $F = \frac{MSS_A}{MSS_W}$

Step 8: Summary of ANOVA

Table 3.2: Summary of ANOVA

Source of variance	Df	S.S.	M.S.S.	F Ratio
Among the Groups	k-1	SS_A	$\frac{SS_A}{K-1}$	$\frac{MSS_A}{MSS_W}$
Within the groups (Error Variance)	N-K	SS_W	$\frac{SS_W}{N-k}$	
Total	N-1			

The obtained F-ratio in Table 3.2, furnishes a comprehensive or overall test of the significance of the difference among means of the groups. A significant "F" does not tell us which mean differ significantly from others.

If F-ratio is not significant, the difference among means is insignificant. The existing or observed differences in the means are due to chance factors or some sampling fluctuations.

To decide whether obtain F-ratio is significant, we are taking the help of F-table [Appendix Table D].

The obtained F-ratio is compared with the F-value given in the table keeping in mind two degrees of freedom k-1 which is also known as greater degree of freedom or df_1 and N-k, which is known as smaller degree of freedom or df_2. Thus, while testing the significance of the F-ratio, two situations may arise.

The obtained F-Ratio is insignificant: When the obtained F-ratio is found less than the value of F-ratio given in F-table [Appendix Table D and E] for corresponding lower degrees of freedom df_1 that is, k−1 and higher degree of freedom df that is, (df=N−K) at .05 and .01 level of significance, it is found to be significant or not significant. Thus, the null hypothesis is rejected retained. There is no reason for further testing, as none of the mean difference will be significant.

When the obtained F-ratio is found higher than the value of F-ratio given in F-table [Appendix Table D and E] for its corresponding df_1 and df_2 at .05 level of .01 level, it is said to be significant. In such condition, we have to proceed further to test the separate differences among the two means, by applying t-test of significance. This further procedure of testing significant difference between the two means is known as post-hoc test or post ANOVA test of difference.

Q18. Enumerate the steps of one-way analysis of variance.
Ans. The steps of one-way analysis of variance are as follows:
Step 1: Set up null hypothesis.
Step 2: Set the raw scores in table form as shown in the two illustrations.
Step 3: Square the individual scores of all the sets and write the same in front of the corresponding raw score.
Step 4: Obtain all the sum of raw scores and the squares of raw scores. Write them at the end of each column.
Step 5: Obtain grand sums of raw scores as and square of raw square as $\sum x^2$.
Step 6: Calculate correction term by using the formula

$$Cx = \frac{\sum x^2}{N} \text{ Or } Cx = \frac{\left(\sum x_1 + \sum x_2 + \sum x_3 + \ldots + \sum x_k^2\right)}{n_1 + n_2 + n_3 + \ldots + n_k}$$

Step 7: Calculate sum of squares, i.e. SS_T by using the formula:
$$SS_T = \sum x^2 - Cx$$

Step 8: Calculate sum of squares among the groups, i.e. SS_A by using the formula:
$$SS_A = \frac{\sum x^2}{n} - Cx$$

Or $SS_A = \frac{\left(\sum x_1^2\right)^2}{n_1} + \frac{\left(\sum x_2^2\right)^2}{n_2} + \frac{\left(\sum x_3^2\right)^2}{n_3} + \ldots + \frac{\left(\sum x_k^2\right)^2}{n_k} - Cx$

Step 9: Calculate sum of squares within the groups, i.e. SS_W by using the formula: $SS_W = SS_T - SS_A$.

Step 10: Calculate the degrees of freedom as
Greater degree of freedom, i.e. $df_1 = k - 1$ (where k is number of groups)
Smaller degree of freedom, i.e. $df_2 = N - k$ (where N is the total number in the group)

Step 11: Find the value of mean sum of squares of two variances as:
Mean sum of squares between the groups $MSS_A = \frac{SS_A}{k-1}$

Mean sum of squares within the groups $MSS_W = \dfrac{SS_W}{N-K}$

Step 12: Prepare summary table of analysis of variance.
Step 13: Evaluate obtained F-ratio with the F-ratio value given in F-table keeping in mind df_1 and df_2.
Step 14: Retain or reject the null hypothesis framed as in Step 1.
Step 15: If F-ratio is found insignificant and null hypothesis is retained, stop further calculation, and interpret the results accordingly. If F-ratio is found significant and null hypothesis is rejected, go for further calculations and use post-hoc comparison, find the t-values and interpret the results accordingly.

Q19. Why F-ratio test and t-ratio test are complementary to each other?

Ans. The F-ratio test and t-ratio test are complementary to each other, because 't' is followed when 'F' value is significant for the specification of inferences.

F-test is followed, when t-value is not found significant. Because within groups, variance is not evaluated by t-test. It evaluates only the difference between variance.

There is a fixed relation between 't' and 'F'. The 'F' is the square of 't', while 't' is a square root of 'F'.

$F = t^2$ or $t = \sqrt{F}$

Q20. State the merits and limitations of analysis of variance.
Or
Discuss the advantages and disadvantages of ANOVA.
[June-2015, Q.No.-9]

Ans. The analysis of variance technique has the following merits and limitations:

Merits:
(1) It is the improved technique over the t-test or z-test. It evaluates both types of variances, i.e. 'between' and 'within'.
(2) This technique is used for ascertaining the difference among several groups or treatments at a time. It is an economical device.
(3) It can involve more than one variable in studying their main effects and interaction effects.
(4) In some of the experimental design, e.g. simple random design and levels X-treatment designs are based on one-way analysis of variance.
(5) If 't' is not significant, F-test must be followed to analyse the difference between two means.

Limitations:
(1) The analysis of variance techniques is based on certain assumptions, e.g. normality and homogeneity of the variances among the groups. The departure of the data from these assumptions may affect adversely on the inferences.
(2) The F-value provides global findings of difference among groups, but it cannot specify the inference. Therefore, for

complete analysis of variance, the t-test is followed for specifying the statistical inference.

(3) It is a time-consuming process and requires the knowledge and skills of arithmetical operations as well the high vision for interpretations of the results.

(4) For the use of F-test, the statistical table of F-value is essential because without it, results cannot we interpreted.

Q21. State the assumption underlying the analysis of variance.

Ans. The method of analysis of variance has a number of assumptions. The failure of the observations or data to satisfy these assumptions, leads to the invalid inferences. The following are the main assumptions of analysis of variance.

The distribution of the dependent variable in the population under study is normal.

There exists homogeneity of variance i.e. the variance in the different sets of scores do not differ beyond chance, in other words $\sigma_1 = \sigma_2 = \sigma_3 = \ldots \sigma_k$. The samples of different groups are selected from the population by using random method of sample selection.

There is no significant difference in the means of various samples or groups taken from a population.

Q22. Discuss the two-way analysis of variance.

Ans. In two-way analysis of variance, usually the two independent variables are taken simultaneously. It has two main effects and one interactional or joint effect on dependent variable. In such condition, we have to use analysis of variance in two ways, i.e. vertically as well as horizontally or we have to use ANOVA, column and row wise. Suppose we are interested to study the intelligence, i.e. I.Q. level of boys and girls studying in VIII class in relation to their level of socio economic status (SES). In such condition, we have the following 3 x 2 design as shown in the table 3.3.

Illustration:

Table 3.3: SES, Intelligence and Gender factors

Groups	Levels of SES			
	High	Average	Low	Total
Boys	M_{HB}	M_{AB}	M_{LB}	M_B
Girls	M_{HG}	M_{AG}	M_{LG}	M_G
Total	M_H	M_A	M_L	M

In the table above,

M: Mean of intelligence scores.

$M_{HB}, M_{AB}, \& M_{LB}$: Mean of intelligence scores of boys belonging to different levels of SES, i.e. high, average and low respectively.

$M_{HG}, M_A, \& M_{LG}$: Mean of intelligence scores of girls belonging to different levels of SES respectively.

$M_H, M_A, \& M_L$: Mean of the intelligence scores of students belonging to different levels of SES respectively.

M_B, M_G : Mean of the intelligence scores of boys and girls respectively.

From the above 3×2 contingency table, it is clear, first we have to study the significant difference in the means column wise or vertically, i.e. to compare the intelligence level of the students belonging to different categories of socio-economic status (High, Average and Low).

Secondly, we have to study the significant difference in the means row wise or horizontally, i.e. to compose the intelligence level of the boys and girls.

Then we have to study the interactional or joint effect of sex and socio-economic status on intelligence level, i.e. we have to compare the significant difference in the cell means of columns and rows.

We have more than two groups, and to study the independent as well as interaction effect of the two variables, viz. socio-economic status and sex on dependent variable, viz. intelligence in terms of I.Q., we have to use two-way analysis of variance, i.e. to apply analysis of variance column and row wise.

Therefore, in two-way analysis of variance technique, the following type of effects are to be tested:
- Significance of the effect of A variable on D.V.
- Significance of the effect of B variable on A.V.
- Significance of the interaction effect of A x B variables on D.V.

In two-way analysis of variance, the format of summary table after applying the analysis of variance is as under:

Table 3.4: Summary of two-way ANOVA

Source of variance	df	SS	MSS	F Ratio
Among the Groups				
Between the group A	$k_a - 1$	SS_A	MSS_A	$F_1 = \dfrac{MSS_A}{MSS_W}$
Between the Group B	$K_b - 1$	SS_B	MSS_B	$F_2 = \dfrac{MSS_B}{MSS_W}$
Interrelation $A \times B$	$(k_a - 1)(k_b - 1)$	$SS_{A \times B}$	$MSS_{A \times B}$	$F_3 = \dfrac{MSS_{A \times B}}{MSS_W}$
Within the groups (Error Variance)	$N - K_a - k_b$			
Total	$N - 1$			

For interpretation of the obtained F-ratios, we have to evaluate each F-ratio value with the F-ratio given in F-table [Appendix Table D and E] keeping in view the corresponding greater and smaller df and the level of confidence. There may be two possibilities.

All the obtained F-ratios may be found insignificant even at .05 level. This shows that there is no independent (i.e. individual) as well as interaction (i.e. joint) effect of the two independent variables on dependant variable. Hence, null hypothesis will retain. There is no need to do further calculations.

All the three obtained F-ratio's may be found significant either at .05 level of significance or at .01 level of significance. This shows that there is a significant independent (i.e. individual) as well as interactional (i.e. joint) effect of the independent variables on the dependant variable. Therefore, the null hypothesis is rejected. In such condition, if the two independent variables have more than two levels, i.e. three or four, we have to go for further calculations and use post-hoc comparisons by finding out various t-values by pairing the groups.

Similarly, the significant interactional effect will also be studied further by applying t-test of significance or by applying graphical method.

At least one or two obtained F-ratio will be found significant either at .05 level of significance or at .01 level of significance. Thus, the null hypothesis may partially be retained. In such condition too, we have to do further calculations, by making post-hoc comparisons and use t-test of significance, if the independent variables have more than two levels.

Q23. Discuss the merits and demerits of two-way ANOVA.
Ans. The merits and demerits of two-way analysis of variance are as follows:

Merits:
 (1) This technique is used to analyse two types of effects, viz. main effects and Interaction Effects.
 (2) More than two factors effects are analysed by this technique.
 (3) For analysing the data obtained on the basis of factorial designs, this technique is used.
 (4) This technique is used to analyse the data for complex experimental studies.

Demerits:
 (1) When there are more than two classifications of a factor(s) of study, F-ratio value provides global picture of difference among the main treatment effects. The inference can be specified by using t-test in case when F-ratio is found significant for a treatment.
 (2) This technique also follows the assumptions on which one-way analysis of variance is based. If these assumptions are not fulfilled, the use of this technique may give us spurious results.
 (3) This technique is difficult and time consuming.
 (4) As the number of factors are increased in a study, the complexity of analysis in increased and interpretation of results become difficult.
 (5) This technique requires high-level arithmetical and calculative ability. Similarly, it also requires high level of imaginative and logical ability to interpret the obtained results.

Solved Practical Problems

Q1. A reading ability test was administered on the sample of 200 cases studying in IX class. The mean and standard deviation of the reading ability test score was obtained 60 and 10 respectively. Find how many cases lie in between the scores 40 and 70. Assume that reading ability scores are normally distributed.

Ans. Given: N = 200
M = 60
$\sigma = 10$
$X_1 = 40$ and
$X_2 = 70$

To find the required no. of cases, first we have to find out the total percentage of cases lie in between Mean and 40 and mean and 70.

$$Z = \frac{X - M}{\sigma}$$

$$\therefore Z_1 = \frac{40 - 60}{10} = -\frac{20}{10}$$

or $z_1 = -2\sigma$

Similarly $z_2 = \frac{70 - 60}{10} = +\frac{10}{10}$

or $z_2 = +1\sigma$

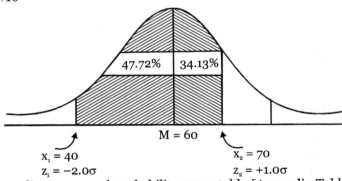

According to normal probability curve table [Appendix Table B] the area of the curve in between M and -2σ is 47.72% and in between M and $+1\sigma$ is 34.13%.

∴ The total area of the curve in between -2σ to $+1\sigma$ is = 47.72 + 34.13 = 81.85%

Therefore, the total no. of cases in between the two scores 40 and 70 are

$$= \frac{81.85 \times 200}{100} = 163.7 \text{ or } 164$$

Thus, total no. of cases who got scores in between 40 and 70 are = 164.

Q2. An IQ test was conducted on 500 students of class X. The mean and SD was found 100 and 16 respectively. Find how many students of the class X having IQ below 80 and above 120.

Ans. Given: M = 100

$\sigma = 16$

$X_1 = 80$ and $X_2 = 120$

To find the required no. of cases first we have to find z scores of the raw scores $X_1 = 80$ and $X_2 = 120$ by using the formula

$$z = \frac{X - M}{\sigma}$$

$$z_1 = \frac{80 - 100}{16} = -\frac{20}{16}$$

or $z_1 = -1.25\sigma$

Similarly,

$$z_2 = \frac{120 - 100}{16} = +\frac{20}{16}$$

or $z_2 = +1.25\sigma$

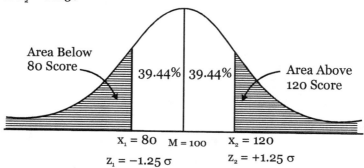

According to NPC table [Appendix Table B] the total percentage of area of the curve lie in between Mean to 1.25σ is = 39.44.

According to the properties of N.P.C. the 50% area lies below to the mean i.e. in left side and 50% area lie above to the mean i.e. in right side.

Thus the total area of NPC curve below M = (100) is = 50 − 39.44 = 10.56

Similarly the total area of NPC curve above M = (100) is = 50 − 39.44 = 10.56

Therefore, total cases below to the I.Q. $80 = \frac{10.56 \times 500}{100} = 52.8 = 53$ Approx.

Similarly Total cases above to the I.Q. $120 = \frac{10.56 \times 500}{100} = 52.8 = 53$ Approx.

Thus, in the group of 500 students of X class there are total 53 students having I.Q. below 80. Similarly, there are 53 students who have I.Q. above 120.

Q3. An adjustment test was administered on a sample of 500 students of class VIII. The mean of the adjustment scores of the total sample obtained was 40 and standard deviation obtained was 8, what percentage of cases lie between the score 36 and 48, if the distribution of adjustment scores is normal in the universe.

Ans. Given: N = 500

M = 40

σ = 8

To find the required percentage of cases, first we have to find out the z scores for the raw scores (X) 36 and 48, by using the formula.

$$z = \frac{X - M}{\sigma}$$

$$z_1 = \frac{36 - 40}{8} = -\frac{4}{8}$$

or $z_1 = -0.5\sigma$

$$z_2 = \frac{48 - 40}{8} = +\frac{8}{8}$$

or $z_2 = +1\sigma$

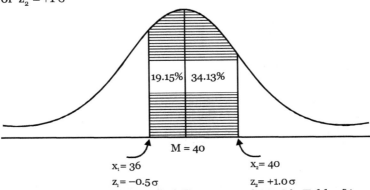

$x_1 = 36$ $\qquad$ $M = 40$ $\qquad$ $x_2 = 40$

$z_1 = -0.5\sigma$ $\qquad\qquad$ $z_2 = +1.0\sigma$

According to Normal Probability curve (N.P.C.) Table [Appendix Table B] the total area of the curve lie in between M to +1σ is 34.13 and in between M to –0.5σ is 19.15.

∴ The total area of the curve in between –0.5σ to +1σ is 19.15 + 34.13 = 53.28

Thus, the total percentage of students who got scores in between 36 and 48 on the adjustment test is 53.28

Q4. In a group of 60 students of class X, Sumit got 75% marks in board examination. If the mean of whole class marks is 50

and S.D. is 10. Find the percentile rank of the Sumit in the class.

Ans. Given: N= 60
M= 50
σ =10

We have to find out the total percentage of cases (i.e. the area of N.P.C.) lie below to the point X = 75.

To find the total required area (shaded part) of the curve, it is essential first to know the area of the curve lie in between the points 50 and 75.

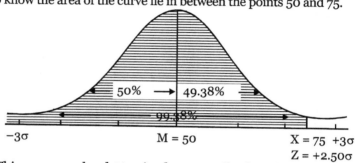

This area can be determined very easily, by taking up the help of N.P.C. Table [Appendix Table B] if we know the value of z of score 75.

$$z = \frac{X-M}{\sigma}$$

$$z = \frac{75-50}{10} = \frac{25}{10}$$

or $= +2.50 \, \sigma$

According to NPC Table [Appendix Table B] the area of the curve lies M and +2.50 σ is 49.38.

In the present problem we have determined 49.38% area lies right to the mean and 50% area lies to the left of the Mean.

Thus, according to the definition of percentile the total area of the curve lies below to the point X = 75 is
= 50 + 49.38%
= 99.38% or 99% Approx

Therefore, the percentile rank of the Sumit in the class is 99th. In other words, Sumit is the topper student in the class, remaining 99% students lie below to him.

Q5. An intelligence test was administered on a large group of student of class VIII. The mean and standard deviation of the scores was obtained 65 and 15 respectively. On the basis intelligence test if the Ramesh's percentile rank in the class is 80, find what is the score of the Ramesh, he got on the test?

Ans. Given: M = 65
σ =15 and PR = 80

As per definition of percentile rank, the 30% area of the curve lie from mean to the point P_{80} and 50% are lie to the left side of the mean.

The z value of the 30% area of the curve lie in between M and P_{80} is = +0.85 σ according to NPC table [Appendix table B]

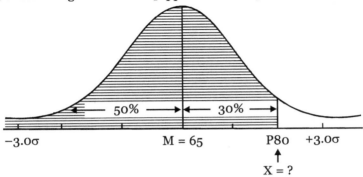

We know that $z = \dfrac{X - M}{\sigma}$

or $+0.85 = \dfrac{X - 65}{15}$

or X = 65 + 15 × 0.85
= 65 + 12.75
= 77.75 or 78 Approx.

Thus, Ramesh's intelligence score on the test is = 78.

Q6. **An achievement test of mathematics was administered on a group of 75 students of class VIII. The value of mean and standard deviation was found 50 and 10 respectively. Find limits of the scores in which middle 60% students lies.**

Ans. Given: N = 75

M = 50

σ = 10

As per given condition (middle 60% cases), 30%-30% cases lie left and right to the mean value of the group as shown in the figure.

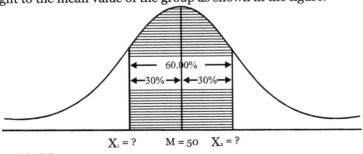

$z = \dfrac{X - M}{\sigma}$

According to the NPC table [Appendix Table B] the value of z_1 and z_2 of the 30% area is $\pm 0.84\sigma$

Therefore by using formula

$$z_1 = \frac{X_1 - M}{\sigma}$$

$$-0.84 = \frac{X_1 - 50}{10}$$

or $X_1 = 50 - 0.84 \times 10$

$= 41.60$ or 42

Similarly,

$$z_2 = \frac{X_2 - M}{\sigma}$$

$$0.84 = \frac{X_2 - 50}{10}$$

or $X_2 = 50 + 0.84 \times 10$

$= 58.4$ or 58

Thus, $X_1 = 42$

$X_2 = 58$

Therefore, the middle 60% cases of the entire group (75 students) got marks on achievement test of mathematics in between $42 - 58$.

Q7. **A group of 1000 applicants who wishes to take admission in a psychology course. The selection committee decided to classify the entire group into five sub-categories A, B, C, D and E according to their academic ability of last qualifying examination. If the range of ability being equal in each sub category, calculate the number of applicants that can be placed in groups ABCD and E.**

Ans. Given: N = 1000

We know that the base line of a normal distribution curve is considered extend from -3σ to $+3\sigma$ that is range of 6σ.

Dividing this range by 5 (the five subgroups) to obtain σ distance of each category, i.e. the z value of the cutting point of each category as shown in the figure given below:

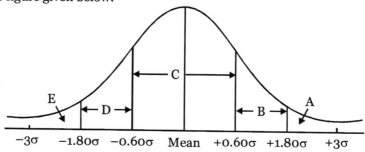

$$\therefore z = \frac{6\sigma}{5} = \pm 1.20\sigma$$

(It is to be noted here that the entire group of 1000 cases is divided into five categories. The number of subgroups is odd number. In such condition the middle group or middle category (c) will lie equally to the centre i.e. M of the distribution of scores. In other words, the number of cases of "c" category or middle category remain half to the left area of the curve from the point of mean and half of the right area of the curve from the mean.

$$\therefore \text{ the limits of "c" category is} = \frac{1.2\sigma}{2} = \pm 0.60\,\sigma$$

i.e. the "c" category will remain on NPC curve in between the two limits -0.6σ to $+0.6\sigma$

Now,

The limits of B category
Lower limit = $+0.6\sigma$
and Upper limit = $0.60\sigma + 1.20\sigma$
or = $+1.80\sigma$
The limits of A category
Lower limit = $+1.8\sigma$
and Upper limit = $+3\sigma$ and above
Similarly, the limits of D category
Upper limit = -6σ
Lower limit = $(-0.60\sigma) + (-1.20\sigma)$
or = -1.80σ
The limits of E category
Upper limit = -1.8σ
Lower limit = -3σ and below

(i) The total % area of the NPC for A category:
According to NPC Table [Appendix Table B] the total % of area in between

Mean to $+1.80\sigma$ is = 46.41
∴ The total % of area of the NPC for A category is = 50 − 46.41 = 3.59

(ii) The total % Area of the NPC for B category:
According to NPC Table [Appendix Table B] the total % of Area in between

Mean and $+0.60\sigma$ is = 22.57
∴ The total % area of NPC for B category is = 46.41 − 22.57 = 23.84

(iii) The total % area of the NPC for C category:
According to NPC table the total % area of NPC in between

M and $+0.60\sigma$ is = 22.57

Similarly the total % area of NPC in between M and -0.06σ is also = 22.57

∴ The total % area of NPC for C category is = 22.57 + 22.57 = 45.14

(iv) In similar way the total % area of NPC for D category is = 23.84

(v) The total % area of NPC for E category is = 3.59

Thus, the total number of applicants (N = 1000) in:

A category is $= \dfrac{3.59 \times 1000}{100} = 35.9 = 36$

B category is $= \dfrac{23.84 \times 1000}{100} = 238.4 = 238$

C category is $= \dfrac{45.14 \times 1000}{100} = 451.4 = 452$

D category is $= \dfrac{23.84 \times 1000}{100} = 238.4 = 238$

E category is $= \dfrac{3.59 \times 1000}{100} = 35.9 = 36$

Total = 1000

Q8. A company wants to classify the group of salesman into four categories as Excellent, Good, Average and Poor on the basis of the sale of a product of the company, to provide incentive to them. If the number of salesman in the company is 100, their average sale of the product per week is ₹10,00,000 and standard deviation is ₹500/-. Find the number of salesman to place as Excellent, Good, Average and Poor.

Ans. As per property of the N.P.C. total area of the curve is 6σ over a range of -3σ to $+3\sigma$.

According to the problem, the total area of the curve is divided into four categories.

Therefore, area of each category is $6\sigma/4 = \pm 1.5\sigma$. It means the distance of each category from the mean on the curve is 1.5σ respectively.

The distance of each category is shown in the figure.

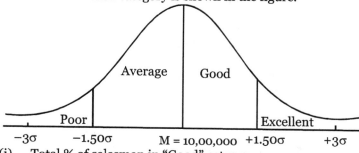

(i) Total % of salesman in "Good" category

According to N.P.C. Table [Appendix Table B] the Total area of the curve lies in between Mean and $+1.5\sigma$ is = 43.32%

∴ The total % of salesman in "Good" category is 43.32%

(ii) Total % of salesman in "Average" category
Total area of the curve lies in between Mean and -1.5σ is also = 43.32%

∴ The total % of salesman in Average category is = 43.32

(iii) Total % of salesman in "Excellent" category
The total area of the curve from Mean to $+3\sigma$ and above is
= 50% .... (As per properties of Normal Curve)
∴ The total % of salesman in the category Excellent is = 50 – 43.32 = 6.68%

(iv) Total % of salesman in "Poor" category
The total area of the curve from Mean to -3σ and below is
= 50% .... (As per properties of Normal Curve)
∴ The total % of the salesman in the poor category is = 50 – 43.32 = 6.68%

Thus,

(i) The number of salesman should place in "Excellent" category
$$= \frac{6.68 \times 100}{100} = 6.68 \text{ or } 7$$

(ii) The number of salesman should place in "Good" category
$$= \frac{43.32 \times 100}{100} = 43.32 \text{ or } 43$$

(iii) The number of salesman should place in "Average" category
$$= \frac{43.32 \times 100}{100} = 43.32 \text{ or } 43$$

(iv) The number of salesman should place in "Poor" category
$$= \frac{6.68 \times 100}{100} = 6.68 \text{ or } 7$$

Total = 100

Q9. A numerical ability test was administered on 300 graduate boys and 200 graduate girls. The boys Mean score is 26 with S.D. (σ) of 6. The girls' mean score is 28 with S.D (σ) of 8. Find the total number of boys who exceed the mean of the girls and total number of girls who got score below to the mean of boys.

Ans. Given: For Boys, N = 300, M = 26 and $\sigma = 6$

For Girls, N = 200, M = 28 and $\sigma = 8$

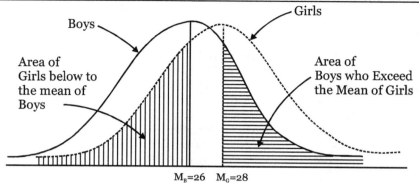

$M_B=26$ $M_G=28$
$\sigma_B=6.0$ $\sigma_G=8.0$

(1) The z score of X (28) is $=\dfrac{28-26}{6}=\dfrac{2}{6}$

or $=+0.33\,\sigma$

According to NPC Table [Appendix Table B] the total % of area of the NPC from M
$= 26$ to $+ 0.33\,\sigma$ is $= 12.93$

∴ The total % of cases above to the point 28 is $= 50 - 12.93 = 37.07$

Thus, the total number of boys above to the point 28 (mean of the girls) is

$=\dfrac{37.07\times 300}{100}=111.21=111$

(2) The z score of X = 26 is $=\dfrac{26-28}{8}=-\dfrac{2}{8}=-0.25\,\sigma$

According to the NPC table the total % of area of the curve in between M = 28 and $-0.25\,\sigma$ is $= 9.87$

∴ Total % of cases below to the point 26 is $= 50 - 9.87 = 40.13$

Thus, the total number of girls below to the point 26 (mean of the boys) is $=\dfrac{40.13\times 200}{100}=80.26=80$

Therefore,
(1) The total number of boys who exceed the mean of the girls in numerical ability is $= 111$
(2) The total number of girls who are below to the mean of the boys is $= 80$.

Q10. **A reasoning test was administered on a sample of 225 boys of age group 15+ years. The mean of the scores obtained on the test is 40 and the standard deviation is 12. Determine how dependable the mean of sample is.**

Ans. Given: N=225, M=40 and $\sigma = 12$

We know that standard error of the mean, when N>30 is determined by using the formula:

$$S.E._M = \sigma/\sqrt{N}$$
$$S.E._M = 12/\sqrt{225}$$
$$= 12/15 = 0.80$$
Or $S.E_M = 0.80$
i.e. $= 0.80$

Interpretation of the Result: As per properties of Normal Distribution, in 95% cases the sample means will lie within the range of ±1.96 in to the M_{pop} (NPC table Appendix Table B). Conversely out of 100, the 99 sample means having equal size, will be within the range of ±2.57 (2.57 ×0.80) of the M_{pop}.

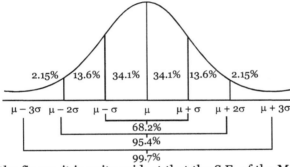

From the figure, it is quite evident that the S.E. of the M=40. Sample of 225 having $\sigma = 12$ lie within the acceptable region of the N.P.C.(Normal Probability curve). Thus, the sample mean obtained is quite trustworthy with the confidence of 95% probability. There are only 5% chances that the sample mean obtained will lie in the area of the rejection of M.P.C.

In simplest term, we can say that, there is 95% probability the maximum possibility of the standard error of the sample mean (40) is ±1.57 (1.96×0.80) which is less than the value of T=1.96 at .05 level of confidence for df=224 (N-1) Thus, the obtained sample mean (40) is quite dependable to its M_{pop} with the confidence level of 95%.

Q11. A randomly selected group of 17 students were given a word cancellation test. The mean and S.D. obtained for cancelling the words per minute is 58 and 8 respectively. Determine how far sample mean is acceptable to represent the Mean of the population?

Ans. Given: N=17 M=58 and $\sigma=8$

In the problem, the size of sample is less than 30. Therefore, to find the standard error of sample mean is

$$S.E_M = \frac{\sigma}{\sqrt{N-1}}$$

$$S.E_M = \frac{8}{\sqrt{17-1}}$$

$$= \frac{8}{\sqrt{16}}$$
$$= 8/4 = 2$$

In the "t" table [Appendix Table C] at .01 level, the value of "t" for 16 df is 2.92 and the obtained value of t = 2.00, which is less in comparison to the "t" value given in the table. Therefore, the obtained sample mean (58) is quite trustworthy and representing its Mean population by 99% confidence. There is only one chance out of 100, that sample mean is low or high.

Q12. One language test was given to 400 boys of VIII class, the mean of their performance is 56 and the standard deviation is 14. What will be the Mean of the population of 99% level of confidence?

Ans. Given: N=400 M=56 and σ=14

We know that Mpop at .01 level or at 99% confidence level is

Mpop .01 or $M.01 = M \pm 2.58\sigma_M$

In this problem, the values of Mean and N are known and the value of σ_M is unknown. The value of σ_M can be determined by using the formula.

$$\sigma_M = \frac{\sigma}{\sqrt{N}}$$

$$\therefore \sigma_M = \frac{14}{\sqrt{400}} = \frac{14}{20}$$

Or $\sigma_M = 0.70$

Thus, $\overline{M}.01 = 56 \pm 2.58 \times 0.70$
= 56±1.806
= 54.194 - 57.806
Or $\overline{M}.01 = 54 - 58$

The Mean of the population at 99% level of confidence will be within the limits 54 to 58. In other words, there are 99% chances that the Mean of the population lie within the range 54-58 scores. There is only 1% chance that mean of the population lie beyond this limit.

Q13. A randomly selected group of 26 VI grade students having a weight of 35 kg and S.D. = 10 kg. How well does this value estimate the average weight of all VI grade students at .99 and .95 level of confidence?

Ans. Given: N =26 M = 35 kg and σ=10 kg.

In this problem the given sample size is below 30, therefore, to have the standard error of sample mean we will use the formula:

$S_M = 2.0$
$N - 1 = 26 - 1$
df = 25

(i) Fiduciary limits of M at .01 level of confidence
By consulting the t table, level of confidence, the value of "t" for 25 df is 2.79

Thus, the Fiduciary limit of M at .01 or 99% level is

$= \overline{M} \pm 2.79\ \sigma_M$
$= 35 \pm 2.79 \times 2.00$
$= 35 \pm 5.58$
$\therefore \overline{M}_{.01} = 29.42 - 40.58 = (11.16)$

(ii) The fiduciary limits of $\overline{M}$ at .05 level of confidence in the t table [Appendix table C] t-value of 0.5 level of confidence for 25 df is 2.06

$M_{0.05} = M \pm 2.06\ \sigma_M$
$= 35 \pm 2.06 \times 2.0$
$= 35 \pm 4.12$
Or $M_{0.05} = 30.88 - 39.12$

(i) Thus, The Fiduciary Limits of $M_{.01} = 29.42 - 38.58$
(ii) The Fiduciary Limits of $M_{.05} = 30.88 - 39.12$

Q14. **If the standard deviation of a certain population (σ) is 20. How many cases would require in a sample in order that standard error of the mean should not miss by 2.**

Ans. Given: $\sigma = 20$ and $S.E._M = 2$

$S.E._M = \dfrac{\sigma}{\sqrt{N}}$

$\therefore 2 = \dfrac{20}{\sqrt{N}}$

Or $\sqrt{N} = \dfrac{20}{2} = 10$

Or $N = (10)^2$

Or $N = 100$

If the standard error of the sample mean should not be more than 2 in such condition the maximum sample size should be 100, i.e. N = 100.

Q15. **The standard deviation of the intelligence scores of an adolescent population is 16. If the maximum acceptable standard error of the mean of the sample should not miss by 1.90, what should be the best sample size at 99% level of confidence?**

Ans. Given: $\sigma = 16, S.E._M = 1.90$

As know that the z value of 99% cases is 2.58

It means due to chance factors the sample mean would deviate from M_{pop} by $2.58\sigma_M$. Further in keeping view the measurement and other uncontrolled factors, the measured error in the sample mean we would like to accept is 1.90.

Therefore, the maximum error in the sample which we would like to select from the parent population is

$$S.E_M = \sigma \times \frac{2.58}{\sqrt{N}} \text{ Or } \sqrt{N} = \frac{\sigma \times 2.58}{S.E_M}$$

$$\text{Or } N = \left(\frac{\sigma \times 2.58}{S.E_M}\right)^2$$

$$\therefore N = \left(\frac{16 \times 2.58}{1.90}\right)^2$$

Or N = 472

To have a representative sample up to the level of 99% to the parent population, it is good to have a sample size more than 472 cases.

Q16. An Intelligence test was administered on the two groups of Boys and Girls. These two groups were drawn from the two populations independently by using random method of sample selection. After administration of the test, the following statistics was obtained:

Groups:	N	M	σ
Boys:	65	52	13
Girls:	60	48	12

Determine the difference between the mean values of Boys and Girls significant?

Ans. In the given problem, the two samples are quite large and independent. Therefore, to test the significance difference in the mean values of Boys and Girls, first we have to determine the null hypothesis which is

$$H_0 = M_B = M_G \text{ i.e.}$$

There is no significant difference in the mean value of the Boys and Girls and the two groups are taken from the same population

$$C.R. = \frac{M_1 \sim M_2 - 0}{\sigma D} = \frac{(M_1 \sim M_2)}{\sqrt{\frac{\sigma_1^2}{N_1} + \frac{\sigma_2^2}{N_2}}}$$

$$C.R. = \frac{(52-48)}{\sqrt{\frac{13^2}{65} + \frac{12^2}{60}}}$$

$$= \frac{4}{\sqrt{\frac{169}{65} + \frac{144}{60}}} = \frac{4}{\sqrt{5}}$$

Or C.R. = 1.79

$$df = (N_1 - 1) + (N_2 - 1)$$
$$= (65 - 1) + (60 - 1)$$
$$= 123$$

To test the null hypothesis, which is framed, we will use two tail test. In the "t" distribution table [Appendix Table C] at 123 df the "t" value at .05 level and .01 level is 1.98 and 2.62 respectively (The "t" table has 100 and

125 df, but df 123 is not given, therefore nearest of 123 i.e. 125df is considered). The obtained t value (1.79) is much less than these two values, hence it is not significant and null hypothesis is accepted at any level of significance.

Interpretation of the Results: Since our null hypothesis is retained, we can say that Boys and Girls do not differ significantly in their level of intelligence. Whatever difference is observed in the obtained mean values of two samples is due to chance factors and sampling fluctuations. Thus, we can say with 99% level of confidence that no sex difference exists in the intelligence level of the population.

Q17. An attitude test regarding a vocational course was given to 10 urban boys and 5 rural boys. The obtained scores are as under:

Urban Boys (x1) = 6, 7, 8, 10, 15, 16, 9, 10, 10, 9
Rural Boys (x2) = 4, 3, 2, 1, 5

Determine at .05 level of significance that there a significant difference in the attitude of boys belonging to rural and urban areas in relation to a vocational course?

Ans. $H_0 = b_1 = b_2 : H_1 = b_1 \neq b_2$

Level of significance = .05

For acceptance or rejection of null hypothesis at .05 level of significance, the two tail test is used.

Thus,

Urban Boys			Rural Boys		
X_1	d_1 (X_1-M_1)	d_1^2	X_2	d_2 (X_2-M_2)	d_2^2
6	−4	16	4	+1	1
7	−3	9	3	0	0
8	−2	4	2	−1	1
10	0	0	1	−2	4
15	+5	25	5	+2	4
16	+6	36			
9	−1	1			
10	0	0			
10	0	0			
9	−1	1			
$\Sigma X_1=100$		$\Sigma d_1^2=92$	$\Sigma X_2=15$		$\Sigma d_2^2=10$

$M_1 = \Sigma X_1 / N$

= 100/10

M_2=10

$M_2 = \Sigma X_2/N$

M_2=15/5=3

We know that

$$t = \frac{M_1 \sim M_2}{\sqrt{\frac{\sum d_1^2 + \sum d_2^2}{N_1 + N_2 - 2} \times \frac{N_1 + N_2}{N_1 N_2}}} = \frac{10-3}{\sqrt{\frac{92+10}{10+5-2} \times \frac{10+5}{10 \times 5}}}$$

$$= \frac{7}{\sqrt{7.8 \times 0.30}} = \frac{7}{\sqrt{2.34}} = \frac{7}{1.52}$$

Or t = 4.6

$$df = (N_1 - 1) + (N_2 - 1)$$
$$= 9 + 4$$
$$= 13$$

In "t" distribution table [Appendix Table C], the t value for 13 df at .05 level is 2.16. The obtained t value 4.6 is much greater than this value. Hence, null hypothesis is rejected.

Interpretation of the Result: Our null hypothesis is rejected at .05 level of significance for 13 df. Thus, we can say that in 95% cases significant difference in the attitude of the urban and rural boys regarding a vocational course. There are only 5% chances out of 100 that the two groups have same attitude towards a vocational course.

Q18. Music interest test was administered on 15 + years did boys and girls sample taken independently from the two populations. The following statistics was obtained:

	Mean	S.D.	N
Girls	40.39	8.69	30
Boys	35.81	8.33	25

Is the mean difference is in favour of girls?

Ans. $H_0 = b_1 = b_2$

$H_1 = b_1 \neq b_2$

In the given problem, the row scores of the two groups are not given. Therefore, we will use the following formula for testing of the difference of means of two uncorrelated sample means:

$$t = \frac{M_1 \sim M_2}{\sqrt{\frac{\sigma_1^2 (N_1 - 1) + \sigma_2^2 (N_2 - 1)}{N_1 + N_2 - 2} \times \frac{N_1 + N_2}{N_1 \times N_2}}}$$

$$t = \frac{40.39 - 35.81}{\sqrt{\frac{(8.69)^2 (30-1) + (8.33)^2 (25-1)}{30+25-2} \times \frac{30+25}{30 \times 25}}}$$

$$= \frac{4.58}{\sqrt{\frac{75.516 \times 29 + 69.389 \times 24}{53} \times \frac{55}{750}}}$$

$$= \frac{4.58}{\sqrt{72.74 \times 0.73}} = \frac{4.58}{2.309}$$

Normal Distribution

Or t = 1.98

$df = (N_1 - 1) + (N_2 - 1) = 53$

In the t distribution table [Appendix Table C] for 53 df the t value at .05 level is 2.01. Our calculated t value 1.98 is less than this value. Therefore, the null hypothesis is retained.

Interpretation of the Results: Since our null hypothesis is accepted at .05 level of significance. Therefore, it can be said that in 95 cases out of 100, there is no significant difference in the mean values of boys and girls regarding their interest in music. There are only 5% chances that the two groups do not have equal interest in music. Hence, with 95% confidence, we can say that both boys and girls have equal interest in music. Whatever difference is deserved in the mean values of the groups is by chance or due to sampling of fluctuations.

Q19. An Intelligence test was administered on a group of 400 students twice after an interval of 2 months. The data obtained are as under:

	M	S.D
Testing –I:	25	8
Testing –II:	30	5
N:	400	
r_{12} :	0.65	

Test if there is a significant difference in the means of intelligence scores obtained in two testing conditions.

Ans. $H_0 \Rightarrow b_1 = b_2$ and $H_1 \Rightarrow b_1 \neq b_2$

$$\therefore t = \frac{M_1 \sim M_2}{\sqrt{\sigma M_1^2 + \sigma M_2^2 - 2r_{12}\sigma M_1 \sigma M_2}}$$

According the formula all values are given except S.E of means ($\sum M$). Therefore, first we have to calculate standard errors of the means of the two sets of scores:

$$\therefore \sigma M_1 = \frac{\sigma_1^2}{\sqrt{N_1}} = \frac{8^2}{\sqrt{400}} = \frac{64}{20}$$

Or $\sigma M_1 = 3.20$

Similarly

$$\sigma M_2 = \frac{\sigma_2^2}{\sqrt{N_2}} = \frac{5^2}{\sqrt{400}} = \frac{25}{20}$$

Or $\sigma M_2 = 1.25$

Thus,

$$t = \frac{30 - 25}{\sqrt{(3.20)^2 + (1.25)^2 - 2 \times .65 \times 3.20 \times 1.25}}$$

$$= \frac{5}{\sqrt{10.24 + 1.5625 - 5.20}}$$

$$= \frac{5}{\sqrt{6.6025}} = \frac{5}{2.57}$$

t = 1.95
df = N-1 = 400-1
df = N-1 = 400-1 (is same i.e. the single group is tested in two different time intervals)
df = 399

According to "t" distribution table [Appendix Table C] the value of t for 399 df at .01 level is 2.59. Our calculated value of t is 1.95, which is smaller than the value of t given in "t" distribution table. Hence, the obtained t value is not significant even at .05 level. Therefore, our null hypothesis is retained at .01 level of significance.

Interpretation of the Results: Since the obtained t value is found insignificant level for 399 df; thus the difference in the mean values of the intelligence scores of a group, tested after an interval of two months is not significant in 99 conditions out of 100, there is only 1% hence that the difference in two means is significant at .01 level.

Q20. In a vocational training course, an achievement test was administered on 100 students at the time of admission. After training of one year, the same achievement test was administered. The results obtained are as under:

	M	σ
Before Training:	52.50	7.25
After Training:	58.70	5.30

r_{12} : 0.50

Is the gain, after training significant?

Ans. $H_0 = b_1 = b_2$ (The gain after training is insignificant)

$H_1 = b_1 \neq b_2$

Here we will use one tail test rather to use two tail test. Because we are interested in gain due to training, not in the loss. That is we are interested in one side of the B.P.C which is +ve side.

The formula of testing the difference between two large correlated means is:

$$t = \frac{M_1 \sim M_2}{\sqrt{\sigma M_1^2 + \sigma M_2^2 - 2r_{12}\sigma M_1 \sigma M_2}}$$

where

$$\sigma M_1 = \frac{\sigma_1}{\sqrt{N}} = \frac{7.25}{\sqrt{100}} = \frac{7.25}{10}$$

Or $\sigma M_1 = .725$

and $\sigma M_2 = \frac{\sigma_2}{\sqrt{N}} = \frac{5.30}{\sqrt{100}} = \frac{5.30}{10}$

Or $\sigma M_2 = .53$

$$t = \frac{58.70 - 52.50}{\sqrt{(.725)^2 + (.53)^2 - 2 \times .50 \times .725 \times .53}}$$

$$= \frac{6.2}{\sqrt{0.4223}} = \frac{6.2}{.65}$$

t = 9.54
df = (100-1)
= 99

In the 't' distribution table [Appendix Table C] at .02 level the t value for 99 df is 2.36 and out obtained t value is 9.54, which is much greater than the "t" value of the table. Thus, the obtained t value is significant at 99% level of significance. Therefore, our null hypothesis is rejected.

Interpretation of the Results: Since the obtained "t" value is found significant at .02 level for 99df. Thus, we can say that gain on the achievement test made by the students after training is highly significant. Therefore, we can say with 99% confidence that given vocational training is quite effective. There is only 1 chance out of 100, the vocational training is ineffective.

Q21. The achievement test scores of 10 students, before and after practice, are given below. Does practice make a significant difference in achievement test scores?

Individuals   : 1 2 3 4 5 6 7 8 9 10
Achievement scores:
(i) before practice : 72 67 90 97 84 92 65 75 80 69
(ii) after practice : 120 81 110 103 109 137 115 82 110 89

Ans. N = 10

Table for t test of achievement scores by the difference method, using the mean difference.

Individuals	Achievement test scores		D $(X_2 - X)_1$	$(D - M_D)$ d	d^2
	before practice $(X)_1$	after practice $(X)_2$			
1	72	120	+48	+21.5	462.25
2	67	81	+14	−12.5	156.25
3	90	110	+20	−6.5	42.25
4	97	103	+6	−20.5	420.25
5	84	109	+25	−1.5	2.25
6	92	137	+45	+18.5	342.25
7	65	115	+50	+23.5	552.25
8	75	82	+7	−19.5	330.25
9	80	110	+30	+3.5	12.25
10	69	89	+20	−6.5	42.25
			$\Sigma D = 265$		$\Sigma d^2 = 2412.50$

$$MD = \frac{\Sigma D}{N} = \frac{265}{10} = 26.5$$

$$SD = \sqrt{\frac{\Sigma d^2}{N-1}} = \sqrt{\frac{2412.50}{10-1}} = 16.37$$

$$SE_{DM} = \frac{SD}{\sqrt{N}} = \frac{16.37}{\sqrt{10}} = 5.177$$

$$\therefore t = \frac{MD}{SE_{DM}} = \frac{26.5}{5.177} = 5.119, \; df = N - 1 = 10 - 1 = 9$$

The t store, computed by any of the two methods is then compared with the two-tail critical t scores (df = 9) for different levels of significant (Table C of Appendix).

$t_{.05(9)} = 2.262; \; t_{.02(9)} = 2.821; \; t_{.01(9)} = 3.250; \; t_{.001(9)} = 4.781$

As the computed t exceeds even the critical $t_{.001}$, the probability P of correctness of the H_0 is lower than 0.001 and is considered too low. So, the H_0 cannot be retained, and it is inferred that practice produces a significant difference in achievement test scores (P < 0.001).

Q22. In a study of intelligence, a group of 5 students of class IX studying each in Arts, Commerce and Science stream were selected by using random method of sample selection. An intelligence test was administered to them and the scores obtained are as under. Determine, whether the three groups differ in their level of intelligence.

S.No.	Arts Group Intelligence scores	Commerce Group Intelligence scores	Science Group Intelligence scores
1	15	12	12
2	14	14	15
3	11	10	14
4	12	13	10
5	10	11	10

Ans. k = 3 (i.e. 3 groups), n = 5 (i.e. each group having 5 cases), N = 15 (i.e. the total number of units in the group)

Null hypothesis $H_0 = \mu_1 = \mu_2 = \mu_3$

i.e. the students of IX class studying in Arts, Commerce and Science stream do not differ in their level of intelligence.

Thus,

Arts Group		Comm. Group		Science Group	
x_1	x_1^2	x_2	x_2^2	x_3	x_3^2
15	225	12	144	12	144
14	196	14	196	15	225
11	121	10	100	14	196
12	144	13	169	10	100
10	100	11	121	10	100
$\Sigma x_1 = 62$	$\Sigma x_1^2 = 786$	$\Sigma x_2 = 60$	$\Sigma x_2^2 = 730$	$\Sigma x_3 = 61$	$\Sigma x_3^2 = 765$
5		5		5	
12.40		12.00		12.20	

Step 1: Correction term

$$Cx = \frac{(\Sigma x)^2}{N} = \frac{(\Sigma x_1 + \Sigma x_2 + \Sigma x_3 \ldots \ldots \Sigma x_k)^2}{n_1 + n_2 + n_3 \ldots \ldots n_k} = \frac{(62+60+61)^2}{5+5+5} = \frac{(183)^2}{15}$$

Or Cx = 2232.60

Step 2: SS_T (Sum of squares of total) $= \Sigma x^2 - Cx$

$$\text{Or} = \left(\Sigma x_1^2 + \Sigma x_2^2 + \Sigma x_3^2 \ldots \ldots \Sigma x_k^2\right) - \frac{(\Sigma x)^2}{N}$$

= (786+730+765) − 2232.60
= 2281.00 − 2232.60
$SS_T = 48.40$

Step 3: SS_A (Sum of squares among the groups) $= \Sigma \frac{(\Sigma x)^2}{N} - Cx$

$$\text{Or} = \frac{(\Sigma x_1)^2}{n_1} + \frac{(\Sigma x_2)^2}{n_2} + \frac{(\Sigma x_3)^2}{n_3} + \ldots \ldots + \frac{(\Sigma x_k)^2}{n_k} - Cx$$

$$= \frac{(62)^2}{5} + \frac{(60)^2}{5} + \frac{(61)^2}{5} - 2232.60$$
$$= 2233.00 - 2232.60$$
Or $SS_A = 0.40$

Step 4: SS_W (Sum of squares within the groups) $= SS_T - SS_A$
Or $= 48.40 - 0.40$
$SS_W = 48.00$

Step 5: MSS_A (Mean sum of squares among the groups)
$$MSS_A = \frac{SS_A}{k-1} = \frac{0.40}{3-1} = \frac{0.40}{2}$$
Or $MSS_A = 0.20$

Step 6: MSS_W (Mean sum of squares within the groups)
$$= \frac{SS_W}{N-K} = \frac{48}{15-3} = \frac{48}{12}$$
$MSS_W = 4.00$

Step 7: F Ratio $= \dfrac{MSS_A}{MSS_W} = \dfrac{0.20}{4.00} = 0.05$

Step 8: Summary of ANOVA

Summary of ANOVA

Source of variance	df	SS	MSS	F Ratio
Among the Groups	(k-1) 3-1 = 2	0.40	0.20	0.05
Within the Groups	(N-k) 15-3 = 12	48.00	4.00	
Total	14			

From F table [Appendix Table D] for 2 and 12 df at .05 level, the F value is 3.88. Our calculated F value is .05, which is very low than the F value given in the table. Therefore, the obtained F ratio is not significant at .05 level of significance for 2 and 12 df. Thus, the null hypothesis (H_0) is accepted.

Interpretation of Results: Because null hypothesis is rejected at .05 and .01 level of significance therefore with 99% confidence it can be said that the students studying in Arts, Commerce and Science stream do not differ significantly in their level of intelligence.

Q23. An experimenter wanted to study the relative effects of four drugs on the physical growth of rats. The experimenter took a group of 20 rats of same age group, from same species and randomly divided them into four groups, having five rats in each group. The experimenter then gave 4 drops of corresponding drug as a one doze to each rat of the concerned group. The physical growth was measured in terms of weight. After one month treatment, the gain in weight is given below.

Determine if the drugs are effective for physical growth? Find out if the drugs are equally effective and determine, which drug is more effective in comparison to other one.

Observations (Gain in weight in ounce)

Group A (Drug P)	Group B (Drug Q)	Group C (Drug R)	Group D (Drug S)
4	9	2	7
5	10	6	7
1	9	6	4
0	6	5	2
2	6	2	7

Ans. Given k = 4, n = 5, N = 20 and Scores of 20 rats in terms of weight
Null hypothesis $H_0 = \mu_1 = \mu_2 = \mu_3$

i.e. All the four drugs are equally effective for the physical growth of the rats.
Therefore:

Group A		Group B		Group C		Group D	
X_1	X_1^2	X_2	X_2^2	X_3	X_3^2	X_4	X_4^2
4	16	9	81	2	4	7	49
5	25	10	100	6	36	7	49
1	1	9	81	6	36	4	16
0	0	6	36	5	25	2	4
2	4	6	36	2	4	7	49
$\Sigma X_1 = 12$	$\Sigma X_1^2 = 46$	$\Sigma X_2 = 40$	$\Sigma X_2^2 = 334$	$\Sigma X_3 = 21$	$\Sigma X_3^2 = 105$	$\Sigma X_4 = 27$	$\Sigma X_4^2 = 167$
5		5		5		5	
2.40		8.0		4.20		5.40	

Step 1: Correction Term $Cx = \dfrac{(\Sigma x)^2}{N} = \dfrac{(12+40+21+27)^2}{20} = \dfrac{(100)^2}{20}$

= 500.00

Step 2: Sum of Squares of total $SS_T = \Sigma x^2 - Cx$
= (46+334+105+187) − 500.00 = 152

Step 3: Sum of Squares Among groups $SS_A = \Sigma \dfrac{(\Sigma x)^2}{n} - Cx$

$= \left(\dfrac{(12)^2}{5} + \dfrac{(40)^2}{5} + \dfrac{(21)^2}{5} + \dfrac{(27)^2}{5} \right) - 500.00$

= 82.80

Step 4: Sum of Squares Within groups $SS_W = SS_T - SS_A$
= 152 − 82.80
= 69.20

Step 5: Summary of ANOVA

Summary of ANOVA

Source of variance	df	SS	MSS	F Ratio
Among Groups	4−1 = 3	82.80	$\frac{82.80}{3} = 27.60$	$\frac{27.60}{4.32} = 6.39$
Within Groups (Error variance)	14−4 = 16	69.20	$\frac{69.20}{16} = 4.32$	
Total	19			

In F table [Appendix Table D and E] $F_{.05}$ for 3 and 16 df = 3.24 and

$F_{.01}$ for 3 and 16 df = 5.29

Our obtained F ratio (6.39) is greater than the F value at .01 level of significance for 3 and 16 df. Thus, the obtained F ratio is significant at .01 level of confidence. Therefore, the null hypothesis is rejected at .01 level of confidence. i.e. the drugs P, Q, R, S are not equally effective for physical growth.

In the given problem it is also to be determined which drug is comparatively more effective. Thus, we have to make post-hoc comparisons.

For post-hoc comparisons, we apply 't' test of significance. The common formula of 't' test is:

$$t = \frac{M_1 \sim M_2}{S.E._{DM}}$$

Here $S.E._{DM} = S.D._W \sqrt{\frac{1}{n_1} + \frac{1}{n_2}}$

Where $S.D._W$ or $\sigma_W = \sqrt{MSS_W}$

i.e. $S.D._W$ is the within groups S.D. and n_1 and n_2 are the size of the samples or groups being compared.

In the given problem the means of four groups A, B, C and D are ranging from 2.40 ounce to 8.00 ounce, and the mean difference from 5.60 to 1.20. To determine the significance of the difference between any two selected means we must compute 't' ratio by dividing the given mean difference by its $S.E._{DM}$. The resulting t is then compared with the 't' value given in 't' table [Appendix Table C] keeping in view the df of within the groups i.e. df_W. Thus, in this way for four groups we have to calculate 6, 't' values as given below:

Step 6: Standard deviation of within the groups

$SD_W = \sqrt{MSS_W} = \sqrt{4.32} = 2.08$

Step 7: Standard Error of Difference of Mean $(S.E._{DM})$

$S.E._{DM} = SD_W \sqrt{\frac{1}{n_1} + \frac{1}{n_2}}$

$$20.8\sqrt{\frac{1}{5}+\frac{1}{5}}$$
$$= 1.31$$

(All the groups have same size therefore the value of $SE._{DM}$ for the two groups will remain same)

Step 8: Comparison of the means of the various pairs of groups.

Group A vs B
$$t = \frac{M_A - M_B}{S.E_{DM}} = \frac{8.0 - 2.40}{1.31} = \frac{5.60}{1.31} = 4.28 \text{ (Significant at .01 level for 16 df)}.$$

Group A vs C
$$t = \frac{4.20 - 2.40}{1.31} = \frac{1.80}{1.31} = 1.37 \text{ (Insignificant at .05 level for 16 df)}.$$

Group A vs D
$$t = \frac{5.40 - 2.40}{1.31} = \frac{3.0}{1.31} = 2.29 \text{ (Significant at .05 level for 16 df)}.$$

Group B vs C
$$t = \frac{8.0 - 4.90}{1.31} = \frac{3.80}{1.31} = 2.90 \text{ (Significant at .05 level for 16 df)}.$$

Group B vs D
$$t = \frac{8.0 - 5.40}{1.31} = \frac{2.60}{1.31} = 1.98 \text{ (Insignificant at .05 level for 16 df)}.$$

Group C vs D
$$t = \frac{5.40 - 4.20}{1.31} = \frac{1.20}{1.31} = 0.92 \text{ (Insignificant at .05 level for 16 df)}.$$

Results: Out of 6 't' values, only 3 t values are found statistically significant. Among these three, one value is found significant at .01 level, while the two values are found significant at .05 level of significance. From these 't' values, it is quite clear that the group B is better in physical growth in comparison to the group A and C, similarly group D is found better in comparison to Group A. The group B&D and groups C&D are found almost equal in their physical growth.

Interpretation of the Results: Since the group B is found better in physical growth of the rats in comparison to group A at 99% confidence level and at 95% confidence level it is found better in case of group C. But the group B and D are found approximately equally good in physical growth. Therefore, the drug Q and S are effective for physical growth in comparison to the drugs P and R. Further, the drug Q is comparatively more effective than the other drugs P, R and S respectively.

Q24. A researcher wanted to study the effect of anxiety and types of personality (Extroverts and Introverts) on the academic achievement of the undergraduate students. For the purpose, he has taken a sample of 20 undergraduates by using random method of sample selection. He administered related test and found following observations in relation to the academic achievement of the students.

Level of Anxiety

	Groups	High anxiety	Low anxiety
Type of Personality	Extroverts	12 13 14 15 14	14 14 13 15 15
	Introverts	14 16 16 16 15	11 10 12 12 16

Determine the independent as well as interactional effect of anxiety and types of personality on the academic achievement of the undergraduates.

Ans. Given,

Two independent variables
- type of personality having two levels, viz. extroverts and introverts
- Anxiety it has also two level, viz. high anxiety and low anxiety.

Dependent variable scores
Academic achievement scores.
Number of groups i.e. k = 4.
Number of units in each cell i.e. n = 5.
Total no. of units i.e. N = 20.

H_0 : "There is no significant effect of types of personality and level of anxiety on academic achievement."

For convenience, the given 2 x 2 table is rearranged as under:

S. N.	Extroverts				Introverts			
	High Anxiety		Low Anxiety		High Anxiety		Low Anxiety	
	x_1	x_1^2	x_2	x_2^2	x_3	x_3^2	x_4	x_4^2
1	12	144	14	196	14	196	11	121
2	13	169	14	196	16	256	10	100
3	14	196	13	169	16	256	12	144
4	15	225	15	225	16	256	12	144
5	14	196	15	225	15	225	16	256
Sums	68	930	71	1011	77	1189	61	765
n	5		5		5		5	
Mean	13.60		14.20		15.40		12.20	

Step 1: Correction Term $C_x = \dfrac{(\sum x)^2}{N}$

$= \dfrac{(68+71+77+61)^2}{20} = \dfrac{(277)^2}{20}$

$= 3836.45$

Step 2: Sum of Squares of Total $SS_T = \sum x^2 - C_x$
= 930+1011+1189+765 − 3836.45
= 58.55

Step 3: Sum of Squares Among the Groups

$$SS_A = \sum \frac{(\sum x)^2}{n} - C_x$$

$$= \frac{(68)^2}{5} + \frac{(71)^2}{5} + \frac{(77)^2}{5} + \frac{(61)^2}{5} - 3836.45$$

= 26.55

Step 4: Sum of squares Between the A Groups (i.e. between types of personality)

$$SS_{BTP} = \frac{(\sum x_1 + \sum x_2)^2}{n_1 + n_2} + \frac{(\sum x_3 + \sum x_4)^2}{n_3 + n_4} - C_x$$

$$= \frac{(68+71)^2}{5+5} + \frac{(77+61)^2}{5+5} - 3836.45$$

= 3836.50 − 3836.45
= .05

Step 5: Sum of squares Between the B Groups (i.e. Between level of Anxiety)

$$SS_{Anx} = \frac{(\sum x_1 + \sum x_3)^2}{n_1 + n_2} + \frac{(\sum x_2 + \sum x_4)^2}{n_3 + n_4} - C_x$$

$$= \frac{(68+77)^2}{5+5} + \frac{(71+61)^2}{5+5} - 3836.45$$

= 8.45

Step 6: Sum of squares of Interaction
$SS_{AxB} = SS_A - SS_{BTP} - SS_{BAnx}$

i.e. SS_{AxB} = Sum of squares Among the Groups − Sum of Squares Between Type of Personality − Sum of Squares Between Anxiety Levels.

SS_{AxB} = 26.55 − 0.05 − 8.45
= 18.05

Step 7: Sum of Squares within the Groups
$SS_W = SS_T - SS_A - SS_B$
= 58.55 − 26.55
= 32.00

Summary of Two-way ANOVA

Source of variance	df	Sum of Squares (SS)	Mean SS (MSS)	F Ratio
Among the Groups	$(k-1)$ $(4-1 = 3)$	(26.55)	$\frac{SS_A}{df} = \frac{26.55}{3} = 8.85$	$\frac{8.85}{2} = 4.425$
Between the Groups- SS_{B_1} (Types of personality)	(k_1-1) $2 - 1 = 1$	0.05	$\frac{SS_{B_1}}{df} = \frac{0.5}{1} = 0.5$	$\frac{.05}{2} = .025$
SS_{B_2} (Anxiety levels)	(k_2-1) $2 - 1 = 1$	8.45	$\frac{SS_{B_2}}{df} = \frac{8.45}{1} = 8.45$	$\frac{8.45}{2} = 4.225$
$SS_{A \times B}$	$(k_1-1)(k_2-1)$ $1 \times 1 = 1$	18.05	$\frac{SS_{B_1 \times SSB_1}}{df} = \frac{18.05}{1} = 18.05$	$\frac{18.05}{2} = 9.025$
Within the Groups	$(N-k)$ $20 - 4 = 16$	32.00	$\frac{SS_W}{df} = \frac{32}{16} = 2$	
Total	19			

In the F table for 1 and 16 df, the F value at .01 and .05 level are 8.53 and 4.49 respectively.

Our calculated F values for type of personality and anxiety are smaller than the table F value 4.49.

Therefore, the obtained F ratio values are not significant even at .05 level of significance. Hence, the null hypotheses is in relation to Type of Personality and Anxiety are retained.

In case of interaction effect the obtained F ratio value 9.025 is found higher than the F value given in table at .01 level of significance. Thus, the F for interaction effect is significant at .01 level. Hence, null hypothesis for interaction effect is rejected.

Interpretation of the Results: Since our null hypotheses are accepted at .05 and .01 level of significance, for type of personality, therefore it can be said that there is no independent as well as interactional effect of Types of Personality and levels of Anxiety on the academic achievement of the students. In other words it can be said that the students who are either Extroverts or Introverts are equally good in their academic performance.

Similarly, the anxiety level of the students do not cause any significant variation in the academic achievement of the students.

But the students having different type of personality and have different level of anxiety, their academic achievement varies in 99% cases. From the mean values, it is evident that the students who are Extroverts and have low level of anxiety are comparatively good in their academic achievement (M = 14.20).

In the case of Introverts those who have high level of anxiety are better in their academic achievement (M = 15.40) in comparison to others.

Non-Parametric Statistics

An Overview

Statistics is of great importance in the field of psychology. The human behaviour which is so unpredictable and cannot be so easily measured or quantified, through statistics attempts are made to quantify the same. For analysis of information about human behaviour, we use both parametric and non-parametric statistics. Non-parametric statistics is defined to be a function on a sample that has no dependency on a parameter. Its interpretation does not depend on the population fitting any parametric distributions. Non-parametric statistics are distribution free statistics and can be used for small samples as well as kind of distribution. It has many tests which are equivalent to the parametric test. For instance, for testing like mean, we have Mann Whitney U-test, for Pearson 'r' we have Kendall's *Tau* and so on. The non-parametric tests are available for single sample, matched pair sample, two samples and k samples.

Q1. What are the aspects to be kept in mind before we decide to apply parametric or non-parametric tests?
Or
Discuss the level of measurement with suitable examples.
[Dec-2013, Q.No.-5]
Or
Describe the different scales of measurement with suitable examples. [June-2015, Q.No.-8]

Ans. The aspects to be kept in mind before we decide to apply parametric or non-parametric tests are as follows:

(1) **Level of Measurement:** When deciding which statistical test to use, it is important to identify the level of measurement associated with the dependent variable of interest. Generally, for the use of a parametric test, a minimum of interval level measurement is required. Non-parametric techniques can be used with all levels of measurement, and are most frequently associated with nominal and ordinal level data.

(i) **Nominal Data:** The first level of measurement is nominal, or categorical. Nominal scales are usually composed of two mutually exclusive named categories with no implied ordering: yes or no, male or female. Data are placed in one of the categories, and the numbers in each category are counted (also known as frequencies). The key to nominal level measurement is that there are no numerical values assigned to the variables. Given that no ordering or meaningful numerical distances between numbers exist in nominal measurement, we cannot obtain the coveted 'normal distribution' of the dependent variable. Descriptive research in the health sciences would make use of the nominal scale often when collecting demographic data about target populations.

Example of an item using a nominal level measurement scale

(a) Does your back problem affect your employment status?

☐Yes ☐No

(b) Are you limited in how many minutes you are able to walk continuously with or without support (i.e. cane)?

☐Yes ☐No

(ii) **Ordinal Data:** The second level of measurement, which is also frequently associated with non-parametric statistics, is the ordinal scale (also known as rank-order). Ordinal level measurement gives us a quantitative 'order' of variables, in mutually exclusive categories, but no indication as to the value of the differences between the positions (squash ladders, army ranks). As such, the difference between positions in the ordered scale cannot be assumed to be equal. Examples of ordinal scales in health science research include pain scales, stress scales and functional scales. One could estimate that someone with a score of 5 is in more pain, more stressed or more functional than someone with a score of 3, but not by how much. There are a number of non-parametric techniques available to test hypotheses about differences between groups and relationships among variables, as well as descriptive statistics relying on rank ordering. Table below provides an example of an ordinal level item from the Oswestry Disability Index.

Table 4.1: Walking (Intensity of pain in terms of the ability to walk)

S. No.	Description	Intensity
(1)	Pain does not prevent me walking any distance	Lowest intensity of pain
(2)	Pain prevents me from walking more than 2 kilometres	Some level of intensity of pain
(3)	Pain prevents me from walking more than 1 kilometre	Moderate intensity of pain
(4)	Pain prevents me from walking more than 500 meters	High intensity of pain
(5)	I can only walk using a stick or crutches	Very high intensity of pain

(4) **Interval and Ratio Data:** Interval level data is usually a minimum requirement for the use of parametric techniques. This type of data is also ordered into mutually exclusive categories, but in this case, the divisions between categories are equidistant. The only difference between interval data and ratio data is the presence of a meaningful zero point. In interval level measurement, zero does not represent the absence of value. As such, we cannot say that one point is two times larger than another. For example, 100 degrees Celsius is not two times hotter than 50 degrees because zero does not represent the complete absence of heat.

Ratio is the highest level of measurement and provides the most information. The level of measurement is characterised by equal intervals between variables, and a meaningful zero point. Examples of ratio level measurement include weight, blood pressure and force. It is important to note that in health science research, we often use multi-item scales, with individual items being either nominal or ordinal.

(5) **Sample Size:** Adequate sample size is another of the assumptions underlying parametric tests. In a large number of research studies, we do use small sample size and in certain

cases, we just use one case study and observe that case over a period of time. Sometimes, we take small sample sizes from a certain place and such samples are known as convenience samples and limited funding. Thus, the assumption of large sample size is often violated by such studies using parametric statistical techniques.

The sample size required for a study has implications for both choices of statistical techniques and resulting power. It has been shown that sample size is directly related to researchers' ability to correctly reject a null hypothesis (power). As such, small sample sizes often reduce power and increase the chance of a type II error. It has been found that by using non-parametric techniques with small sample sizes, it is possible to gain adequate power. However, there does not seem to be a consensus among statisticians regarding what constitutes a small sample size. Many statisticians argue that if the sample size is very small, there may be no alternative to using a non-parametric statistical test, but the value of 'very small' is not delineated. It has been suggested by Wampold et al. (1990), that the issue of sample size is closely related to the distribution of the dependent variable, given that as sample size increases, the sampling distribution approaches normal (n>100).

At the same time, one can state that if the distribution of the dependant variable resembles closely the normal distribution, then it will amount to the sampling distribution of the mean being approximately normal. For other distributions, 30 observations might be required. Furthermore, in regard to decision about the statistical technique to be used, there is no clear cut choice but one can choose a technique depending on the nature of the data and sample size. Thus, even the choice of parametric or non-parametric tests depends on the nature of the data, the sample size, level of measurement, the researcher's knowledge of the variables' distribution in the population, and the shape of the distribution of the variable of interest. If, in doubt, the researcher should try using both parametric and non-parametric techniques.

(6) **Normality of the Data:** According to Pett (1997), in choosing a test, we must consider the shape of the distribution of the variable of interest. In order to use a parametric test, we must assume a normal distribution of the dependent variable. However, in real research situations, things do not come packaged with labels detailing the characteristics of the population of origin. Sometimes it is feasible to base assumptions of population distributions on empirical evidence, or past experience. However, often sample sizes are too small, or experience too limited to make any reasonable assumptions about the population parameters. Generally, in practice, one is only able to say that a sample appears to come from say, a skewed, very peaked or very flat population. Even when one has precise measurement (ratio scale), it may be irrational to assume a normal distribution, because this implies a certain degree of symmetry and spread.

Non-parametric statistics are designed to be used when we know nothing about the distribution of the variable of interest. Thus, we can apply non-parametric techniques to data from which the variable of interest does not belong to any specified distribution (i.e. normal distribution). Although there are many variables in existence that are normally distributed, such as weight, height and strength, this is not true of all variables in social or health sciences.

The incidence of rare disease and low prevalence conditions are both non-normally distributed populations. However, it seems that most researchers using parametric statistics often just 'assume' normality. Micceri et al. (1989) states that the naïve assumption of normality appears to characterise research in many fields.

However, empirical studies have documented non-normal distributions in literature from a variety of fields. Micceri et al. (1989) investigated the distribution in 440 large sample achievement and psychometric measures. It was found that all of the samples were significantly non-normal ($p<0.01$).

It was concluded that the underlying tenets of normality assuming statistics appeared to be fallacious for the commonly used data in these samples. It is likely that if a similar study, investigating the nature of the distributions of data were to be conducted with some of the measures commonly used in health science research, a similar result would ensue, given that not all variables are normally distributed.

Q2. When do we use the non-parametric statistics?
Or
What are the problems for which non-parametric statistics is used?

Ans. It can sometimes be difficult to assess whether a continuous outcome follows a normal distribution and, thus, whether a parametric or nonparametric test is appropriate. For each of the main parametric techniques, there is a non-parametric test available. Also, experiments with the data would also determine which test provides the best power, and the greatest level of significance. In general, these tests fall into the following categories:

(1) **Differences between Independent Groups:** When we have two samples that we want to compare concerning their mean value for some variable of interest, we would use the t-test for independent samples. The non-parametric alternatives for this test are the Wald-Wolfowitz runs test, the Mann-Whitney U-test, and the Kolmogorov-Smirnov two-sample test.

If we have multiple groups, we would use analysis of variance like ANOVA/MANOVA. The non-parametric equivalents to this method are the Kruskal-Wallis analysis of ranks and the Median test.

(2) **Differences between Dependent Groups:** If we want to compare two variables measured in the same sample, we would customarily use the t-test for dependent samples. For example, we want to compare the math skills of students just at the beginning of the year and again at the end of the year, we would take the scores and use the t-test for such comparison and state that there is a significant difference between the two periods. Non-parametric alternatives to this test are the *Sign* test and *Wilcoxon's matched pairs* test.

If the variables of interest are dichotomous in nature (i.e., "pass" vs. "no pass") then McNemar's Chi-square test is appropriate.

If there are more than two variables that were measured in the same sample, then we would customarily use repeated measures ANOVA.

Non-parametric alternatives to this method are Friedman's two-way analysis of variance and Cochran Q test (if the variable was measured in terms of categories, e.g., "passed" vs. "failed"). Cochran Q is particularly useful for measuring changes in frequencies (proportions) across time.

(3) **Relationships between Variables:** To express a relationship between two variables, one usually computes the correlation coefficient. Non-parametric equivalents to the standard correlation coefficient of Pearson 'r' are Spearman R, Kendall's Tau.

The appropriate non-parametric statistics for testing the relationship between two variables are the Chi-square test, the Phi coefficient and the Fisher exact test. In addition, a simultaneous test for relationships between multiple cases is available, as for example, Kendall coefficient of concordance. This test is often used for expressing inter rater agreement among independent judges who are rating (ranking) the same stimuli.

(4) **Descriptive Statistics:** When one's data are not normally distributed, and the measurements at best contain rank order information, then using non-parametric methods is the best. For example, in the area of psychometrics it is well known that the rated intensity of a stimulus (e.g., perceived brightness of a light) is often a logarithmic function of the actual intensity of the stimulus (brightness as measured in objective units of Lux). In this example, the simple mean rating (sum of ratings divided by the number of stimuli) is not an adequate summary of the average actual intensity of the stimuli. In this example, one

would probably rather compute the geometric mean. Non-parametrics and Distributions will compute a wide variety of measures of location (mean, median, mode, etc.) and dispersion (variance, average deviation, quartile range, etc.) to provide the "complete picture" of one's data.

(5) **Problems and Non-parametric Test:** The four problems for which non-parametric statistics used are as follows:

(i) **Two or more independent groups:** The Mann-Whitney 'U' test and the Kruskal-Wallis one-way analysis of variance (H) provide tests of the null hypothesis that independent samples from two or more groups come from identical populations. Multiple comparisons are available by the Kruskal-Wallis test.

(ii) **Paired observations:** The sign test and Wilcoxon Signed-rank test both test the hypothesis of no difference between paired observations.

(iii) **Randomised blocks:** The Friedman two-way analysis of variance is the non-parametric equivalent of a two-way ANOVA with one observation per cell or a repeated measures design with a single group. Multiple comparisons are available for the Friedman test. Kendall's co-efficient of concordance is a normalisation of the Friedman statistic.

(iv) **Rank correlations:** The Kendall and Spearman rank correlations estimate the correlation between two variables based on the ranks of the observations.

Q3. What are the misconceptions about non-parametric statistic tests?

Ans. Non-parametric statistics have long taken the back seat to parametric statistics, often being portrayed as inferior in practice and teaching. It has been suggested that researchers are hesitant to use these techniques due to fear that peer reviewers may not be completely familiar with these statistics, and therefore, unable to properly interpret and review the results.

The above opinion could be due to the widespread case of limited exposure of researchers and clinicians to this type of statistics.

Non-parametric techniques are often left out of basic statistics courses, and relegated to the last chapter of texts, making them seem less important, while reinforcing the focus on parametric statistics.

Another common misconception concerning non-parametric statistics is that they are restricted in their application. It is thought that there are only a limited number of simple designs that can be analysed using these techniques.

However, there are non-parametric techniques, which span from simple 2-group analysis, to complex structural equation modeling. Basically, for any parametric test, there is a non-parametric equivalent that would be equally, or in some cases, more appropriate for use.

Q4. Explain Mann-Whitney 'U' Test. What are the underlying assumptions of Mann-Whitney U test?

Ans. The Mann-Whitney U test is a non-parametric counterpart of the t-test used to compare the means of two independent populations. This test was developed by Henry B. Mann and D.R. Whitney in 1947. It analyses the degree of separation (or the amount of overlap) between the Experimental (E) and Control (C) groups.

The null hypothesis assumes that the two sets of scores (E and C) are samples from the same population; and therefore, because sampling was random, the two sets of scores do not differ systematically from each other.

The alternative hypothesis, on the other hand, states that the two sets of scores do differ systematically. If the alternative is directional, or one-tailed, it further specifies the direction of the difference (i.e., Group E scores are systematically higher or lower than Group C scores).

Mechanics of the Mann-Whitney U test: The Mann-Whitney U test is commonly known as a ranking test. In this ranking process, the magnitudes of the values are taken into consideration, and accordingly larger values are allocated greater ranks than smaller values. The same is true whenever the data involves both positive and negative numbers, e.g. −5 is allocated a smaller rank than +5. After the data in the two treatment groups have been ranked, the sum of the ranks in each treatment group is calculated. The Mann-Whitney U statistic may then be computed and interpreted in terms of the acceptance or rejection of the null hypothesis.

The Mann-Whitney U statistics is conveniently calculated using the following equation:

$$U_1 = n_1 n_2 + \frac{n_1(n_1 + 1)}{2} - \Sigma R_1$$

where n_1 is the number of values in treatment group 1, n_2 is the number of values in treatment group 2 and ΣR_1 is the sum of the ranks corresponding to treatment group 1.

Alternatively, the notation in the equation may be altered and the Mann-Whitney U statistic may be calculated using the data associated with treatment group 2:

$$U_2 = n_1 n_2 + \frac{n_2(n_2 + 1)}{2} - \Sigma R_2$$

where n_1 is the number of values in treatment group 1, n_2 is the number of values in treatment group 2 and ΣR_2 is the sum of the ranks corresponding to treatment group 2.

Assumptions: The Mann-Whitney U test is based on the following assumptions:

(1) Each sample has been randomly selected from the population it represents;
(2) The two samples are independent of one another;
(3) The original variable observed (which is subsequently ranked) is a continuous random variable. In truth, this assumption, which

variable which represents a discrete random variable; and
(4) The underlying distributions from which the samples derived are identical in shape. The shapes of the underlying population distributions, however, do not have to be normal.

Q5. Discuss the step-by-step procedure for 'U' test for small sample.

Ans. Mann Whitney U Test for Small Sample case (not more than 20 items in each set), use U if the data is:
- in the form of ranks or;
- not normally distributed; and
- there is an obvious difference in the variance of the two groups.

Step 1: Rank the data (taking both groups together) giving rank 1 to the lowest score, and the highest rank to the highest score.

Step 2: Find the sum of the ranks for the smaller sample.

Step 3: Find the sum of the ranks for the larger sample.

Step 4: Find U applying the formula given below:

$$U_1 = n_1 n_2 + \frac{n_1(n_1+1)}{2} - \Sigma R_1$$

and

$$U_2 = n_1 n_2 + \frac{n_2(n_2+1)}{2} - \Sigma R_2$$

Step 5: Look up the smaller of U_1 and U_2 in Mann-Whitney U test [Appendix Table H]. There is a significant difference if the observed value is equal to or more than the table value.

Step 6: Translate the results of the test back in the terms of experiment.

Q6. Discuss the Mann-Whitney 'U' test for analysis of large sample.

Ans. Mann-Whitney 'U' test for large sample is used when the sample sizes are greater than 20. Under these circumstances, it is assumed that the sampling distribution of the Mann-Whitney U statistic approximates to the normal distribution and therefore the standardised normal distribution may be employed to interpret the outcome of the statistical analysis. Under these circumstances, the z value is calculated as before, i.e. the difference between the test value (the Mann-Whitney U statistic) and the mean is divided by the standard deviation:

$$z = \frac{U - (N_1 N_2 / 2)}{\sqrt{(N_1 \times N_2)(N_1 + N_2 + 1)/12}}$$

where U is the calculated Mann-Whitney U statistic (the smaller of the two possible calculated values), N_1 is the sample size of the smaller group and N_2 is the size of the large group.

Q7. Enumerate the steps for computing Mann-Whitney U test in SPSS.

Ans. The Steps for computing Mann-Whitney U test in SPSS are as follows:

Step 1: Choose Analyse
Step 2: Select Non-parametric Tests
Step 3: Select 2 Independent Samples
Step 4: Highlight the test variable and click on the arrow to move this into the Test Variable List box
Step 5: Highlight the grouping variable and click on the arrow to move this into the Grouping Variable box.
Step 6: Click on Define Groups and type in the codes that indicate which group an observation belongs to. Click on Continue.
Step 7: Under Test Type, make sure that Mann-Whitney U is selected.
Step 8: If you want exact probabilities, click on Exact, choose Exact, then Continue Click on OK.

Q8. Explain the concept of Wilcoxon Matched-Pairs Signed-Rank Test.

Ans. The Wilcoxon Matched-Pairs Signed-Ranks test is also a non-parametric analogue of the t-test for matched samples. However, this test is based on richer information than the sign test. Not only are the signs of the difference scores considered, but also their ranks. Nevertheless, since the Wilcoxon matched-pairs signed-ranks test is not based on the magnitude of the difference scores, but is based on their ranking, it makes use of less rich information than the t-test. Despite this loss of information, it may be usefully applied if the distributions of the two sets of related scores are not normal.

Background Information on Wilcoxon Test: The Wilcoxon matched-pairs signed-ranks test (Wilcoxon (1945, 1949)) is a non-parametric procedure employed in a hypothesis testing situation involving a design with two dependent samples. Whenever one or more of the assumptions of the t-test for two dependent samples are saliently violated, the Wilcoxon matched-pairs signed-ranks test (which has less stringent assumptions) may be preferred as an alternative procedure.

The Wilcoxon matched-pairs signed-ranks test is essentially an extension of the Wilcoxon signed-ranks test (which is employed for a single sample design) to a design involving two dependent samples.

In order to employ the Wilcoxon matched-pairs signed ranks test, it is required that each of n subjects (or n pairs of matched subjects) has two interval/ratio scores (each score having been obtained under one of the two experimental conditions).

A difference score is computed for each subject (or pair of matched subjects) by subtracting a subject's score in Condition 2 from his score in Condition 1.

The hypothesis evaluated with the Wilcoxon matched-pairs signed-ranks test is whether in the underlying populations represented by the sampled experimental conditions, the median of the difference scores equals zero.

If a significant difference is obtained, it indicates that there is a high likelihood that the two sampled conditions represent two different populations.

Assumptions: The Wilcoxon matched-pairs signed-ranks test is based on the following assumptions:
(1) The sample of n subjects has been randomly selected from the population it represents;
(2) The original scores obtained for each of the subjects are in the format of interval/ratio data; and
(3) The distribution of the difference scores in the populations represented by the two samples is symmetric about the median of the population of difference scores.

Q9. State the step-by-step procedure for Wilcoxon test for small sample.

Ans. For matched pairs or repeated measures designs in Wilcoxon Test-Small Sample case (not more than 25 pairs of scores), use instead of a correlated t-test if either:
- the differences between treatments can only be ranked in size or
- the data is obviously non-normal or
- there is an obvious difference in the variance of the two groups.

Step 1: Obtain the difference between each pair of reading, taking sign into account;

Step 2: Rank order these differences (ignoring the sign), giving rank 1 to the smallest difference;

Step 3: Obtain T, the sum of the ranks for differences with the less frequent sign;

Step 4: Consulting Table G, if the observed T is equal to or less than the table value then there is a significant difference between two conditions; and

Step 5: Translate the result of the test back in terms of the experiment.

Q10. Discuss the Wilcoxon Test for large sample.

Ans. If the sample size employed in a study is relatively large, i.e. more than 25, the normal distribution can be employed to approximate the Wilcoxon T-statistic. Although sources do not agree on the value of the sample size that justifies employing the normal approximation of the Wilcoxon distribution, they generally state that it should be employed for sample sizes larger than those documented in the Wilcoxon table contained within the source.

Therefore, under these conditions, one can perform a Z-test.

$$Z = \frac{T - \frac{N(N+1)}{4}}{\sqrt{\frac{N(N+1)(2N+1)}{24}}}$$

Q11. Compare the Mann-Whitney 'U' test and Wilcoxon MPSR test with T-test.

Ans. The power efficiency of the Mann-Whitney and Wilcoxon tests, whilst usually somewhat lower than the corresponding t-test, compares very favourably with it. The Mann-Whitney and Wilcoxon tests can be used in situations where the t-test would be inappropriate (e.g., where the assumptions of the t-test obviously do not apply). In other words, they are capable of wider application.

Different statisticians give different advice as to the relative merits of parametric and non-parametric tests. The non-parametric camp claims that their tests are simpler to compute, have fewer assumptions and can be used more widely. The parametric camp claims that their tests are robust with respect to violations of their assumptions and have greater power efficiency.

The strategy recommended here is to use the t-test unless the data is in form of ranks, or where the sample is small and either the distribution is obviously non-normal or there are obviously large differences in variance.

However, if we are particularly pressed for time or have a large number of analyses to do there is particularly nothing inappropriate about using non-parametric statistics, even in cases where t-tests might have been used.

Q12. Discuss the Kruskal Wallis ANOVA test.
Or
Enumerate the assumptions of Kruskal Wallis ANOVA.
Or
Describe the procedure for ANOVA calculations.
Or
When do we use Kruskal Wallis Analysis of variance? What relevant background information do you require on Kruskal Wallis ANOVA test? [Dec-2014, Q.No.-9]

Ans. The Kruskal-Wallis test is a non-parametric alternative to one-way ANOVA. There may be cases where a researcher is not clear about the shape of the population. In this situation, the Kruskal-Wallis test is a non-parametric alternative to one-way ANOVA. One-way ANOVA is based on the assumptions of normality, independent groups and equal population variance. In order to perform one-way ANOVA, it is essential that data is atleast interval scaled. On the other hand, Kruskal-Wallis test can be performed on ordinal data and is not based on the normality assumption of the population. Kruskal-Wallis test is based on the assumption of independency of groups. It is also based on the assumption that individual items are selected randomly.

A researcher has to first draw K independent samples from k different populations. Let these samples of size $n_1, n_2, n_3, ..., n_k$ be from k different populations. These samples are then combined such that $N = n_1 + n_2 + n_3 + ... + n_k$. The next step is to arrange n observations in an ascending order. The smallest value is assigned Rank 1 and the highest value is assigned the highest rank. In case of a tie, average ranks of ties are assigned. Then ranks corresponding to different samples are added. The total of the ranks are denoted by $T_1, T_2, T_3, ..., T_k$. The Kruskal-Wallis statistic is computed by using the following formula Kruskal-Wallis statistic (K).

$$K = \frac{12}{N(N+1)} \left(\sum_{j=1}^{k} \frac{T_j^2}{n_j} \right) - 3(N+1)$$

where,
  k = Number of groups;
  N = Total number of observations (items);
  $T_j = T_1 + T_2 + ...T_k$ (Sum of ranks in groups);
  n = Number of observations (items) in a group.

Here, it is important to note that the K value is approximately χ^2 distributed with k – 1 degrees of freedom, as long as n_j is not less than 5 items for any group.

The null and alternative hypotheses for the Kruskal-Wallis test can be stated as below:
  H_0 : The k different populations are identical; and
  H_1 : At least one of the k population is different.

Decision rule: Reject H_0, when the calculated k value > χ^2 at k – 1 degrees of freedom and a level of significance, otherwise, accept H_0.

Assumptions: Kruskal Wallis test is based on the following assumptions:
  (1) Each sample has been randomly selected from the population it represents;
  (2) The k samples are independent of one another;
  (3) The dependent variable (which is subsequently ranked) is a continuous random variable. In truth, this assumption, which is common to many non-parametric tests, is often not adhered to, in that such tests are often employed with a dependent variable which represents a discrete random variable; and
  (4) The underlying distributions from, which the samples derived, are identical in shape.

Q13. Discuss the Kruskal Wallis ANOVA test for large sample.

Ans. When the number of sample increases, the table I is unable to give us with the critical values, for example, it gives critical values upto 8 samples when k=3, 4 samples when k=4, and 3 samples when k=5, therefore as the sample increases, table I is not of use for the critical value. In such a case, we resort to chi-square table for getting our information on the critical value taking degrees of freedom (k – 1).

Exact tables of the Kruskal-Wallis distribution: Although an exact probability value can be computed for obtaining a configuration of ranks which is equivalent to or more extreme than the configuration observed in the data evaluated with the Kruskal-Wallis one-way analysis of variance by ranks, the chi-square distribution is generally employed to estimate the latter probability. As the values of k and N increase, the chi-square distribution provides a more accurate estimate of the exact Kruskal-Wallis distribution. Although most sources employ the chi-square approximation regardless of the values of k and N, some sources recommend that exact tables be employed under certain conditions. Beyer (1968), Daniel and Siegel and Castellan (1988) provide exact Kruskal-Wallis probabilities for whenever k=3 and the number of subjects in any of the samples is five or less. Use of the chi-square distribution for small sample sizes will generally result in a slight decrease in the power of the test (i.e., there is a higher likelihood of retaining a false null hypothesis). Thus, for small sample sizes, the tabled critical chi-square value should, in actuality, are a little lower than the value of Table I.

Q14. Explain the Kendall's Rank Order Correlation (Kendall's Tau).

Ans. Kendall's tau (τ) is one of a number of measures of correlation or association. Measures of correlation are not inferential statistical tests, but are, instead, descriptive statistical measures which represent the degree of relationship between two or more variables. Upon computing a measure of correlation, it is a common practice to employ one or more inferential statistical tests in order to evaluate one or more hypotheses concerning the correlation coefficient. The hypothesis stated below is the most commonly evaluated hypothesis for Kendall's tau.

Null Hypothesis

$H_0 : \tau = 0$

(In the underlying population, the sample represents the correlation between the ranks of subjects on Variable X and Variable Y, which is equal to 0.)

Relevant Background Information on Test: Developed by Kendall (1938), tau is a bivariate measure of correlation/association that is employed with rank-order data. The population parameter estimated by the correlation coefficient will be represented by the notation τ (which is the lower case Greek letter tau). As is the case with Spearman's rank-order correlation coefficient rho (ρ), Kendall's tau can be employed to evaluate data in which a researcher has scores for n subjects/objects on two variables (designated as the X and Y variables), both of which are rank-ordered.

Kendall's tau is also commonly employed to evaluate the degree of agreement between the rankings of m = 2 judges for n subjects/objects. As is the case with Spearman's rho, the range of possible values Kendall's tau can assume is defined by the limits − 1 to +1 (i.e., − 1 < r > +1). Although Kendall's tau and Spearman's rho share certain properties in common with one another, they employ a different logic with respect to how they evaluate the degree of association between two variables.

Kendall's tau measures the degree of agreement between two sets of ranks with respect to the relative ordering of all possible pairs of subjects/objects.

One set of rank represents the ranks on the X variable, and the other set represents the ranks on the Y variable.

Specifically, the data are in the form of the following two pairs of observations expressed in a rank-order format:

(1) (R_x, R_y) (which represent the ranks on Variables X and Y, respectively for the 1st subject/object); and

(2) $(R_{xj}, R_{yj'})$ (which represent the ranks on Variables X and Y, respectively for the jth subject/object).

If the sign/direction of the difference $(R_{xi} - R_{yj})$, i.e. a pair of ranks is said to be concordant (i.e. in agreement).

If the sign/direction of the difference $(R_{xi} - R_{xj})$, a pair of ranks is said to be discordant (i.e., disagree).

If $(R_{yi} - R_{yj})$ and/or $(R_{xi} - R_{xj})$ result in the value of zero, a pair of ranks is neither the concordant nor discordant.

Kendall's tau is a proportion, which represents the difference between the proportions of concordant pairs of ranks less the proportion of discordant pairs of ranks.

The computed value of tau will equal to +1 when there is complete agreement among the rankings (i.e., all of the pairs of ranks are concordant), and will equal to −1 when there is complete disagreement among the rankings (i.e., all of the pairs of ranks are discordant).

As a result of the different logic involved in computing Kendall's tau and Spearman's rho, the two measures have different underlying scales, and, because of this, it is not possible to determine the exact value of one measure if the value of the other measure is known.

In spite of the differences between Kendall's tau and Spearman's rho, the two statistics employ the same amount of information, and, because of this, it is equally likely to detect a significant effect in a population.

In contrast to Kendall's tau, Spearman's rho is more commonly discussed in statistics books as a bivariate measure of correlation for ranked data. Two reasons for this are as follows:

(1) The computations required for computing *tau* are more tedious than those required for computing rho; and
(2) When a sample is derived from a bivariate normal distribution, the computed value r_s will generally provide a reasonably good approximation of Pearson r, whereas the value of $\tilde{\tau}$ will not.

Since r_s provides a good estimate of r, r_s^2 can be employed to represent the coefficient of determination (i.e., a measure of the proportion of variability on one variable which can be accounted for by variability on the other variable). One commonly cited advantage of tau over rho is that $\tilde{\tau}$ is an unbiased estimate of the population parameter τ, whereas the value computed for r_s is not an unbiased estimate of the population parameter ρ_s.

Q15. Enumerate the step-by-step calculation of Kendall's *Tau*.

Ans. The procedure for computing the Kendall rank order correlation coefficient is as follows:

(1) Rank the observations on the X-variable from 1 to N.
(2) Rank the observations on the Y-variable from 1 to N.

(3) Arrange the list of N subjects so that the rank of the subjects on variable X are in their natural order, i.e. 1, 2, 3,....N.
(4) Observe the Y ranks in the order in which they occur when X ranks are in natural order.
(5) Determine the value of S, the number of agreements in order minus the number of disagreements in order, for the observed order of the Y ranks.
(6) If there are no ties among either the X or the Y observations, then we use the formula:

$$\tau = \frac{2S}{N(N-1)}$$

Where,
S = Score of agreement − score of disagreement on X and Y
N = Number of objects or individuals ranked on both X and Y
If there are ties then the formula would be:

$$\tau = \frac{2S}{\sqrt{N(N-1)-T_x}\sqrt{N(N-1)-T_y}}$$

Where,
$T_x = \sum t(t-1)$, t being the number of tied observations in each group of the ties on the X-variable;
$T_y = \sum t(t-1)$, t being the number of tied observation in each group of the ties on the Y-variable.

Q16. What are the properties of Chi-square distribution?
Ans. For large sample size, the sampling (probability) distribution of χ^2 can be closely approximated by a continuous curve known as the chi-square distribution. The Greek Letter χ^2 is used to denote this test. The quantity χ^2 describes the magnitude of discrepancy between the observed and expected frequencies. The value of χ^2 is calculated as:

$$\chi^2 = \sum_{i=1}^{n}\left[\frac{(O_i - E_i)^2}{E_i}\right] = \frac{(O_1 - E_1)^2}{E_1} + \frac{(O_2 - E_2)^2}{E_2} + \frac{(O_3 - E_3)^2}{E_3} + \ldots + \frac{(O_n - E_n)^2}{E_n}$$

Where,
O = Observed frequency; and
E = Expected or theoretical frequency.

Important Properties of the Chi-square Distribution:
(1) The chi-square distribution is positively skewed with values between 0 and ∞.
(2) There are many chi-square distributions and they are labelled by the parameter degree of freedom (df). Three such chi-square distributions are shown in Fig. 4.1 with df = 5, 15 and 30, respectively.
(3) The mean and variance of the chi-square distribution are given by μ = df and σ^2 = (2) df. For example, if the chi-square

distribution are given by df = 30, then the mean and variance of that distribution are μ = 30 and σ² = 60.

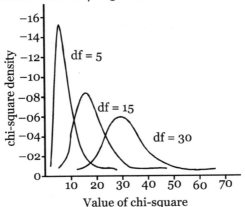

Fig. 4.1: Densities of the chi-square (df = 5, 15, 30) distribution

Q17. What are the conditions for the application of chi-square test?
Or
What is Chi-square test? Explain its conditions.
Or
Write a short note on "Chi-square test".
[Dec-2014, Q.No.-10(a)]

Ans. Chi-square is a statistical test commonly used to compare observed data with data we would expect to obtain according to a specific hypothesis. For example, if, according to Mendel's laws, we expected 10 of 20 offspring from a cross to be male and the actual observed number was 8 males, then we might want to know about the "goodness to fit" between the observed and expected. Were the deviations (differences between observed and expected) the result of chance, or were they due to other factors. How much deviation can occur before us, the investigator, must conclude that something other than chance is at work, causing the observed to differ from the expected. The chi-square test is always testing what scientists call the **null hypothesis,** which states that there is no significant difference between the expected and observed result.

$$\chi^2 = \sum \frac{(O-E)^2}{E}$$

Where,
    O = observed frequency
    E = expected or theoretical frequency

Conditions for the Application of χ^2 Test: The following conditions should be satisfied before applying the x^2 test:
  (1) The constraints on the cell frequencies if any should be linear, i.e., they should not involve square and higher powers of the frequencies such as $\sum O = \sum E = N$.

(2) In the first place N must be reasonably large to ensure the similarity between theoretically correct distribution and our sampling distribution of χ^2, the chi-square statistic. It is difficult to say that constitutes largeness, but as a general rule χ^2 test should not be used when N is less than 50, however few the cells.

(3) No theoretical cell frequency should be small when the expected frequencies are too small, the value of χ^2 will be overestimated and will result in too many rejections of the null hypothesis. To avoid making incorrect inference, a general rule is followed that expected frequency of less than 5 in one cell of a contingency table is too small to use. When the table contains more than one cell with an expected frequency of less than 5 we "pool" the frequencies which are less than 5 with the preceding or succeeding frequency so that the resulting sum is 5 or more. However, in doing so, we reduce the number of categories of data and will gain less information from contingency table.

Q18. What are the limitations of chi-square test?

Ans. In order to prevent the misapplication of the χ^2 test, one has to keep the following limitations of the test in mind:

(1) The chi-square test is highly sensitive to the sample size. As sample size increases, absolute differences become a smaller and smaller proportion of expected value. This means that a reasonably strong association may not come up as significant if the sample size is small. Conversely, in a large sample, we may find statistical significance when the findings are small and insignificant. That is, the findings are not substantially significant, although they are statistically significant.

(2) Chi-square test is also sensitive to small frequencies in the cells of contingency table. Generally, when the expected frequency in a cell of a table is less than 5, chi-square can lead to erroneous conclusions. The rule of thumb here is that if either (i) an expected value in a cell in a 2 × 2 contingency table is less than 5 or (ii) the expected value of more than 20% of the cells in a greater than 2 × 2 contingency table are less than 5, then chi-square test should not be applied. If at all, a chi-square test is applied then appropriately either Yates correction or cell pooling should also be applied.

(3) No directional hypothesis is assumed in chi-square test. Chi-square tests the hypothesis that two attributes/variables are related only by chance. That is if a significant relationship is found, this is not equivalent to establishing the researchers' hypothesis that attribute A causes attribute B or attribute B causes attribute A.

Q19. Enumerate the step-by-step calculation of Chi-square test.

Ans. The step-by-step calculation of Chi-square test is as follows:
    (1)   Write the observed frequencies in column O.
    (2)   Figure the expected frequencies and write them in column E.

Expected Frequencies: When we find the value for chi-square, we determine whether the observed frequencies differ significantly from the expected frequencies. We find the expected frequencies for chi-square in these ways:

    (1)   We hypothesise that all the frequencies are equal in each category. For example, we might expect that half of the enrolling students in class of 200 at Tech College will be identified as women and half as men. We figure the expected frequency by dividing the number in the sample by the number of categories. In this example, where there are 200 enrolling students and two categories, male and female, we divide our sample of 200 by 2, the number of categories, to get 100 (expected frequencies) in each category.

    (2)   We determine the expected frequencies on the basis of some prior knowledge. For example, suppose we have prior knowledge of the frequencies of men and women in each category from last year's in class of Tech College, 60% of the students were men and 40% were women. This year we might expect that 60% of the total would be men and 40% would be women. We find the expected frequencies by multiplying the sample size by each of the hypothesised population proportions. If the total students were 200, we would expect 120 to be men (60% × 200) and 80 to be women (40% × 200).

    (3)   Use the formula to find the chi-square value:

$$\text{Chi Square} = \sum \left[(O-E)^2 / E \right]$$

Where:
O is the Observed Frequency in each category
E is the Expected Frequency in the corresponding category

    (4)   Find the *df*. (N-1)
    (5)   Find the Chi-square table value [Appendix Table F]
    (6)   If chi-square value is *equal to or greater than* the table value, reject the null hypothesis: *differences in your data are not due to chance alone.*

Solved Practical Problems

Q1. Calculate Mann-Whitney U test for the following data given below:

Team A	Team B
72	97
67	76
87	83
46	69
58	56
63	68
84	92
53	88
62	74
77	73
82	65
89	54
	43

Ans. We first rank the ratings from lowest to highest score of the both teams.

Team A		Team B	
Score	Rank (R_1)	Score	Rank (R_2)
72	13	97	25
67	10	76	16
87	21	83	19
46	2	69	12
58	6	56	5
63	8	68	11
84	20	92	24
53	3	88	22
62	7	74	15
77	17	73	14
82	18	65	9
89	23	54	4
		43	1
$N_1 = 12$	$\Sigma R1 = 148$	$N_2 = 13$	$\Sigma R2 = 177$

$$\sum(R_1) = 148$$

$\sum(R_2) = 177$

Calculation of U

$$U_1 = n_1 n_2 + \frac{n_1(n_1+1)}{2} - \sum R_1$$

$U_1 = (12)(13) + [12(12+1)/2] - 148$

$U_1 = 156 + 78 - 148 = 86$

$U_2 = (12)(13) + [13(13+1)/2] - 177$

$U_2 = 156 + 91 - 175 = 70$

The critical value of U for $n_1 = 12$ and $n_2 = 13$, two-tailed $\alpha = 0.05$, is 41.

Since the smaller obtained value of $U_1(U_2 = 70)$ is larger than the table value, the null hypothesis is accepted. And we conclude that there is no significant difference in the ratings given by the two assessment teams.

Q2. A researcher wished to evaluate the effectiveness of micro-teaching and simulation in developing certain teaching skills among student-teachers of a teacher training institution. He divided all the 40 students teachers of the college into two groups A and B by randomly assigning 20 to each of the groups. Group A was trained in various skills of teaching through micro-teaching and the Group B was trained through simulation technique. After a period of two months training, the student teachers were rated in the teaching skills by supervisors. The rating scores of the student teachers are given below:

Group A	Group B
90	46
78	42
75	65
72	61
75	64
83	82
73	69
80	66
74	56
67	48
63	68
45	44
55	85
84	83
89	71
77	87
70	76
58	50
47	59
92	79

Ans.

Group A	Rank	Group A	Rank
90	39	46	4
78	29	42	1
75	25.5	65	15
72	22	61	12
75	25.5	64	14
83	33.5	82	32
73	23	69	19
80	31	66	16
74	24	56	9
67	17	48	6
63	13	68	18
45	3	44	2
55	8	85	36
84	35	83	33.5
89	38	71	21
77	28	87	37
70	20	76	27
58	10	50	7
47	5	59	11
92	40	79	30
$N_1 = 20$	$\Sigma R_1 = 496.50$	$N_2 = 20$	$\Sigma R_2 = 350.50$

All rating scores are ranked from lowest to highest and the Mann Whitney U test is used to test the null hypothesis at the .05 level of significance using the following formulae:

$$U_1 = n_1 n_2 + \frac{n_1(n_1+1)}{2} - \Sigma R_1$$

$$U_1 = (20)(20) + \frac{(20)(21)}{2} - 469.50 = 140.50$$

$$U_2 = (20)(20) + \frac{(20)(21)}{2} - 350.50 = 259.50$$

Using the equation $U_1 = N_1 N_2 - U_2$, we check

140.50 = 400 − 259.50
140.50 = 140.50

$$Z = \frac{U - \frac{N_1 N_2}{2}}{\sqrt{\frac{(N_1)(N_2)(N_1 + N_2 + 1)}{12}}}$$

$$Z = \frac{140.50 - \frac{400}{2}}{\sqrt{\frac{(20)(20)(41)}{12}}} - 1.61$$

Since the obtained Z value of –1.61 does not exceed the Z critical value of 1.96 for a two-tailed test at 0.05 level, the null hypothesis is retained and it may be concluded that micro-teaching approach and simulation technique are equally effective in developing certain teaching skills among the student teachers.

Q3. Use Wilcoxon's signed-rank test to see if there is a difference between the number of days until the collection of an account receivable before and after a new collection policy. Use the 0.05 level of significance.

Before (X):	30	28	34	35	40	42	33	38	34	45	28	27	25	41	36
After (Y):	32	29	33	32	37	43	40	41	37	44	27	33	30	38	36

Ans. Let us take hypothesis H_0 : There is no difference between the number of days before and after a new collection policy in the accounts receivable.

And H_1 : There is a difference between the two.

Determination of Signed Ranks:

X	Y	d = X – Y	|d|	Ranks (R) |d| (± ignored)	Signed Ranks	
					R^+	R^-
30	32	–2	2	6	-	6
28	29	–1	1	3	-	3
34	33	1	1	3	3	-
35	32	3	3	9	9	-
40	37	3	3	9	9	-
42	43	–1	1	3	-	3
33	40	–7	7	14	-	14
38	41	–3	3	9	-	9
34	37	–3	3	9	-	9
45	44	1	1	3	3	-
28	27	1	1	3	3	-
27	33	–6	6	13	-	13
25	30	–5	5	12	-	12
41	38	3	3	9	9	-
36	36	-	-	-	-	-
Total				n = 14	$\Sigma R^+ = 36$	$\Sigma R^- = 69$

From the above table, it must be seen that the total number of ranks = n = 14 (n ≤ 25).

Since n < 25, the test statistic is given by
T = smaller of two sums of the signed ranked = 36

Looking at Wilcoxon's T-table at 5 per cent level for a two tailed test at n=14, we get the critical value of T=21

Since the calculated value of T is greater than its critical value, null hypothesis is accepted. It means that there is no significance difference between the number of days before and after a new collection policy.

Q4. Suppose a group of 26 delinquent children were initially rated for their social adjustment by a psychiatrist and then sent to a juvenile jail. After they were rated by a psychiatrist for social adjustment and then their initial and final adjustment rating scores were compared. The rating data are given in the following table:

50	47
54	52
62	63
39	31
56	52
51	42
58	51
60	49
48	42
46	42
42	40
53	56
40	36
51	50
56	42
60	48
57	47
43	48
45	37
52	39
61	60
62	52
48	42
39	45
41	42
39	40

Using Wilicoxon sign ranked test to test the rating score of children.

Ans.

Final adjustment score	Initial adjustment score	d	Rank of d	Rank with less frequent sign
50	47	3	7.5	
54	52	2	5.5	
62	63	−1	−2.5	2.5
39	31	8	17.5	

contd..

Final adjustment score	Initial adjustment score	d	Rank of d	Rank with less frequent sign
56	52	4	10	
51	42	9	19	
58	51	7	16	
60	49	11	23	
48	42	6	14	
46	42	4	10	
42	40	2	5.5	
53	56	−3	−7.5	7.5
40	36	4	10	
51	50	1	2.5	
56	42	14	26	
60	48	12	24	
57	47	10	21	
43	48	−5	−12	12
45	37	8	17.5	
52	39	13	25	
61	60	1	2.5	
62	52	10	21	
48	42	6	14	
39	45	−6	−14	14
41	42	−1	−2.5	2.5
39	49	−10	−21	21

The null hypothesis that there was no difference between in initial and final adjustment rating scores of the group was tested at .05 level of significance. Since the direction of the difference is not predicted, a two tailed region of rejection is appropriated.

T, the smaller of the sum of the like signed ranks
= 2.5 + 7.5 + 12 + 14 + 2.5 + 21 = 59.5
By using the following formula:

$$Z = \frac{T - \frac{N(N+1)}{4}}{\sqrt{\frac{N(N+1)(2N+1)}{24}}}$$

$$Z = \frac{59.5 - \frac{(26)(26+1)}{4}}{\sqrt{\frac{26(26+1)(2(26)+1)}{24}}} = 2.95$$

Since the obtained Z-value of 2.95 exceeds the Z critical value of 1.96 for a two-tailed test at the 0.05 level, the null hypothesis is rejected. We may conclude that the environment in the juvenile jail has considerably improved the social adjustment of delinquent children.

Q5. A researcher wanted to study the stress level of employees in public and private sector organisations. The scores of the employees are given as follows: [Dec-2012, Q.No.-10]

Public sector	Private sector
116	100
110	112
99	116
112	108
118	104
97	105
110	98
90	108
94	121
115	125
	110
	117
	106
	116
	118
	120
$N_2 = 10$	$N_1 = 16$

with the help of 'U' test find out whether scores of the two groups differ significantly or not.

Critical value of U for $N_1 = 16$ and $N_2 = 10$ is 48

Ans. Rank the rating from lowest to highest

Private sector	Rank	Public sector	Rank
100	6	116	19
112	15.5	110	13
116	19	99	5
108	10.5	112	15.5
104	7	118	22.5
105	8	97	3
98	4	110	13
108	10.5	90	1
121	25	94	2
125	26	115	17

110	13		
117	21		
106	9		
116	19		
118	22.5		
120	24		
N= 16	ΣR= 240	N= 10	ΣR=111

$\sum R_1 = 240$

$\sum R_2 = 111$

$U_1 = n_1 n_2 + \dfrac{n_1(n_1+1)}{2} - \sum R_1$

$= (16)(10) + \dfrac{16(16+1)}{2} - 240$

$U = 160 + \dfrac{272}{2} - 240$

$= 160 + 136 - 240$

$= 56$

$U_2 = n_1 n_2 + \dfrac{n_2(n_2+1)}{2} - \sum R_2$

$= (16)(10) + \dfrac{10(10+1)}{2} - 111$

$= 160 + \dfrac{110}{2} - 111$

$= 104$

The critical value of U for $n_1 = 16$ and $n_2 = 10$ is 48.

Since the smallest obtained value of U, i.e. 56 is larger than the table value, the null hypothesis is accepted. We can conclude that there is no significant difference in the scores of two groups.

Q6. In a study, 12 participants were divided into three groups of 4 each, they were subjected to three different conditions, A (Low Noise), B(Average Noise), and C(Loud Noise). They were given a test and the errors committed by them on the test were noted and are given in the table below:

Participant No.	Condition A (Low Noise)	Participant No.	Condition B (Average Noise)	Participant No.	Condition C (Loud Noise)
1	3	5	2	9	10
2	5	6	7	10	8
3	6	7	9	11	7
4	3	8	8	12	11

The researcher wishes to know whether these three conditions differ amongst themselves and there are no assumptions of the probability.

Ans. We should rank all the numbers in the entire data set from smallest to largest (using all samples combined); in the case of ties, we use the average of the ranks that the values would have normally been given.

Condition A	Ranks T_1	Condition B	Ranks T_2	Condition C	Ranks T_3
3	2.5	2	1	10	11
5	4	7	6.5	8	8.5
6	5	9	10	7	6.5
3	2.5	8	8.5	11	12
	$\Sigma T_1 = 14$		$\Sigma T_2 = 26$		$\Sigma T_3 = 38$

$\Sigma T_1 = 14$

$\Sigma T_2 = 26$

$\Sigma T_3 = 38$

$$K = \frac{12}{N(N+1)} \left(\sum_{j=1}^{k} \frac{T_j^2}{n_j} \right) - 3(N+1)$$

N = 12

$n_j = n_k = n_l = 4$

$K = [12/12(12+1)] [(14^2/4) + (26^2/4) + (38^2/4)] - 3(12+1)$

K = [12/156] [49 + 169 + 361] − 39

K = (0.0769 × 579) − 39

K = 44.525 − 39

K = 5.525

Since the groups are three and number of items in each group are 4, therefore looking in Kruskal-Wallis Appendix Table I (k=3, sample size of 4, 4, 4) it can be seen that the critical value is 5.692 (α = 0.05).

Since the critical value is more than the actual value we accept the null hypothesis that all the three conditions A (Low Noise), B(Average Noise), and C(Loud Noise), do not differ from each other, therefore, in the said experiment there was no differences in the group's performance based on the noise level.

Q7. A state court administrator asked the 24 court coordinators in the state's three largest counties to rate their relative need for training in case flow management on a Likert scale (1 to 7).

1 = no training need

7 = critical training need

Training Need of Court Coordinators

County A	County B	County C
3	7	4
1	6	2
3	5	5
1	7	1
5	3	6
4	1	7
4	6	
2	4	
	4	
	5	

Ans. Rank order the total groups' Likert scores from lowest to highest.

County A		County B		County C	
Rating	Rank	Rating	Rank	Rating	Rank
3	8	7	23	4	12
1	2.5	6	20	2	5.5
3	8	5	16.5	5	16.5
1	2.5	7	23	1	2.5
5	16.5	3	8	6	20
4	12	1	2.5	7	23
4	12	6	20		
2	5.5	4	12		
		4	12		
		5	16.5		
	$\Sigma T_1 = 67$		$\Sigma T_2 = 153.5$		$\Sigma T_3 = 79.5$

$$K = \frac{12}{N(N+1)}\left(\sum_{j=1}^{k}\frac{T_j^2}{n_j}\right) - 3(N+1)$$

K = [12/24 (24+1)] [4489/8 + 23562.25/10 + 6320.25/6] − 3(24 + 1)
K = (0.02)(3970.725) − (75)
K = 4.42
df = (k − 1) = (3 − 1) = 2

Interpretation: The critical chi-square table [Appendix Table F] value of K for $\alpha = 0.05$, and df = 2, is 5.991

Since 4.42 < 5.991, the null hypothesis is accepted. There is no difference in the training needs of the court coordinators in the three counties.

Q8. Find out the Tau value for the following data:

Ans. Step 1: Ranking the data of X and Y

	A	B	C	D
X	6	8	5	2
Y	8	4	9	6

	A	B	C	D
X	3	4	2	1
Y	3	1	4	2

Step 2: Rearrange the data of X in order of 1 to N

	D	C	A	B
X	1	2	3	4
Y				

Step 3: Put the corresponding score of Y in order of X and Determine number of agreements and disagreements

	D	C	A	B
X	1	2	3	4
Y	2	4	3	1

To calculate S we need number of agreements and disagreements. This can be calculated by using the Y scores, starting from left and counting the number of ranks to its right that are larger, these are agreements in order. We subtract from this the number of ranks to its right that are smaller- these are the disagreements in order. If we do this for all the ranks and then sum the results we obtain S:

Y	2	4	3	1	Total
	2	+	+	−	+1
		4	−	−	−2
			3	−	−1
				1	0
				Grand Total = S	−2

Step 4: Calculate τ

$$\tau = \frac{2S}{N(N-1)}$$

$$\tau = \frac{2(-2)}{4(4-1)}$$

$$\tau = \frac{-4}{12}$$

$$\tau = -0.33$$

Thus, $\tau = -0.33$ is a measure of the agreement between the preference of X and Y.

Q9. Calculate the Tau value for the following data:

Subject	A	B	C	D	E	F	G	H	I	J	K	L
Status striving rank	3	4	2	1	8	11	10	6	7	12	5	9
Yielding rank	1.5	1.5	3.5	3.5	5	6	7	8	9	10.5	10.5	12

Ans. Rearrange X and observe the scores of corresponding Y scores to calculate S.

Subject	D	C	A	B	K	H	I	E	L	G	F	J	
Status striving rank	1	2	3	4	5	6	7	8	9	10	11	12	
Yielding rank	3.5	3.5	1.5	1.5	10.5	8	9	5	12	7	6	10.5	Total
		3.5	-	-	+	+	+	+	+	+	+	+	6
			3.5	-	-	+	+	+	+	+	+	+	+	6
				1.5	0	+	+	+	+	+	+	+	+	8
					1.5	+	+	+	+	+	+	+	8
						10.5	-	-	-	+	-	-	0	-4
							8	+	-	+	-	-	+	0
								9	-	+	-	-	+	-1
									5	+	+	+	+	4
										12	-	-	-	-3
											7	-	+	0
												6	+	1
													10.5	0
													S =	Grand Total	25

There are no ties among the scores on social status striving, i.e. in the X ranks and thus $T_x = 0$

On Y scores there are three sets of tied ranks. Two subjects are tied at 1.5, two subjects at 3.5, and two subjects' at 10.5 ranks. In each of these cases T = 2, the number of tied observations. Thus, may be computed as:

$T_Y = \sum t(t-1)$
$= 2(2-1) + 2(2-1) + 2(2-1)$
$= 6$

With $T_x = 0$, $T_y = 6$, $S = 25$, and $N = 12$, we may determine the value of T by using formula:

$$\tau = 2S / \left[\sqrt{N(N-1) - T_x} \sqrt{N(N-1) - T_y} \right]$$

$$\tau = (2 \times 25) / \sqrt{12(12-1) - 0} \sqrt{12(12-1) - 6}$$

$$= 0.39$$

Q10. A sample of 200 people with a particular disease was selected. Out of these, 100 were given a drug and the others were not given any drug. The results are as follows:

Number of People

	Drug	No Drug	Total
Cured	65	55	120
Not Cured	35	45	80
Total	100	100	200

Test whether the drug is effective or not.

Ans. We take the null hypothesis that the drug is not effective in curing the disease. Applying χ^2 test:

The expected cell frequencies are computed as follows:

$$E_{11} = \frac{R_1 C_1}{N} = \frac{120 \times 100}{200} = 60$$

$$E_{12} = \frac{R_1 C_2}{N} = \frac{120 \times 100}{200} = 60$$

$$E_{21} = \frac{R_2 C_1}{N} = \frac{80 \times 100}{200} = 40$$

$$E_{22} = \frac{R_2 C_2}{N} = \frac{80 \times 100}{200} = 40$$

The table of expected frequencies is as follows:

60	60	120
40	40	80
100	100	200

O	E	$(O-E)^2$	$(O-E)^2/E$
65	60	25	0.417
35	40	25	0.625
55	60	25	0.417
45	40	25	0.625
			$S[(O-E)^2/E] = 2.084$

Arranging the observed frequencies with their corresponding frequencies in the following table, we get:

$$\chi^2 = \sum \frac{(O-E)^2}{E} = 2.084$$

$v = (r-1)(c-1) = (2-1)(2-1) = 1$

For $v = 1$, $\chi^2_{0.05} = 3.84$

The calculated value of χ^2 is less than the table value. The hypothesis is accepted. Hence, the drug is not effective in curing the disease.

Q11. A random sample of 400 persons was selected from each of three age groups and each person was asked to specify which of three types of TV programmes was preferred. The results are shown in the following table.

Age Group	Types of Programme			Total
	A	B	C	
Under 30	120	30	50	200
30 - 40	10	75	15	100
45 and above	10	30	60	100
Total	140	135	125	400

Test the hypothesis that the population are homogeneous with respect the types of television programmes they prefer.

Ans. We take the hypothesis that the populations are homogeneous with respect to different types of television programmes they prefer.

$$E_{11} = \frac{140 \times 200}{400} = 70 \quad E_{21} = \frac{135 \times 200}{400} = 67.5$$

$$E_{12} = \frac{140 \times 100}{400} = 35 \quad E_{22} = \frac{135 \times 100}{400} = 33.75$$

$$E_{13} = \frac{140 \times 100}{400} = 35 \quad E_{23} = \frac{135 \times 100}{400} = 33.75$$

$$E_{31} = \frac{125 \times 200}{400} = 62.5$$

$$E_{32} = \frac{125 \times 100}{400} = 31.25$$

$$E_{33} = \frac{125 \times 100}{400} = 31.25$$

Applying χ^2 test:

O	E	$(O-E)^2$	$(O-E)^2/E$
120	70.00	2500.00	35.7143
10	35.00	625.00	17.8571
10	35.00	625.00	17.8571
30	67.50	1406.25	20.8333
75	33.75	1701.56	50.4166
30	33.75	14.06	0.4166
50	62.50	156.25	2.5000
15	31.25	264.06	8.4499
60	31.25	826.56	26.4499
			$\Sigma[(O-E)^2/E] = 180.4948$

$$\chi^2 = \sum \frac{(O-E)^2}{E}$$

The table value of χ^2 for 4 d.f. at 5% level of significance is 9.488.

The calculated value of χ^2 is much greater than the table value. We reject the hypothesis and conclude that the populations are not homogeneous with respect to the types of TV programmes preferred.

Q12. Two researchers adopted different sampling techniques while investigating the same group of students to find the number of students falling in different intelligence levels. The results are as follows:

Researcher	No. of students in each level				Total
	Below average	Average	Above average	Genius	
X	86	60	44	10	200
Y	40	33	25	2	100
Total	126	93	69	12	300

Would you say that the sampling techniques adopted by the two researchers are significantly different? (Given 5% value of for 3 d.f. and 4 d.f are 7.82 and 9.49 respectively).

Ans. We set up the null hypothesis that the data obtained are independent of the sampling techniques adopted by the two researchers. In other words, the null hypothesis is that there is no significant difference between the sampling techniques used by the two researchers for collecting the required data.

Here, we have a 4 × 2 contingency table and d.f. = (4 – 1) × (2 – 1) = 3 × 1 = 3. Hence, we need to compute only 3 independent expected frequencies and the remaining expected frequencies can be obtained by subtraction from the marginal totals.

Under the null hypothesis of independence we have:

$$E(86) = \frac{126 \times 200}{300} = 84$$

$$E(60) = \frac{93 \times 200}{300} = 62$$

$$E(44) = \frac{69 \times 200}{300} = 46$$

$$E(40) = \frac{126 \times 100}{300} = 42$$

$$E(33) = \frac{93 \times 100}{300} = 31$$

$$E(25) = \frac{69 \times 100}{300} = 23$$

Thus, the table of expected frequencies can now be completed as:

Expected Frequencies:

Researcher	No. of students in each level				Total
	Below average	Average	Above average	Genius	
X	84	62	46	8	200
Y	42	31	23	4	100
Total	126	93	69	12	300

O	E	(O – E)	(O – E)^2	(O – E)^2/E
86	84	2	4	0.048
60	62	–2	4	0.064
44	46	–2	4	0.087
10	8	2	4	0.500
40	42	–2	4	0.095
33	31	2	4	0.129
25	23	2	4	0.174
2	4	–2	4	1.000
300	300	Σ(O–E) = 0		Σ[(O – E)^2/E] = 2.097

$$\therefore \chi^2 = \sum \left[\frac{(O-E)^2}{E} \right] = 2.097$$

d.f. = (4 - 1) × (2 - 1) = 3 × 1 = 3 and $\chi^2_{0.005}$ for 3 d.f.

= 7.82

Since calculated value less than table value, it is not significant. Hence, null hypothesis may be expected at 5% level of significance and we may conclude that the sampling techniques adopted by the two investigators do not differ significantly.

Q13. Calculate Chi square from following:

	Right	Wrong
fo	80%	20%
fe	50%	50%

Ans. Applying χ^2 test:

	O	E	(O – E)	(O – E)²	(O – E)²/E
Right	80	50	30	900	18
Wrong	20	50	–30	900	18
					$\Sigma[(O-E)^2/E] = 36$

$$\chi^2 = \sum \frac{(O-E)^2}{E} = 36$$

df = (2 – 1) × (2 – 1) = 1
[∵ df = (No. of rows – 1) × (No. of column – 1)]
For df = 1, $\chi^2_{0.05}$ = 3.84

The calculate value of χ^2 is more than the table value. The hypothesis is rejected.

Read GPH books and score excellent marks.

Appendix Tables

Table (A): t- Distribution table (One tail and two tails)

cum. prob one-tail two tails	$t_{.50}$ 0.50 1.00	$t_{.75}$ 0.25 0.50	$t_{.80}$ 0.20 0.40	$t_{.85}$ 0.15 0.30	$t_{.90}$ 0.10 0.20	$t_{.95}$ 0.05 0.10	$t_{.975}$ 0.025 0.05	$t_{.99}$ 0.01 0.02	$t_{.995}$ 0.005 0.01	$t_{.999}$ 0.001 0.002	$t_{.9995}$ 0.0005 0.001
1	0.000	1.000	1.376	1.963	3.078	6.314	12.71	31.82	63.66	318.31	636.62
2	0.000	0.816	1.061	1.386	1.886	2.920	4.303	6.965	9.925	22.327	31.599
3	0.000	0.765	0.978	1.250	1.638	2.353	3.182	4.541	5.841	10.215	12.924
4	0.000	0.741	0.941	1.190	1.533	2.132	2.776	3.747	4.604	7.173	8.610
5	0.000	0.727	0.920	1.156	1.476	2.015	2.571	3.365	4.032	5.893	6.869
6	0.000	0.718	0.906	1.134	1.440	1.943	2.447	3.143	3.707	5.208	5.959
7	0.000	0.711	0.896	1.119	1.415	1.895	2.365	2.998	3.499	4.785	5.408
8	0.000	0.706	0.889	1.108	1.397	1.860	2.306	2.896	3.355	4.501	5.041
9	0.000	0.703	0.883	1.100	1.383	1.833	2.262	2.821	3.250	4.297	4.781
10	0.000	0.700	0.879	1.093	1.372	1.812	2.228	2.764	3.169	4.144	4.587
11	0.000	0.697	0.876	1.088	1.363	1.796	2.201	2.718	3.106	4.025	4.437
12	0.000	0.695	0.873	1.083	1.356	1.782	2.179	2.681	3.055	3.930	4.318
13	0.000	0.694	0.870	1.079	1.350	1.771	2.160	2.650	3.012	3.852	4.221
14	0.000	0.692	0.868	1.076	1.345	1.761	2.145	2.624	2.977	3.787	4.140
15	0.000	0.691	0.866	1.074	1.341	1.753	2.131	2.602	2.947	3.733	4.073
16	0.000	0.690	0.865	1.071	1.337	1.746	2.120	2.583	2.921	3.686	4.015
17	0.000	0.689	0.863	1.069	1.333	1.740	2.110	2.567	2.898	3.646	3.965
18	0.000	0.688	0.862	1.067	1.330	1.734	2.101	2.552	2.878	3.610	3.922
19	0.000	0.688	0.861	1.066	1.328	1.729	2.093	2.539	2.861	3.579	3.883
20	0.000	0.687	0.860	1.064	1.325	1.725	2.086	2.528	2.845	3.552	3.850
21	0.000	0.686	0.859	1.063	1.323	1.721	2.080	2.518	2.831	3.527	3.819
22	0.000	0.686	0.858	1.061	1.321	1.717	2.074	2.508	2.819	3.505	3.792
23	0.000	0.685	0.858	1.060	1.319	1.714	2.069	2.500	2.807	3.485	3.768
24	0.000	0.685	0.857	1.059	1.318	1.711	2.064	2.492	2.797	3.467	3.745
25	0.000	0.684	0.856	1.058	1.316	1.708	2.060	2.485	2.787	3.450	3.725
26	0.000	0.684	0.856	1.058	1.315	1.706	2.056	2.479	2.779	3.435	3.707
27	0.000	0.684	0.855	1.057	1.314	1.703	2.052	2.473	2.771	3.421	3.690
28	0.000	0.683	0.855	1.056	1.313	1.701	2.048	2.467	2.763	3.408	3.674
29	0.000	0.683	0.854	1.055	1.311	1.699	2.045	2.462	2.756	3.396	3.659
30	0.000	0.683	0.854	1.055	1.310	1.697	2.042	2.457	2.750	3.385	3.646
40	0.000	0.681	0.851	1.050	1.303	1.684	2.021	2.423	2.704	3.307	3.551
60	0.000	0.679	0.848	1.045	1.296	1.671	2.000	2.390	2.660	3.232	3.460
80	0.000	0.678	0.846	1.043	1.292	1.664	1.990	2.374	2.639	3.195	3.416
100	0.000	0.677	0.845	1.042	1.290	1.660	1.984	2.364	2.626	3.174	3.390
1000	0.000	0.675	0.842	1.037	1.282	1.646	1.962	2.330	2.581	3.098	3.300
z	0.000	0.674	0.842	1.036	1.282	1.645	1.960	2.326	2.576	3.090	3.291
	0%	50%	60%	70%	80%	90%	95%	98%	99%	99.8%	99.9%
	Confidence Level										

Table (B): Normal Possibility Curve Table

	0.00	0.01	0.02	0.03	0.04	0.05	0.06	0.07	0.08	0.09
0.0	0.0000	0.0040	0.0080	0.0120	0.0160	0.0199	0.0239	0.0279	0.0319	0.0359
0.1	0.0398	0.0438	0.0478	0.0517	0.0557	0.0596	0.0636	0.0675	0.0714	0.0753
0.2	0.0793	0.0832	0.0871	0.0910	0.0948	0.0987	0.1026	0.1064	0.1103	0.1141
0.3	0.1179	0.1217	0.1255	0.1293	0.1331	0.1368	0.1406	0.1443	0.1480	0.1517
0.4	0.1554	0.1591	0.1628	0.1664	0.1700	0.1736	0.1772	0.1808	0.1844	0.1879
0.5	0.1915	0.1950	0.1985	0.2019	0.2054	0.2088	0.2123	0.2157	0.2190	0.2224
0.6	0.2257	0.2291	0.2324	0.2357	0.2389	0.2422	0.2454	0.2486	0.2517	0.2549
0.7	0.2580	0.2611	0.2642	0.2673	0.2704	0.2734	0.2764	0.2794	0.2823	0.2852
0.8	0.2881	0.2910	0.2939	0.2967	0.2995	0.3023	0.3051	0.3078	0.3106	0.3133
0.9	0.3159	0.3186	0.3212	0.3238	0.3264	0.3289	0.3315	0.3340	0.3365	0.3389
1.0	0.3413	0.3438	0.3461	0.3485	0.3508	0.3531	0.3554	0.3577	0.3599	0.3621
1.1	0.3643	0.3665	0.3686	0.3708	0.3729	0.3749	0.3770	0.3790	0.3810	0.3830
1.2	0.3849	0.3869	0.3888	0.3907	0.3925	0.3944	0.3962	0.3980	0.3997	0.4015
1.3	0.4032	0.4049	0.4066	0.4082	0.4099	0.4115	0.4131	0.4147	0.4162	0.4177
1.4	0.4192	0.4207	0.4222	0.4236	0.4251	0.4265	0.4279	0.4292	0.4306	0.4319
1.5	0.4332	0.4345	0.4357	0.4370	0.4382	0.4394	0.4406	0.4418	0.4429	0.4441
1.6	0.4452	0.4463	0.4474	0.4484	0.4495	0.4505	0.4515	0.4525	0.4535	0.4545
1.7	0.4554	0.4564	0.4573	0.4582	0.4591	0.4599	0.4608	0.4616	0.4625	0.4633
1.8	0.4641	0.4649	0.4656	0.4664	0.4671	0.4678	0.4686	0.4693	0.4699	0.4706
1.9	0.4713	0.4719	0.4726	0.4732	0.4738	0.4744	0.4750	0.4756	0.4761	0.4767
2.0	0.4772	0.4778	0.4783	0.4788	0.4793	0.4798	0.4803	0.4808	0.4812	0.4817
2.1	0.4821	0.4826	0.4830	0.4834	0.4838	0.4842	0.4846	0.4850	0.4854	0.4857
2.2	0.4861	0.4864	0.4868	0.4871	0.4875	0.4878	0.4881	0.4884	0.4887	0.4890
2.3	0.4893	0.4896	0.4898	0.4901	0.4904	0.4906	0.4909	0.4911	0.4913	0.4916
2.4	0.4918	0.4920	0.4922	0.4925	0.4927	0.4929	0.4931	0.4932	0.4934	0.4936
2.5	0.4938	0.4940	0.4941	0.4943	0.4945	0.4946	0.4948	0.4949	0.4951	0.4952
2.6	0.4953	0.4955	0.4956	0.4957	0.4959	0.4960	0.4961	0.4962	0.4963	0.4964
2.7	0.4965	0.4966	0.4967	0.4968	0.4969	0.4970	0.4971	0.4972	0.4973	0.4974
2.8	0.4974	0.4975	0.4976	0.4977	0.4977	0.4978	0.4979	0.4979	0.4980	0.4981
2.9	0.4981	0.4982	0.4982	0.4983	0.4984	0.4984	0.4985	0.4985	0.4986	0.4986
3.0	0.4987	0.4987	0.4987	0.4988	0.4988	0.4989	0.4989	0.4989	0.4990	0.4990

Table (C): t-Distribution

Degrees of Freedom	Probability (P)			
	0.10	0.05	0.02	0.01
1	t = 6.34	t = 12.71	t = 31.82	t = 63.66
2	2.92	4.30	6.96	9.92
3	2.35	3.18	4.54	5.84
4	2.13	2.78	3.75	4.60
5	2.02	2.57	3.36	4.03
6	1.94	2.45	3.14	3.71
7	1.90	2.36	3.00	3.50
8	1.86	2.31	2.90	3.36
9	1.83	2.26	2.82	3.25
10	1.81	2.23	2.76	3.17
11	1.80	2.20	2.72	3.11
12	1.78	2.18	2.68	3.06
13	1.77	2.16	2.65	3.01
14	1.76	2.14	2.62	2.98
15	1.75	2.13	2.60	2.95
16	1.75	2.12	2.58	2.92
17	1.74	2.11	2.57	2.90
18	1.73	2.10	2.55	2.88
19	1.73	2.09	2.54	2.86
20	1.72	2.09	2.54	2.84
21	1.72	2.08	2.52	2.83
22	1.72	2.07	2.51	2.82
23	1.71	2.07	2.50	2.81
24	1.71	2.06	2.49	2.80
25	1.71	2.06	2.48	2.79
26	1.71	2.06	2.48	2.78
27	1.70	2.05	2.47	2.77
28	1.70	2.05	2.47	2.76
29	1.70	2.04	2.46	2.76
30	1.70	2.04	2.46	2.75
35	1.69	2.03	2.44	2.72
40	1.68	2.02	2.42	2.71
45	1.68	2.02	2.41	2.69
50	1.68	2.01	2.40	2.68
60	1.67	2.00	2.39	2.66
70	1.67	2.00	2.38	2.65
80	1.66	1.99	2.38	2.64
90	1.66	1.99	2.37	2.63
100	1.66	1.98	2.36	2.63
125	1.66	1.98	2.36	2.62
150	1.66	1.98	2.35	2.61
200	1.65	1.97	2.35	2.60
300	1.65	1.97	2.34	2.59
400	1.65	1.97	2.34	2.59
500	1.65	1.96	2.33	2.59
1000	1.65	1.96	2.33	2.58
∞	1.65	1.96	2.33	2.58

Table (D): Critical Value of F-Distribution (5% level of significance)

df2/df1	1	2	3	4	5	6	7	8	9
1	161.4476	199.5000	215.7073	224.5832	230.1619	233.9860	236.7684	238.8827	240.5433
2	18.5128	19.0000	19.1643	19.2468	19.2964	19.3295	19.3532	19.3710	19.3848
3	10.1280	9.5521	9.2766	9.1172	9.0135	8.9406	8.8867	8.8452	8.8123
4	7.7086	6.9443	6.5914	6.3882	6.2561	6.1631	6.0942	6.0410	5.9988
5	6.6079	5.7861	5.4095	5.1922	5.0503	4.9503	4.8759	4.8183	4.7725
6	5.9874	5.1433	4.7571	4.5337	4.3874	4.2839	4.2067	4.1468	4.0990
7	5.5914	4.7374	4.3468	4.1203	3.9715	3.8660	3.7870	3.7257	3.6767
8	5.3177	4.4590	4.0662	3.8379	3.6875	3.5806	3.5005	3.4381	3.3881
9	5.1174	4.2565	3.8625	3.6331	3.4817	3.3738	3.2927	3.2296	3.1789
10	4.9646	4.1028	3.7083	3.4780	3.3258	3.2172	3.1355	3.0717	3.0204
11	4.8443	3.9823	3.5874	3.3567	3.2039	3.0946	3.0123	2.9480	2.8962
12	4.7472	3.8853	3.4903	3.2592	3.1059	2.9961	2.9134	2.8486	2.7964
13	4.6672	3.8056	3.4105	3.1791	3.0254	2.9153	2.8321	2.7669	2.7144
14	4.6001	3.7389	3.3439	3.1122	2.9582	2.8477	2.7642	2.6987	2.6458
15	4.5431	3.6823	3.2874	3.0556	2.9013	2.7905	2.7066	2.6408	2.5876
16	4.4940	3.6337	3.2389	3.0069	2.8524	2.7413	2.6572	2.5911	2.5377
17	4.4513	3.5915	3.1968	2.9647	2.8100	2.6987	2.6143	2.5480	2.4943
18	4.4139	3.5546	3.1599	2.9277	2.7729	2.6613	2.5767	2.5102	2.4563
19	4.3807	3.5219	3.1274	2.8951	2.7401	2.6283	2.5435	2.4768	2.4227
20	4.3512	3.4928	3.0984	2.8661	2.7109	2.5990	2.5140	2.4471	2.3928
21	4.3248	3.4668	3.0725	2.8401	2.6848	2.5727	2.4876	2.4205	2.3660
22	4.3009	3.4434	3.0491	2.8167	2.6613	2.5491	2.4638	2.3965	2.3419
23	4.2793	3.4221	3.0280	2.7955	2.6400	2.5277	2.4422	2.3748	2.3201
24	4.2597	3.4028	3.0088	2.7763	2.6207	2.5082	2.4226	2.3551	2.3002
25	4.2417	3.3852	2.9912	2.7587	2.6030	2.4904	2.4047	2.3371	2.2821
26	4.2252	3.3690	2.9752	2.7426	2.5868	2.4741	2.3883	2.3205	2.2655
27	4.2100	3.3541	2.9604	2.7278	2.5719	2.4591	2.3732	2.3053	2.2501
28	4.1960	3.3404	2.9467	2.7141	2.5581	2.4453	2.3593	2.2913	2.2360
29	4.1830	3.3277	2.9340	2.7014	2.5454	2.4324	2.3463	2.2783	2.2229
30	4.1709	3.3158	2.9223	2.6896	2.5336	2.4205	2.3343	2.2662	2.2107
40	4.0847	3.2317	2.8387	2.6060	2.4495	2.3359	2.2490	2.1802	2.1240
60	4.0012	3.1504	2.7581	2.5252	2.3683	2.2541	2.1665	2.0970	2.0401
120	3.9201	3.0718	2.6802	2.4472	2.2899	2.1750	2.0868	2.0164	1.9588
inf	3.8415	2.9957	2.6049	2.3719	2.2141	2.0986	2.0096	1.9384	1.8799

10	12	15	20	24	30	40	60	120	INF
241.8817	243.9060	245.9499	248.0131	249.0518	250.0951	251.1432	252.1957	253.2529	254.3144
19.3959	19.4125	19.4291	19.4458	19.4541	19.4624	19.4707	19.4791	19.4874	19.4957
8.7855	8.7446	8.7029	8.6602	8.6385	8.6166	8.5944	8.5720	8.5494	8.5264
5.9644	5.9117	5.8578	5.8025	5.7744	5.7459	5.7170	5.6877	5.6581	5.6281
4.7351	4.6777	4.6188	4.5581	4.5272	4.4957	4.4638	4.4314	4.3985	4.3650
4.0600	3.9999	3.9381	3.8742	3.8415	3.8082	3.7743	3.7398	3.7047	3.6689
3.6365	3.5747	3.5107	3.4445	3.4105	3.3758	3.3404	3.3043	3.2674	3.2298
3.3472	3.2839	3.2184	3.1503	3.1152	3.0794	3.0428	3.0053	2.9669	2.9276
3.1373	3.0729	3.0061	2.9365	2.9005	2.8637	2.8259	2.7872	2.7475	2.7067
2.9782	2.9130	2.8450	2.7740	2.7372	2.6996	2.6609	2.6211	2.5801	2.5379
2.8536	2.7876	2.7186	2.6464	2.6090	2.5705	2.5309	2.4901	2.4480	2.4045
2.7534	2.6866	2.6169	2.5436	2.5055	2.4663	2.4259	2.3842	2.3410	2.2962
2.6710	2.6037	2.5331	2.4589	2.4202	2.3803	2.3392	2.2966	2.2524	2.2064
2.6022	2.5342	2.4630	2.3879	2.3487	2.3082	2.2664	2.2229	2.1778	2.1307
2.5437	2.4753	2.4034	2.3275	2.2878	2.2468	2.2043	2.1601	2.1141	2.0658
2.4935	2.4247	2.3522	2.2756	2.2354	2.1938	2.1507	2.1058	2.0589	2.0096
2.4499	2.3807	2.3077	2.2304	2.1898	2.1477	2.1040	2.0584	2.0107	1.9604
2.4117	2.3421	2.2686	2.1906	2.1497	2.1071	2.0629	2.0166	1.9681	1.9168
2.3779	2.3080	2.2341	2.1555	2.1141	2.0712	2.0264	1.9795	1.9302	1.8780
2.3479	2.2776	2.2033	2.1242	2.0825	2.0391	1.9938	1.9464	1.8963	1.8432
2.3210	2.2504	2.1757	2.0960	2.0540	2.0102	1.9645	1.9165	1.8657	1.8117
2.2967	2.2258	2.1508	2.0707	2.0283	1.9842	1.9380	1.8894	1.8380	1.7831
2.2747	2.2036	2.1282	2.0476	2.0050	1.9605	1.9139	1.8648	1.8128	1.7570
2.2547	2.1834	2.1077	2.0267	1.9838	1.9390	1.8920	1.8424	1.7896	1.7330
2.2365	2.1649	2.0889	2.0075	1.9643	1.9192	1.8718	1.8217	1.7684	1.7110
2.2197	2.1479	2.0716	1.9898	1.9464	1.9010	1.8533	1.8027	1.7488	1.6906
2.2043	2.1323	2.0558	1.9736	1.9299	1.8842	1.8361	1.7851	1.7306	1.6717
2.1900	2.1179	2.0411	1.9586	1.9147	1.8687	1.8203	1.7689	1.7138	1.6541
2.1768	2.1045	2.0275	1.9446	1.9005	1.8543	1.8055	1.7537	1.6981	1.6376
2.1646	2.0921	2.0148	1.9317	1.8874	1.8409	1.7918	1.7396	1.6835	1.6223
2.0772	2.0035	1.9245	1.8389	1.7929	1.7444	1.6928	1.6373	1.5766	1.5089
1.9926	1.9174	1.8364	1.7480	1.7001	1.6491	1.5943	1.5343	1.4673	1.3893
1.9105	1.8337	1.7505	1.6587	1.6084	1.5543	1.4952	1.4290	1.3519	1.2539
1.8307	1.7522	1.6664	1.5705	1.5173	1.4591	1.3940	1.3180	1.2214	1.0000

Table (E): Critical Values of F-Distribution (1% level of significance)

d2	d_1								
	1	2	3	4	5	6	7	8	9
1	4052	4999.5	5403	5625	5764	5859	5928	5982	6022
2	98.50	99.00	99.17	99.25	99.30	99.33	99.36	99.37	99.39
3	34.12	30.82	29.46	28.71	28.24	27.91	27.67	27.49	27.35
4	21.20	18.00	16.69	15.98	15.52	15.21	14.98	14.80	14.66
5	16.26	13.27	12.06	11.39	10.97	10.67	10.46	10.29	10.16
6	13.75	10.92	9.78	9.15	8.75	8.47	8.26	8.10	7.98
7	12.25	9.55	8.45	7.85	7.46	7.19	6.99	6.84	6.72
8	11.26	8.65	7.59	7.01	6.63	6.37	6.18	6.03	5.91
9	10.56	8.02	6.99	6.42	6.06	5.80	5.61	5.47	5.35
10	10.04	7.56	6.55	5.99	5.64	5.39	5.2	5.06	4.94
11	9.65	7.21	6.22	5.67	5.32	5.07	4.89	4.74	4.63
12	9.33	6.93	5.95	5.41	5.06	4.82	4.64	4.50	4.39
13	9.07	6.70	5.74	5.21	4.86	4.62	4.44	4.30	4.14
14	8.86	6.51	5.56	5.04	4.69	4.46	4.28	4.14	4.03
15	8.68	6.36	5.42	4.89	4.56	4.32	4.14	4.00	3.89
16	8.53	6.23	5.29	4.77	4.44	4.20	4.03	3.89	3.78
17	8.40	6.11	5.18	4.67	4.34	4.10	3.93	3.79	3.68
18	8.29	6.01	5.09	4.58	4.25	4.01	3.84	3.71	3.60
19	8.18	5.93	5.01	4.50	4.17	3.94	3.77	3.63	3.52
20	8.10	5.85	4.94	4.43	4.10	3.87	3.70	3.56	3.46
21	8.02	5.78	4.87	4.37	4.04	3.81	3.64	3.51	3.40
22	7.95	5.72	4.82	4.31	3.99	3.76	3.59	3.45	3.35
23	7.88	5.66	4.76	4.26	3.94	3.71	3.54	3.41	3.30
24	7.82	5.61	4.72	4.22	3.90	3.67	3.50	3.36	3.26
25	7.77	5.57	4.68	4.18	3.85	3.63	3.46	3.32	3.22
26	7.72	5.53	4.64	4.14	3.82	3.59	3.42	3.29	3.18
27	7.68	5.49	4.60	4.11	3.78	3.56	3.39	3.26	3.15
28	7.64	5.45	4.57	4.07	3.75	3.53	3.36	3.23	3.12
29	7.60	5.42	4.54	4.04	3.73	3.50	3.33	3.20	3.09
30	7.56	5.39	4.51	4.02	3.70	3.47	3.30	3.17	3.07
40	7.31	5.18	4.31	3.83	3.51	3.29	3.12	2.99	2.89
60	7.08	4.98	4.13	3.65	3.34	3.12	2.95	2.82	2.72
120	6.85	4.79	3.95	3.48	3.17	2.96	2.79	2.66	2.56
inf	6.63	4.61	3.78	3.32	3.02	2.80	2.64	2.51	2.41

				d1					
10	12	15	20	24	30	40	60	120	inf
6056	6106	6157	6209	6235	6261	6287	6313	6339	6366
99.40	99.42	99.43	99.45	99.46	99.47	99.47	99.48	99.49	99.50
27.23	27.05	26.87	26.69	26.60	26.50	26.41	26.32	26.22	26.13
14.55	14.37	14.20	14.02	13.93	13.84	13.75	13.65	13.56	13.46
10.05	9.89	9.72	9.55	9.47	9.38	9.29	9.20	9.11	9.02
7.87	7.72	7.56	7.40	7.31	7.23	7.14	7.06	6.97	6.88
6.62	6.47	6.31	6.16	6.07	5.99	5.91	5.82	5.74	5.65
5.81	5.67	5.52	5.36	5.28	5.20	5.12	5.03	4.95	4.86
5.26	5.11	4.96	4.81	4.73	4.65	4.57	4.48	4.40	4.31
4.85	4.71	4.56	4.41	4.33	4.25	4.17	4.08	4.00	3.91
4.54	4.40	4.25	4.10	4.02	3.94	3.86	3.78	3.69	3.60
4.30	4.16	4.01	3.86	3.78	3.70	3.62	3.54	3.45	3.36
4.10	3.96	3.82	3.66	3.59	3.51	3.43	3.34	3.25	3.17
3.94	3.80	3.66	3.51	3.43	3.35	3.27	3.18	3.09	3.00
3.80	3.67	3.52	3.37	3.29	3.21	3.13	3.05	2.96	2.87
3.69	3.55	3.41	3.26	3.18	3.10	3.02	2.93	2.84	2.75
3.59	3.46	3.31	3.16	3.08	3.00	2.92	2.83	2.75	2.65
3.51	3.37	3.23	3.08	3.00	2.92	2.84	2.75	2.66	2.57
3.43	3.30	3.15	3.00	2.92	2.84	2.76	2.67	2.58	2.49
3.37	3.23	3.09	2.94	2.86	2.78	2.69	2.61	2.52	2.42
3.31	3.17	3.03	2.88	2.80	2.72	2.64	2.55	2.46	2.36
3.26	3.12	2.98	2.83	2.75	2.67	2.58	2.50	2.40	2.31
3.21	3.07	2.93	2.78	2.70	2.62	2.54	2.45	2.35	2.26
3.17	3.03	2.89	2.74	2.66	2.58	2.49	2.40	2.31	2.21
3.13	2.99	2.85	2.70	2.62	2.54	2.45	2.36	2.27	2.17
3.09	2.96	2.81	2.66	2.58	2.50	2.42	2.33	2.23	2.13
3.06	2.93	2.78	2.63	2.55	2.47	2.38	2.29	2.20	2.10
3.03	2.90	2.75	2.60	2.52	2.44	2.35	2.26	2.17	2.06
3.00	2.87	2.73	2.57	2.49	2.41	2.33	2.23	2.14	2.03
2.98	2.84	2.70	2.55	2.47	2.39	2.30	2.21	2.11	2.01
2.80	2.66	2.52	2.37	2.29	2.20	2.11	2.02	1.92	1.80
2.63	2.50	2.35	2.20	2.12	2.03	1.94	1.84	1.73	1.60
2.47	2.34	2.19	2.03	1.95	1.86	1.76	1.66	1.53	1.38
2.32	2.18	2.04	1.88	1.79	1.70	1.59	1.47	1.32	1.00

Table (F): Critical Values of Chi-square Distribution

df \ area	.995	.990	.975	.950	.900	.750
1	0.00004	0.00016	0.00098	0.00393	0.01579	0.10153
2	0.01003	0.02010	0.05064	0.10259	0.21072	0.57536
3	0.07172	0.11483	0.21580	0.35185	0.58437	1.21253
4	0.20699	0.29711	0.48442	0.71072	1.06362	1.92256
5	0.41174	0.55430	0.83121	1.14548	1.61031	2.67460
6	0.67573	0.87209	1.23734	1.63538	2.20413	3.45460
7	0.98926	1.23904	1.68987	2.16735	2.83311	4.25485
8	1.34441	1.64650	2.17973	2.73264	3.48954	5.07064
9	1.73493	2.08790	2.70039	3.32511	4.16816	5.89883
10	2.15586	2.55821	3.24697	3.94030	4.86518	6.73720
11	2.60322	3.05348	3.81575	4.57481	5.57778	7.58414
12	3.07382	3.57057	4.40379	5.22603	6.30380	8.43842
13	3.56503	4.10692	5.00875	5.89186	7.04150	9.29907
14	4.07467	4.66043	5.62873	6.57063	7.78953	10.16531
15	4.60092	5.22935	6.26214	7.26094	8.54676	11.03654
16	5.14221	5.81221	6.90766	7.96165	9.31224	11.91222
17	5.69722	6.40776	7.56419	8.67176	10.08519	12.79193
18	6.26480	7.01491	8.23075	9.39046	10.86494	13.67529
19	6.84397	7.63273	8.90652	10.11701	11.65091	14.56200
20	7.43384	8.26040	9.59078	10.85081	12.44261	15.45177
21	8.03365	8.89720	10.28290	11.59131	13.23960	16.34438
22	8.64272	9.54249	10.98232	12.33801	14.04149	17.23962
23	9.26042	10.19572	11.68855	13.09051	14.84796	18.13730
24	9.88623	10.85636	12.40115	13.84843	15.65868	19.03725
25	10.51965	11.52398	13.11972	14.61141	16.47341	19.93934
26	11.16024	12.19815	13.84390	15.37916	17.29188	20.84343
27	11.80759	12.87850	14.57338	16.15140	18.11390	21.74940
28	12.46134	13.56471	15.30786	16.92788	18.93924	22.65716
29	13.12115	14.25645	16.04707	17.70837	19.76774	23.56659
30	13.78672	14.95346	16.79077	18.49266	20.59923	24.47761

.500	.250	.100	.050	.025	.010	.005
0.45494	1.32330	2.70554	3.84146	5.02389	6.63490	7.87944
1.38629	2.77259	4.60517	5.99146	7.37776	9.21034	10.59663
2.36597	4.10834	6.25139	7.81473	9.34840	11.34487	12.83816
3.35669	5.38527	7.77944	9.48773	11.14329	13.27670	14.86026
4.35146	6.62568	9.23636	11.07050	12.83250	15.08627	16.74960
5.34812	7.84080	10.64464	12.59159	14.44938	16.81189	18.54758
6.34581	9.03715	12.01704	14.06714	16.01276	18.47531	20.27774
7.34412	10.21885	13.36157	15.50731	17.53455	20.09024	21.95495
8.34283	11.38875	14.68366	16.91898	19.02277	21.66599	23.58935
9.34182	12.54886	15.98718	18.30704	20.48318	23.20925	25.18818
10.34100	13.70069	17.27501	19.67514	21.92005	24.72497	26.75685
11.34032	14.84540	18.54935	21.02607	23.33666	26.21697	28.29952
12.33976	15.98391	19.81193	22.36203	24.73560	27.68825	29.81947
13.33927	17.11693	21.06414	23.68479	26.11895	29.14124	31.31935
14.33886	18.24509	22.30713	24.99579	27.48839	30.57791	32.80132
15.33850	19.36886	23.54183	26.29623	28.84535	31.99993	34.26719
16.33818	20.48868	24.76904	27.58711	30.19101	33.40866	35.71847
17.33790	21.60489	25.98942	28.86930	31.52638	34.80531	37.15645
18.33765	22.71781	27.20357	30.14353	32.85233	36.19087	38.58226
19.33743	23.82769	28.41198	31.41043	34.16961	37.56623	39.99685
20.33723	24.93478	29.61509	32.67057	35.47888	38.93217	41.40106
21.33704	26.03927	30.81328	33.92444	36.78071	40.28936	42.79565
22.33688	27.14134	32.00690	35.17246	38.07563	41.63840	44.18128
23.33673	28.24115	33.19624	36.41503	39.36408	42.97982	45.55851
24.33659	29.33885	34.38159	37.65248	40.64647	44.31410	46.92789
25.33646	30.43457	35.56317	38.88514	41.92317	45.64168	48.28988
26.33634	31.52841	36.74122	40.11327	43.19451	46.96294	49.64492
27.33623	32.62049	37.91592	41.33714	44.46079	48.27824	50.99338
28.33613	33.71091	39.08747	42.55697	45.72229	49.58788	52.33562
29.33603	34.79974	40.25602	43.77297	46.97924	50.89218	53.67196

Table (G): Table of critical values of T in the Wilcoxon matched pairs-signed ranks test

N	Level of significance for one-tailed test		
	.025	.01	.005
	Level of significance for two-tailed test		
	.05	.02	.01
6	0	-	-
7	2	0	-
8	4	2	0
9	6	3	2
10	8	5	3
11	11	7	5
12	14	10	7
13	17	13	10
14	21	16	13
15	25	20	16
16	30	24	20
17	35	28	23
18	40	33	28
19	46	38	32
20	52	43	38
21	59	49	43
22	66	56	49
23	73	62	55
24	81	69	61
25	89	77	68

Appendix Tables

Table (H): Table of critical values of U in the Mann-Whitney Test Statistic

n_2	α	n_1																	
		3	4	5	6	7	8	9	10	11	12	13	14	15	16	17	18	19	20
3	.05	-	0	0	1	1	2	2	3	3	4	4	5	5	6	6	7	7	8
	.01	-	0	0	0	0	0	0	0	0	1	1	1	2	2	2	2	3	3
4	.05	-	0	1	2	3	4	4	5	6	7	8	9	10	11	11	12	13	14
	.01	-	-	0	0	0	1	1	2	2	3	3	4	5	5	6	6	7	8
5	.05	0	1	2	3	5	6	7	8	9	11	12	13	14	15	17	18	19	20
	.01	-	-	0	1	1	2	3	4	5	6	7	7	8	9	10	11	12	13
6	.05	1	2	3	5	6	8	10	11	13	14	16	17	19	21	22	24	25	27
	.01	-	0	1	2	3	4	5	6	7	9	10	11	12	13	15	16	17	18
7	.05	1	3	5	6	8	10	12	14	16	18	20	22	24	26	28	30	32	34
	.01	-	0	1	3	4	6	7	9	10	12	13	15	16	18	19	21	22	24
8	.05	2	4	6	8	10	13	15	17	19	22	24	26	29	31	34	36	38	41
	.01	-	1	2	4	6	7	9	11	13	15	17	18	20	22	24	26	28	30
9	.05	2	4	7	10	12	15	17	20	23	26	28	31	34	37	39	42	45	48
	.01	0	1	3	5	7	9	11	13	16	18	20	22	24	27	29	31	33	36
10	.05	3	5	8	11	14	17	20	23	26	29	33	36	39	42	45	48	52	55
	.01	0	2	4	6	9	11	13	16	18	21	24	26	29	31	34	37	39	42
11	.05	3	6	9	13	16	19	23	26	30	33	37	40	44	47	51	55	58	62
	.01	0	2	5	7	10	13	16	18	21	24	27	30	33	36	39	42	45	48
12	.05	4	7	11	14	18	22	26	29	33	37	41	45	49	53	57	61	65	69
	.01	1	3	6	9	12	15	18	21	24	27	31	34	37	41	44	47	51	54
13	.05	4	8	12	16	20	24	28	33	37	41	45	50	54	59	63	67	72	76
	.01	1	3	7	10	13	17	20	24	27	31	34	38	42	45	49	53	56	60
14	.05	5	9	13	17	22	26	31	36	40	45	50	55	59	64	67	74	78	83
	.01	1	4	7	11	15	18	22	26	30	34	38	42	46	50	54	58	63	67
15	.05	5	10	14	19	24	29	34	39	44	49	54	59	64	70	75	80	85	90
	.01	2	5	8	12	16	20	24	29	33	37	42	46	51	55	60	64	69	73
16	.05	6	11	15	21	26	31	37	42	47	53	59	64	70	75	81	86	92	98
	.01	2	5	9	13	18	22	27	31	36	41	45	50	55	60	65	70	74	79
17	.05	6	11	17	22	28	34	39	45	51	57	63	67	75	81	87	93	99	105
	.01	2	6	10	15	19	24	29	34	39	44	49	54	60	65	70	75	81	86
18	.05	7	12	18	24	30	36	42	48	55	61	67	74	80	86	93	99	106	112
	.01	2	6	11	16	21	26	31	37	42	47	53	58	64	70	75	81	87	92
19	.05	7	13	19	25	32	38	45	52	58	65	72	78	85	92	99	106	113	119
	.01	3	7	12	17	22	28	33	39	45	51	56	63	69	74	81	87	93	99
20	.05	8	14	20	27	34	41	48	55	62	69	76	83	90	98	105	112	119	127
	.01	3	8	13	18	24	30	36	42	48	54	60	67	73	79	86	92	99	105

Table (I): Table of critical values of K in the Kruskal-Wallis test

K = 3					K=4						K = 5						
Sample Size			α=0.05	α=0.01	Sample Size				α=0.05	α=0.01	Sample Size					α=0.05	α=0.01
2	2	2	-	-	2	2	1	1	-	-	2	2	1	1	1	-	-
3	2	1	-	-	2	2	2	1	5.679	-	2	2	2	1	1	6.750	-
3	2	2	4.714	-	2	2	2	2	6.167	6.667	2	2	2	2	1	7.133	7.533
3	3	1	5.143	-	3	1	1	1	-	-	2	2	2	2	2	7.418	8.291
3	3	2	5.361	-	3	2	1	1	-	-	3	1	1	1	1	-	-
3	3	3	5.600	7.200	3	2	2	1	5.833	-	3	2	1	1	1	6.583	-
4	2	1	-	-	3	2	2	2	6.333	7.133	3	2	2	1	1	6.800	7.600
4	2	2	5.333	-	3	3	1	1	6.333	-	3	2	2	2	1	7.309	8.127
4	3	1	5.208	-	3	3	2	1	6.244	7.200	3	2	2	2	2	7.682	8.682
4	3	2	5.444	6.444	3	3	2	2	6.527	7.636	3	3	1	1	1	7.111	-
4	3	3	5.791	6.745	3	3	3	1	6.600	7.400	3	3	2	1	1	7.200	8.073
4	4	1	4.967	6.667	3	3	3	2	6.727	8.015	3	3	2	2	1	7.591	8.576
4	4	2	5.455	7.036	3	3	3	3	7.000	8.538	3	3	2	2	2	7.910	9.115
4	4	3	5.598	7.144	4	1	1	1	-	-	3	3	3	1	1	7.576	8.424
4	4	4	5.692	7.654	4	2	1	1	5.833	-	3	3	3	2	1	7.769	9.051
5	2	1	5.000	-	4	2	2	1	6.133	7.000	3	3	3	2	2	8.044	9.505
5	2	2	5.160	6.533	4	2	2	2	6.545	7.391	3	3	3	3	1	8.000	9.451
5	3	1	4.960	-	4	3	1	1	6.178	7.067	3	3	3	3	2	8.200	9.876
5	3	2	5.251	6.909	4	3	2	1	6.309	7.455	3	3	3	3	3	8.333	10.20
5	3	3	5.648	7.079	4	3	2	2	6.621	7.871							
5	4	1	4.985	6.955	4	3	3	1	6.545	7.758							
5	4	2	5.273	7.205	4	3	3	2	6.795	8.333							
5	4	3	5.656	7.445	4	3	3	3	6.984	8.659							
5	4	4	5.657	7.760	4	4	1	1	5.945	7.909							
5	5	1	5.127	7.309	4	4	2	1	6.386	7.909							
5	5	2	5.338	7.338	4	4	2	2	6.731	8.346							
5	5	3	5.705	7.578	4	4	3	1	6.635	8.231							
5	5	4	5.666	7.823	4	4	3	2	6.874	8.621							
5	5	5	5.780	8.000	4	4	3	3	7.038	8.876							
6	1	1	-	-	4	4	4	1	6.725	8.588							
6	2	1	4.822	-	4	4	4	2	6.957	8.871							
6	2	2	5.345	6.655	4	4	4	3	7.142	9.075							
6	3	1	4.855	6.873	4	4	4	4	7.235	9.287							

Must Read   अवश्य पढ़ें

GULLYBABA PUBLISHING HOUSE PVT. LTD.

New Syllabus Based

100% Guidance for IGNOU EXAM

IGNOU HELP BOOKS

BAG, BCOMG, BSCG, BA (Hons.) M.A., M.COM, BCA, B.ED., M.ED, AND OTHER SUBJECTS

IAS, PCS, UGC & All University Examinations

Chapterwise Researched
QUESTIONS & ANSWERS
Solved papers & very helpful for your assignments preparation

Hindi & English Medium

GULLYBABA PUBLISHING HOUSE PVT. LTD.
2525/193, 1st Floor, Onkar Nagar-A, Tri Nagar, Delhi-110035,
(From Kanhaiya Nagar Metro Station Towards Old Bus Stand)
Email : Hello@gullybaba.com
Web : www.gullybaba.com

Join us on Facebook at Gph Book
For any Guidance & Assistance Call:
9350849407

WE'D LOVE IT IF YOU'D LIKE US!
/gphbooks

We're now on Facebook!
Like our page to stay on top of the useful, greatest headlines & exciting rewards.

Our other awesome Social Handles:

gphbooks
For awesome & informative videos for IGNOU students

9350849407
Order now through WhatsApp

gphbooks
We are in pictures

gphbook
Words you get empowered by

Question Papers

Statistics in Psychology : MPC-006
December, 2012

Note: *(i) Answer any five questions.*
(ii) Each question carries 10 marks.
(iii) Use of simple calculator may be permitted.

Q1. Discuss in detail parametric tests and highlight their assumptions.

Ans. Parametric tests normally involved data expressed in absolute numbers or value rather than ranks. The parametric test operates under certain conditions which are not ordinarily tested and assumed to hold valid. The meaningfulness of the results of a parametric test depends on the validity of the assumptions. Proper interpretation of parametric test based on normal distribution also assumes that the scene being analysed result from measurement in at least an interval scale. Tests like t, z and f are called parametric statistical tests. t-tests is used to determine if the scores of two groups differ on a single variable. The parametric test like t-test and f-test are considered to be quite robust and are appropriate even when some assumptions are not met. Parametric tests are useful as these tests are most powerful for testing the significance of trustworthiness of the computed sample statistics. However, their use is based upon certain assumptions.

The principal assumptions on which parametric tests are based include independence of the observations, normality of the underlying population distributions, and homogeneity of the population variances across groups (for multiple group procedures). Additional assumptions may be required for some parametric procedures, such as linearity of regression (Pearson product-moment correlation), homoscedasticity (simple and multiple regression), homogeneity of regression slopes (univariate and multi-variate analysis of covariance), and sphericity/compound symmetry and homogeneity of treatment-difference variances (univariate and multivariate repeated measures). The principal assumptions for multivariate statistics include independence of the observations, multivariate normal distributions for all dependent variables, and homogeneity of the variance-covariance (dispersion) matrices across groups.

Q2. Calculate rank correlation coefficient for the following scores obtained by employees on Emotional Intelligence (EI) and Leadership [L]

$$EI = \frac{A \quad B \quad C \quad D \quad E \quad F \quad G \quad H \quad I \quad J \quad K}{85 \quad 75 \quad 70 \quad 68 \quad 65 \quad 60 \quad 58 \quad 56 \quad 55 \quad 45 \quad 80}$$

L = 90 74 70 65 64 62 60 48 50 86 82

Ans. Same as Chapter-2, Q.No.-11 (Practical Problems)

Q3. Explain the concept of hypothesis testing and highlight the errors in hypothesis testing.

Ans. Refer to Chapter-1, Q.No.-18 and Q.No.-22

Q4. Discuss in detail the setting up of the level of confidence or significance.

Ans. The experimenter has to take a decision about the level of confidence or significance at which the hypothesis is going to be tested. At times the researcher may decide to use 0.05 or 5% level of significance for rejecting a null hypothesis (when a hypothesis is rejected at the 5% level it is said that the chances are 95 out of 100, that the hypothesis is not true and only 5 chances out of 100 that it is true). At other times, the researcher may prefer to make it more rigid and therefore, use the 0.01 or 1% level of significance. If a hypothesis is rejected at this level, the chances are 99 out of 100, that the hypothesis is not true and that only 1 chance out of 100 is true. This level on which we reject the null hypothesis, is established before doing the actual experiment (before collecting data).

Now, Refer to Chapter-1, Q.No.-25 and 28

Q5. A group of individuals obtained following scores on two tests A and B. Calculate regression equations for both the tests.

	Individuals				
	1	2	3	4	5
Test A =	8	9	12	11	10
Test B =	10	10	20	18	12

Ans. Same as Chapter-2, Q.No.-18 (Practical Problems)

Q6. A research was conducted to find out the effectiveness of three teaching methods namely, lecture method, group discussion and case study method. For this purpose, three groups of 10 students each, were formed and were assigned one of the teaching methods. The performance of the students is given as follows:

Group 1 [Lecture Method]	Group 2 [Group Discussion]	Group 3 [Case Study]
6	14	10
10	8	7
9	19	8
7	15	6
10	10	5
8	11	7
11	13	9
11	12	13
10	9	11
12	12	8

Using ANOVA find out significance of difference in the performance of three groups.
- Critical values of F = 3.35 at 00.5 level of significance
- Critical values of F = 5.49 at 0.01 level of significance

Ans. Same as Chapter-3, Q.No.-22 (Practical Problems)

Q7. Explain Normal Distribution and highlight its characteristics.
Ans. Refer to Chapter-3, Q.No.-1

Q8. The opinions of 90 educated and 100 uneducated persons were taken on a health related attitude scale. The data collected is given as follows:

	Agree No.	Opinion	Disagree
Educated	14	10	66
Uneducated	27	7	66

With the help of Chi square, find out whether significant difference in opinion exists in terms of the level of education of the persons.
- Critical value of χ^2 = 5.991 at 0.05 level of significance
- Critical value of χ^2 = 9.210 at 0.01 level of significance.

Ans. Same as Chapter-4, Q.No.-12 (Practical Problems)

Q9. Define correlation and discuss product moment coefficient of correlation in detail with suitable example.
Ans. Refer to Chapter-2, Q.No.-1 and Q.No.-7

Q10. A researcher wanted to study the stress level of employees in public and private sector organisations. The scores of the employees are given as follows:

Public sector	Private sector
116	100
110	112
99	116
112	108
118	104
97	105
110	98
90	108
94	121
115	125
	110
	117
	106
	116
	118
	120
N_2 = 10	N_1 = 16

with the help of 'U' test find out whether scores of the two groups differ significantly or not.
- Critical value of U for N_1 = 16 and N_2 = 10 is 48

Ans. Refer to Chapter-4, Q.No.-5 (Practical Problems)

Statistics in Psychology : MPC-006
June, 2013

Note: *(i) Answer any five questions.*
(ii) Each question carries 10 marks.
(iii) Use of simple calculator may be permitted.

Q1. Differentiate between parametric and non-parametric statistics and discuss advantages to non-parametric statistics.
Ans. Refer to Chapter-1, Q.No.-1 and Q.No.-2

Q2. What do you mean by inferential statistics? Discuss advantages and disadvantages of descriptive statistics over inferential statistics.
Ans. Refer to Chapter-1, Q.No.-17 and Q.No.-7

Q3. Find the correlation between two sets of scores from the following data:

Subject	X	Y
A	15	40
B	18	42
C	22	50
D	17	45
E	19	43
F	20	46
G	16	41
H	21	41

Ans. Same as Chapter-2, Q.No.-2 (Practical Problems)

Q4. Write importance of normal distribution. An IQ test was conducted on 500 students of class X. The mean and SD was found 100 and 16 respectively. Find how many students of the class X having IQ below 80 and above 120.
Ans. Refer to Chapter-3, Q.No.-3 and Chapter-3, Q.No.-2 (Practical Problems)

Q5. What do you mean by hypothesis testing? Discuss significance of One - Tailed and Two - Tailed hypothesis testing in research.
Ans. Refer to Chapter-1, Q.No.-18 and Q.No.-28

Q6. Define correlation. In four experiments, the correlations between X and Y were as follows: .60, .20, .70 and .40. The N's were 26, 31, 42 and 35. What is the mean r : the weighted average of these 4r's?
Ans. Refer to Chapter-2, Q.No.-1
  The best estimate of the mean correlation is not the simple mean across studies but a weighted average in which each correlation is weighted

by the number of persons (or other subjects) in that study. Thus, the estimate of the population correlation is

$$\bar{r} = \frac{\Sigma(N_i r_i)}{\Sigma N_i}$$

Thus, $\bar{r} = \dfrac{26 \times .60 + 31 \times .20 + 42 \times .70 + 35 \times .40}{26 + 31 + 42 + 35} = \dfrac{65.2}{134} = .49$

Q7. Write assumptions of Chi square and calculate Chi square from following:

	Right	Wrong
fo	80%	20%
fe	50%	50%

Ans. The chi-square goodness-of-fit test is based on the following assumptions:
    (1) Categorical nominal data are employed in the analysis. This assumption reflects the fact that the test data should represent frequencies for k mutually exclusive categories;
    (2) The data that are evaluated consists of a random sample of n independent observations. This assumption reflects the fact that each observation can only be represented once in the data; and
    (3) The expected frequency of each cell is 5 or greater.
    Now, Refer to Chapter-4, Q.No.-13 (Practical Problems)

Q8. Four groups of 8 students, each having an equal number of boys and girls were randomly selected and assigned to four different conditions of an experiment. Use ANOVA to test the main effects due to conditions of sex, and the interaction of the two.

Boys				Girls			
I	II	III	IV	I	II	III	IV
7	9	12	12	3	4	3	6
0	4	6	14	3	7	7	7
5	5	10	9	2	5	4	6
8	6	6	5	0	2	6	5

Ans. Same as Chapter-3, Q.No.-24 (Practical Problems)

Q9. Write short notes on any two of the following:
(a) Characteristics of variance
Ans. Refer to Chapter-3, Q.No.-16
(b) Importance of alternative hypothesis
Ans. Refer to Chapter-1, Q.No.-23
(c) Importance of standard error of mean.
Ans. Refer to Chapter-3, Q.No.-10

Q10. A group of 10 students was given four trials on a test of physical efficiency. The scores on the I and IV trials are given below. Test whether there was a significant gain from the first to the fourth trials.

Student	Trial - I	Trial - IV
1	15	20
2	16	22
3	17	22
4	20	25
5	25	35
6	30	30
7	17	21
8	18	23
9	10	17
10	12	20

Ans.

Student	Trial (X) I	Trial (X) IV	D (X_2-X_1)	d D-MD	d^2
1	15	20	5	−0.5	0.25
2	16	22	6	0.5	0.25
3	17	22	5	−0.5	0.25
4	20	25	5	−0.5	0.25
5	25	35	10	4.5	20.25
6	30	30	0	−5.5	30.25
7	17	21	4	−1.5	2.25
8	18	23	5	−0.5	0.25
9	10	17	7	1.5	2.25
10	12	20	8	2.5	6.25
			$\Sigma D = 55$		$\Sigma d^2 = 62.5$

$$MD = \frac{\Sigma D}{N} = \frac{55}{10} = 5.5 \qquad SD = \sqrt{\frac{\Sigma d^2}{N-1}} = \sqrt{\frac{62.5}{10-1}} = 2.63$$

Now, calculate the standard error of mean of difference, i.e. SE_{DM}

$$SE_{DM} = \frac{SD}{\sqrt{N}} = \frac{2.63}{\sqrt{10}} = 0.832$$

$$\therefore t = \frac{MD}{SE_{DM}} = \frac{5.5}{0.832} = 6.610$$

df = N − 1 = 10 − 1 = 9

Interpretation: In the "t" distribution table [Appendix table C] for 9 df at 0.01 level the value is 3.25 and our calculate value of t (6.610) is much greater than the table value. Here, the null hypothesis is rejected at 0.01 level of significance. Since our hypothesis is rejected at 0.01 level of significance, therefore we can say that there was a significant gain from the first to the fourth trails.

Statistics in Psychology : MPC-006
December, 2013

Note: *(i) Answer any five questions.*
(ii) Each question carries 10 marks.
(iii) Use of simple calculator may be permitted.

Q1. Define statistics and differentiate between descriptive and inferential statistics.

Ans. The word statistics refers to a special discipline or a collection of procedures and principles useful as an aid in gathering as an aid in gathering and analysing numerical information for the purpose of drawing conclusions and making decisions. Since any numerical figure, or figures, cannot be called statistics owing to many considerations which decide its use, statistical data or mere data is a more appropriate expression to indicate numerical facts.

Different authors have given different definitions to the science of statistics, emphasising different aspects.

Webster defines statistics as "classified facts representing the conditions of the people in a State ... especially those facts which can be stated in numbers or in tables of numbers or in any tabular or classified arrangement". This definition is too narrow and inadequate.

A.L. Bowley Defines statistics as "the science of counting"; the "science of averages", and "the science of measurement of social phenomena, regarded as a whole in all its manifestations".

A.L. Boddington defines statistics as "the science of estimates and probabilities".

Croxton and Cowden defines statistics as "the collection, presentation, analysis and interpretation of numerical data".

Wallis and Roberts define statistics as "the body of methods for making wise decisions in the face of uncertainty".

Descriptive statistics give information that describes the data in some manner. For example, suppose a pet shop sells cats, dogs, birds and fish. If 100 pets are sold and 40 out of the 100 were dogs, then one description of the data on the pets sold would be that 40% were dogs.

This same pet shop may conduct a study on the number of fish sold each day for one month and determine that an average of 10 fish were sold each day. The average is an example of descriptive statistics.

Some other measurements in descriptive statistics answer questions such as 'How widely dispersed is this data?', 'Are there a lot of different values?' or 'Are many of the values the same?', 'What value is in the middle of this data?', 'Where does a particular data value stand with respect with the other values in the data set?'

A graphical representation of data is another method of descriptive statistics. Examples of this visual representation are histograms, bar graphs and pie graphs, to name a few. Using these methods, the data is described by compiling it into a graph, table or other visual representation.

This provides a quick method to make comparisons between different data sets and to spot the smallest and largest values and trends or changes over a period of time. If the pet shop owner wanted to know what type of pet was purchased most in the summer, a graph might be a good medium to compare the number of each type of pet sold and the months of the year.

Inferential Statistics: Now, suppose we need to collect data on a very large population. For example, suppose we want to know the average height of all the men in a city with a population of so many million residents. It isn't very practical to try and get the height of each of man.

This is where inferential statistics come into play. Inferential statistics makes inferences about populations using data drawn from the population. Instead of using the entire population to gather the data, the statistician will collect a sample or samples from the millions of residents and make inferences about the entire population using the sample.

Q2. What do you mean by decision errors? Discuss applications of one-tailed and two - tailed hypothesis tests in statistics.

Ans. Refer to Chapter-1, Q.No.-24(ii) and Q.No.-20

Q3. From the following data, find Rank-Difference Coefficient of correlation:

Student	Score on Test I	Score on Test II
	X	Y
A	10	16
B	15	16
C	11	24
D	14	18
E	16	22
F	20	24
G	10	14
H	8	10
I	7	12
J	9	14
N = 10		

Ans. Refer to Chapter-2, Q.No.-12 (Practical Problems)

Q4. Define regression. Differentiate between linear and multiple regression by citing example.

Ans. Refer to Chapter-2, Q.No.-19, Q.No.-16 and Q.No.-24

Q5. Discuss the level of measurement with suitable examples.

Ans. Refer to Chapter-4, Q.No.-1

Q6. What do you mean by non-parametric statistics? Discuss advantages and disadvantages of non-parametric statistics.

Ans. Refer to Chapter-1, Q.No.-1 and Q.No.-2

Q7. What do you mean by two sample tests? Write step by step procedure for Wilcoxon test for small sample.

Ans. A two-sample test is hypothesis test for answering questions about the mean where the data are collected from two random samples of independent observations, each from an underlying distribution.

For example, a two-sample hypothesis could be used to test if there is a difference in the mean salary between male and female doctors in the Delhi area. A two-sample hypothesis test could also be used to test if the mean number of defective parts produced using assembly line A is greater than the mean number of defective parts produced using assembly line B.

Now, Refer to Chapter-4, Q.No.-9

Q8. What are assumptions of Analysis of Variance? Discuss uses and limitations of ANOVA.

Ans. Refer to Chapter-3, Q.No.-15 and Q.No.-23

Q9. Write short notes on any two of the following:

(a) Type I Error

Ans. Refer to Chapter-1, Q.No.-22

(b) Level of significance

Ans. Refer to Chapter-1, Q.No.-24(i)

(c) Alternative hypothesis

Ans. Refer to Chapter-1, Q.No.-23

Q10. Calculate simple regression from the following raw scores and set up regression for predicting Y from X, and also X from Y.

X	Y	X^2	Y^2	XY
10	12	100	144	120
11	18	121	324	198
12	20	144	400	240
9	10	81	100	90
8	10	64	100	80
50	70	510	1068	728
X	Y	X^2	Y^2	XY
		N = 5		

Ans. Same as Chapter-2, Q.No.-13 (Practical Problems)

Statistics in Psychology : MPC-006
June, 2014

Note: *(i) Answer any five questions.*
(ii) Each question carries 10 marks.
(iii) Use of simple calculator may be permitted.

Q1. Define Parametric and Non-parametric Statistics. Discuss their advantages and disadvantages.

Ans. Refer to Chapter-1, Q.No.-1

Disadvantage of parametric statistics:
- (1) The hypothesis tested by the parametric test may not be more appropriate for research investigation.
- (2) It is not useful to analyse data which are inherently in ranks as well as data whose seemingly numerical score have the strength of ranks.
- (3) Sample made up of observations from several different populations at times cannot be handled by parametric tests.
- (4) Parametric statistical test typically are difficult to learn and to apply than are non-parametric test.
- (5) Parametric statistical test are not valid on very small data sets.

Advantages of parametric statistics:
- (1) Parametric statistics have high statistics efficiency than non-parametric statistics, when sample size is large preferably above 30.
- (2) If all assumptions of parametric statistics are fulfilled, the use of more non-parametric statistics are simply marking of data.
- (3) Parametric statistics tests don't require the data to be converted to a rank-order format.
- (4) Parametric statistics makes it easier to analyse and describe data with central tendencies and data transformations.

Now, Refer to Chapter-1, Q.No.-2

Q2. Discuss in detail the four major statistical techniques for organising the data.

Ans. The four major statistical techniques for organising the data are as follows:
- (1) Classification
- (2) Tabulation
- (3) Graphical Presentation
- (4) Diagrammatical Presentation

Now, Refer to Chapter-1, Q.No.-8, Q.No.-11, Q.No.-12 and Q.No.-13

Question Papers

Q3. Describe the Hypothesis-testing process. What are the implications if you reject or fail to reject the Null Hypothesis?
Ans. Refer to Chapter-1, Q.No.-19 and Q.No.-21

Q4. Delineate the steps in setting up the level of significance.
Ans. Refer to Chapter-1, Q.No.-26

Q5. Describe linear and non-linear relationship with suitable examples.
Ans. Refer to Chapter-2, Q.No.-4

Q6. Define Product moment coefficient of correlation. Calculate "r" for the following data:

S. No.	Set X	Set Y
1	30	25
2	35	30
3	35	35
4	40	40
5	45	55
6	55	50
7	65	70
8	50	60
9	45	45
10	50	40
Total	450	450

Ans. Refer to Chapter-2, Q.No.-7 and Chapter-2, Q.No.-10 (Practical Problems)

Q7. When do we use Kendall "Tau"? Find out Tau value for the following data:

Subject	R_x	R_y
A	1	1
B	2	3
C	3	2
D	4	4

Ans. Refer to Chapter-2, Q.No.-14

Q8. Describe with example, the divergence from Normality (The Non-Normal Distribution).
Ans. Refer to Chapter-3, Q.No.-4

Q9. Discuss the procedure involved in Analysis of Variance. Find out the F-value for the following data:

Group A	Group B	Group C
4	15	6
6	20	10
8	25	12
10	30	15
12	35	20

Ans. Refer to Chapter-3, Q.No.-17
K = 3 (i.e. 3 group), n = 5 (i.e each group having 5 cases), N = 15 (i.e. the total number of units in the group)

Null hypothesis $H_0 = \mu_1 = \mu_2 = \mu_3$, where μ_1, μ_2 and μ_3 denote the group A, B and C respectively.

Thus,

Group A		Group B		Group C	
X_1	X_1^2	X_2	X_2^2	X_2	X_3^2
4	16	15	225	6	36
6	36	20	400	10	100
8	64	25	625	12	144
10	100	30	900	15	225
12	144	35	1225	20	400
$\sum X_1 =$ 40	$\sum X_1^2 =$ 360	$\sum X_2 =$ 125	$\sum X_2^2 =$ 3375	$\sum X_3 =$ 63	$\sum X_3^2 =$ 905
5		5		5	
8		25		12.6	

$$Cx = \frac{(\sum x)^2}{N} = \frac{(\sum x_1 + \sum x_2 + \sum x_3 \ldots \sum x_k)^2}{n_1 + n_2 + n_3 \ldots n_k}$$

$$= \frac{(40+125+63)^2}{5+5+5} = \frac{(228)^2}{15}$$

Cx = 3465.6

SS_T (Sum of square of total) $= \sum x^2 - Cx$
= (360 + 3375 + 905) − 3465.6
= 4640 − 3465.6
= 1174.4

$$SS_A = \sum \frac{(\sum x)^2}{N} - Cx$$

$$= \frac{(40)^2}{5} + \frac{(125)^2}{5} + \frac{(63)^2}{5} - 3465.6$$

$$= \frac{1600}{5} + \frac{15625}{5} + \frac{3969}{5} - 3465.6$$
$$= 320 + 3125 + 793.8 - 3465.6$$
$$= 773.2$$
$$SS_W = SS_T - SS_A$$
$$= 1174.4 - 773.2$$
$$= 401.2$$
$$MSS_A = \frac{SS_A}{K-1} = \frac{773.2}{3-1} = 386.6$$
$$MSS_W = \frac{SS_W}{N-K} = \frac{401.2}{15-3} = 33.43$$
$$F \text{ Ratio} = \frac{MSS_A}{MSS_W} = \frac{386.6}{33.43} = 11.56$$

Summary of ANOVA

Source of variance	df	SS	MSS	F Ratio
Among the Groups	(K-1) 3-1 =2	773.2	386.6	11.56
Within the Groups	(N-K) 15-3 = 12	401.2	33.43	
Total	14			

From F table for 2 and 12 df at .05 level, the F value is 3.88. Our calculated F value is 11.56, which is very higher than the F value given in the table, Therefore, the F ratio is significant at .05 level (of significance for 2 and 12 df. Thus, the null hypothesis H_0 is rejected.

Q10. Write short notes on any two of the following:
(a) Point estimation and Interval estimation
Ans. Refer to Chapter-1, Q.No.-17
(b) Type I and Type II errors
Ans. Refer to Chapter-1, Q.No.-22
(c) Degrees of freedom
Ans. Refer to Chapter-3, Q.No.-9
(d) Variance
Ans. Refer to Chapter-3, Q.No.-16
(e) Points to remember while testing the significance of difference in two means.
Ans. Refer to Chapter-3, Q.No.-14

Statistics in Psychology : MPC-006
December, 2014

Note: *(i) Answer any five questions.*
(ii) Each question carries 10 marks.
(iii) Use of simple calculator may be permitted.

Q1. What are the various assumptions underlying Parametric and non-Parametric Statistics?
Ans. Refer to Chapter-1, Q.No.-1

Q2. Describe briefly the significance of the difference between the means of two independent samples. Find out whether the two groups differ significantly on the IQ scores given below.

Groups	IQ scores	SD
A	120	2.0
B	140	6.0
N = 25		

Ans. Refer to Chapter-1, Q.No.-4

To find out whether the two groups differ significantly on the IQ scores:

Groups	N	IQ Scores	M	S.D
A	25	120	4.8	2
B	25	140	5.6	6

$H_o = b_1 = b_2$
$H_1 = b_1 \neq b_2$

In the given problem, row scores of the two groups are not given. Therefore, we will use the formula for testing of the difference of mean of two uncorrelated sample means:

$$t = \frac{M_1 \sim M_2}{\sqrt{\frac{\sigma_1^2(N_1-1)+\sigma_2^2(N_2-1)}{N_1+N_2-2} \times \frac{N_1+N_2}{N_1 \times N_2}}}$$

$$t = \frac{4.8-5.6}{\sqrt{\frac{(2)^2(25-1)+(6)^2(25-1)}{25+25-2} \times \frac{25+25}{25 \times 25}}}$$

$$= \frac{0.8}{\sqrt{\frac{96+864}{48} \times \frac{50}{625}}}$$

$$= \frac{0.8}{\sqrt{20 \times 0.08}} = \frac{0.8}{1.26}$$
$$= 0.634$$
$$df = (N_1 - 1) + (N_2 - 1)$$
$$= (25 - 1) + (25 - 1) = 48$$

In the t distribution table [Appendix table C] for 48 df the t value at 0.5 level is 2.01. Our calculated t value 0.634 is less than this value. Therefore, the null hypothesis is retained.

Q3. Differentiate between descriptive and Inferential Statistics with suitable examples.
Ans. Refer to Dec-2013, Q.No.-1

Q4. State the various forms of graphical presentation of Data.
Ans. Refer to Chapter-1, Q.No.-12

Q5. How do we determine the strength of relationship between two variables? Find out Rho (Spearman's rank correlation) for the following data:

S. No.	X	Y
1	7	8
2	11	16
3	16	14
4	9	12
5	6	8
6	17	16
7	7	9
8	11	12
9	5	7
10	14	15

Ans. Refer to Chapter-2, Q.No.-1 and Chapter-2, Q.No.-11 (Practical Problems)

Q6. When do we use partial and multiple correlations? Write the regression equation for the following.

Academic achievement	Anxiety
x	y
1	4
3	2
4	1
5	0
8	0

Ans. Refer to Chapter-2, Q.No.-15, Q.No.-18 and Chapter-2, Q.No.-18 (Practical Problems)

Q7. Elucidate the concept of Normal curve and its properties.
Ans. Refer to Chapter-3, Q.No.-1

Q8. Describe standard error of the mean for large and small sample.
Ans. Refer to Chapter-3, Q.No.-8

Q9. When do we use Kruskal Wallis Analysis of variance? What relevant background information do you require on Kruskal Wallis ANOVA test?
Ans. Refer to Chapter-4, Q.No.-12

Q10. Write short notes on any two of the following:
(a) Chi-square test
Ans. Refer to Chapter-4, Q.No.-17
(b) Skewness
Ans. Refer to Chapter-1, Q.No.-16(i)
(c) Variance and Covariance: Building blocks of correlations
Ans. Refer to Chapter-2, Q.No.-6
(d) Regression
Ans. Refer to Chapter-2, Q.No.-19
(e) one-tail and two-tail test.
Ans. Refer to Chapter-1, Q.No.-20

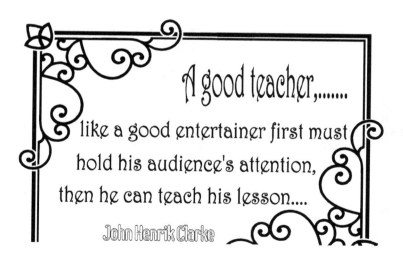

Statistics in Psychology : MPC-006
June, 2015

Note: (i) Answer any five questions.
(ii) Each question carries 10 marks.
(iii) Use of simple calculator may be permitted.

Section–A

Note: Answer any two of the following questions in about 500 words each:

Q1. Discuss the graphical and diagrammatic presentation of data.

Ans. Refer to Chapter-1, Q.No.-12 and Q.No.-13

Q2. Define Correlation and Regression. Find out if a relationship exists between the two groups of data given below with the help of Spearman's Rank coefficient of correlation.

Data 1: 11, 10, 7, 9, 5, 8, 3, 6, 12, 13
Data 2: 4, 3, 2, 20, 13, 12, 11, 10, 6, 5

Ans. Refer to Chapter-2, Q.No.-1, Q.No.-19 and Same as Chapter-2, Q.No.-7 (Practical Problems)

Q3. Define non-parametric statistics. Compute chi-square for the following data:

Age group	Attitude towards Tribals		
	+ve	–ve	Total
11 – 15	25	30	55
16 – 20	20	40	60
21 – 25	10	20	30
26 – 30	35	20	55
Total	90	110	200

χ^2 at 0.01 level = 11.345

Ans. Refer to Chapter-1, Q.No.-1, and Same as Chapter-4, Q.No.-11 (Practical Problems)

Q4. Explain the meaning of variance. Three groups of employees were given training for enhancing communication skills. Three different techniques were used. The scores of their performance test are given as follows. With the help of ANOVA, find out whether significant difference exists in their performance.

Group A	Group B	Group C
6	5	7
3	5	3
7	9	7
1	4	1
3	3	5
5	5	5
3	4	5

Critical value = 0.01, level of significance = 6.01
Ans. Refer to Chapter-3, Q.No.-16 and Same as Chapter-3, Q.No.-22 (Practical Problems)

Section–B
Note: Answer any four of the following questions in about 300 words each:

Q5. Describe the measures of central tendency with hypothetical data.
Ans. Refer to Chapter-1, Q.No.-14

Q6. Explain regression equation with the help of hypothetical data.
Ans. Refer to Chapter-2, Q.No.-19 and Chapter-2, Q.No.-14 (Practical Problems)

Q7. Calculate Mann-Whitney U-test with the help of the following data:
Data 1: 37, 62, 71, 65, 66, 45
Data 2: 42, 61, 70, 63, 72, 47
Ans. Same as Chapter-4, Q.No.-1 (Practical Problems)

Q8. Describe the different scales of measurement with suitable examples.
Ans. Refer to Chapter-4, Q.No.-1

Q9. Discuss the advantages and disadvantages of ANOVA.
Ans. Refer to Chapter-3, Q.No.-20

Section–C
Note: Write short notes on any two of the following in about 100 words each:

Q10. Type I and Type II errors
Ans. Refer to Chapter-1, Q.No.-22

Q11. Linear Regression
Ans. Refer to Chapter-2, Q.No.-16

Q12. Kurtosis
Ans. Refer to Chapter-3, Q.No.-4

Statistics in Psychology : MPC-006
December, 2015

Note : *(i) All sections are compulsory.*
(ii) Use of simple calculator be permitted.

Section—A

Answer any two of the following questions in about 500 words each:

Q1. What is hypothesis testing? Discuss the steps involved in setting up the level of significance with suitable examples.

Ans. Refer to Chapter-1, Q.No.-18 and Q.No.-26

Q2. Define correlation. Find out if relationship exists between the two data given below with the help of Spearman's Rank coefficient of correlation:

Data 1 : 20, 31, 42, 60, 51, 77, 62, 45, 50, 59
Data 2 : 21, 34, 39, 59, 53, 79, 61, 47, 48, 58

Ans. Refer to Chapter-2, Q.No.-1 and Same as Chapter-2, Q.No.-11 (Practical Problems)

Q3. Differentiate between parametric and non-parametric statistics. Compute chi-square for the following data:

For the following question 'Whether cancer is contagious?', the replies given by individuals belonging to low and high Socio-Economic Status (SES) is given below:

	Response		
	Yes	No	Total
Low SES	72	48	120
High SES	34	46	80

Critical value: 0.01, level of significance=6.635

Ans. Refer to Chapter-1, Q.No.-1 and Same as Chapter-4, Q.No.-10 (Practical Problems)

Q4. Explain the term variance. A research was carried out to study the effectiveness of three different methods in enhancing mathematical performance of students. The data based on the performance test is given below. Find out if significant difference exists in the performance of the students with the help of ANOVA.

Group A (Method 1)	Group B (Method 2)	Group C (Method 3)
6	12	10
10	9	7
9	12	8
7	13	6
10	11	5
8	10	7
11	15	9
11	18	13
10	8	11
12	14	8

Critical value=0.01, level of significance=5.49.
Ans. Refer to Chapter-3, Q.No.-16 and Same as Chapter-3, Q.No.-22 (Practical Problems)

Section–B
Answer any four of the following questions in about 300 words each:
Q5. Differentiate between descriptive and inferential statistics.
Ans. Refer to Dec-2013, Q.No.-1
Q6. Compute the regression equation with the help of the following data:
X : 7, 6, 10, 7, 10
Y : 9, 7, 10, 4, 5
Ans. Same as Chapter-2, Q.No.-13 (Practical Problems)
Q7. Calculate Mann-Whitney U test with the help of the following data.
Data 1 : 20, 27, 30, 31, 32, 25
Data 2 : 26, 33, 40, 36, 28, 21
Ans. Same as Chapter-4, Q.No.-1 (Practical Problems)
Q8. Explain divergence in normality with the help of a suitable diagram.
Ans. Refer to Chapter-3, Q.No.-4
Q9. Discuss the merits and demerits of Two-way ANOVA.
Ans. Refer to Chapter-3, Q20

Section–C
Write short notes on any two of the following in about 100 words each:
Q10. Levels of Significance
Ans. Refer to Chapter-1, Q.No.-24(i)
Q11. Linear Relationship
Ans. Refer to Chapter-2, Q.No.-4
Q12. Degree of freedom
Ans. Refer to Chapter-3, Q.No.-9

Statistics in Psychology : MPC-006
June, 2016

Note : *(i) All sections are compulsory.*
(ii) Use of simple calculator be permitted.

Section—A

Answer any two of the following questions in about 450 words each:

Q1. Define parametric and nonparametric statistics. Discuss their assumptions.
Ans. Refer to Chapter-1, Q.No.-1

Q2. Describe divergence of normality with suitable diagrams. Explain the factors causing divergence in normal curve.
Ans. Refer to Chapter-3, Q.No.-4

Q3. A research was carried out to find if significant difference exists in Achievement Motivation Scores obtained by three groups. Using ANOVA, find out if there exists difference in the 3 groups.

Group - I	Group - II	Group - III
4	8	7
4	12	7
6	14	7
2	23	8
4	14	7
4	25	8
5	15	9
2	15	8
3	14	8
4	13	6

Critical value: 5.49 at 0.01 level of significance
3.35 at 0.05 level of significance.

Ans. $H_0 : \mu_1 = \mu_2 = \mu_3$

The mean performance of the sample for Achievement Motivation is statistically equal across all the three groups.

H_1: At least one group Achievement Motivation Scores mean performance is not statistically equal.

In this example,
k=3 (i.e. three groups)
n=10 (i.e. each group is having 10 observations)
N=30 (i.e. the total numbers of observation)
Here,

$df_{between} = k - 1 = 3 - 1 = 2$
$df_{within} = N - k = 30 - 3 = 27$
$df_{total} = N - 1 = 30 - 1 = 29$

S.No.	Group I		Group II		Group III	
	X_1	X_1^2	X_2	X_2^2	X_3	X_3^2
(1)	4	16	8	64	7	49
(2)	4	16	12	144	7	49
(3)	6	36	14	196	7	49
(4)	2	4	23	529	8	64
(5)	4	16	14	196	7	49
(6)	4	16	25	625	8	64
(7)	5	25	15	225	9	81
(8)	2	4	15	225	8	64
(9)	3	9	14	196	8	64
(10)	4	16	13	169	6	36
Σx	38	158	153	2569	75	569
Mean $(\overline{X})$	3.8		15.3		7.5	
$(\Sigma x)^2$	1444		23409		5625	
$\Sigma(\Sigma x)$	38+153+75=266					
$\Sigma(\Sigma x^2)$	158+2569+569=3296					

$SS_B = \sum \frac{(\Sigma x)^2}{n} - \frac{(\Sigma(\Sigma x))^2}{N}$

$= \left(\frac{38^2}{10} + \frac{153^2}{10} + \frac{75^2}{10} \right) - \left(\frac{(38+153+75)^2}{30} \right)$

=3047.8-2358.533
=689.267

$SS_W = \left(\Sigma(X_1^2) - \frac{(\Sigma x_1)^2}{n} \right) + \left(\Sigma(x_2^2) - \frac{(\Sigma x_2)^2}{n} \right) + \left(\Sigma(x_3^2) - \frac{(\Sigma x_3)^2}{n} \right)$

$= \left(158 - \frac{38^2}{10} \right) + \left(2569 - \frac{153^2}{10} \right) + \left(569 - \frac{75^2}{10} \right)$

=13.6+228.1+6.5
=248.2

$MS_B = \frac{SS_B}{df_B} = \frac{689.267}{2} = 344.633$

$MS_W = \frac{SS_W}{df_W} = \frac{248.2}{27} = 9.19$

$$\text{F Ratio} = \frac{MS_B}{MS_W} = \frac{344.633}{9.19} = 37.490$$

Source of Variation	Sum of Squares	Degree of Freedom	Mean Square	F Ratio
Between Sample	689.267	2	344.633	37.490
Within Sample	248.2	27	9.19	
Total	937.467	29		

Critical values of F=5.49 at 0.01 level of significance
Critical values of F=3.35 at 0.05 level of significance

Since it is observed that F(calculated) > F(critical), at 0.01 and 0.05 level of significance, it is then concluded that the null hypothesis is rejected.

Therefore, there is enough evidence to claim that not all 3 population means performance of Achievement Motivation Scores of the three groups are equal, at α = 0.05 & 0.01 significance level.

Q4. Compute regression equation for X and Y based on the data given below:

Individuals	X	Y
A	3	2
B	6	4
C	4	7
D	5	9
E	3	11
F	9	12

Ans.

S.No.	X	Y	X^2	Y^2	XY
(1)	3	2	9	4	6
(2)	6	4	36	16	24
(3)	4	7	16	49	28
(4)	5	9	25	81	45
(5)	3	11	9	121	33
(6)	9	12	81	144	108
Total	30	45	176	415	244

Here,

$n = 6$, $\quad \overline{X} = \dfrac{\Sigma X}{n} = \dfrac{30}{6} = 5 \quad\quad \overline{Y} = \dfrac{\Sigma Y}{n} = \dfrac{45}{6} = 7.5$

$(\Sigma X)^2 = 30 \times 30 = 900 \quad\quad (\Sigma Y)^2 = 45 \times 45 = 2025$

Regression Equation — 'X' on 'Y'

$$S_x = \sum X^2 - \frac{(\sum X)^2}{n} = 176 - \frac{900}{6} = 26$$

$$Cov_{XY} = \sum XY - \frac{(\sum X)(\sum Y)}{n} = 244 - \frac{30 \times 45}{6} = 19$$

$$b = \frac{Cov_{xy}}{S_x} = \frac{19}{26} = 0.73$$

$$a = \overline{Y} - b\overline{X} = 7.5 - (0.73 \times 5) = 3.85$$

$$\hat{Y} = a + bX$$

$$\hat{Y} = 3.85 + 0.73X$$

Section–B

Answer any four of the following questions in about 250 words each:

Q5. Explain the meaning of descriptive statistics. Discuss its advantages and disadvantages.

Ans. Refer to Chapter-1, Q.No.-7

Q6. Calculate Mann – Whitney U - test with the help of the following data :

Group 1 : 38, 64, 66, 70, 46,

Group 2 : 45, 65, 71, 62, 70, 43

Ans.

Group 1	Rank	Group 2	Rank
38	1	45	3
64	6	65	7
66	8	71	11
70	9.5	62	5
46	4	70	9.5
		43	2
$\sum R_1$	28.5	$\sum R_2$	37.5

$$U = n_1 \cdot n_2 + \frac{n_1(n_1+1)}{2} - \sum R_1 \qquad U' = n_1 \cdot n_2 + \frac{n_2(n_2+1)}{2} - \sum R_2$$

$$U = 5 \times 6 + \frac{5(5+1)}{2} - 28.5 \qquad U' = 5 \times 6 + \frac{6(6+1)}{2} - 37.5$$

$$U = 30 \times 15 - 28.5 = 16.5 \qquad U' = 30 + 21 - 37.5 = 13.5$$

$$U = 16.5 \text{ and } U' = 13.5$$

Q7. Compute Chi – square for the following data:

Years of Experience	Organisational Citizenship	
	High	Low
1 – 5 Years	10	15
6 – 10 Years	15	20
11 – 15 Years	20	13

Ans.

Years of Experience		Organisational Citizenship		Total	χ^2
		High	Low		
1 to 5 years	O	10	15	25	
	E	12.10	12.90		
	O-E	-2.10	2.10		
	$(O-E)^2$	4.40	4.40		
	$(O-E)^2/E$	0.36	0.34		0.7
6 to 10 years	O	15	20	35	
	E	16.94	18.06		
	O-E	-1.94	1.94		
	$(O-E)^2$	3.75	3.75		
	$(O-E)^2/E$	0.22	0.21		0.43
11 to 15 years	O	20	13	33	
	E	15.97	17.03		
	O-E	4.03	-4.03		
	$(O-E)^2$	16.26	16.26		
	$(O-E)^2/E$	1.02	0.95		1.97
Total		45	48	93	3.11

$$\chi 2 = \sum \frac{(O-E)^2}{E} = 3.11$$

Q8. Compute Spearman's Rank correlation for the following data:

Data 1 : 34, 45, 54, 34, 23, 43, 45, 45, 43, 45
Data 2 : 43, 45, 54, 34, 34, 43, 43, 23, 34, 43

Ans.

S. No.	X	Y	Rank X	Rank Y	(Rank X)²	(Rank Y)²	(Rank X)(Rank Y)
(1)	34	43	2.5	6.5	6.25	42.25	16.25
(2)	45	45	7.5	9	56.25	81	67.5

(3)	54	54	10	10	100	100	100
(4)	34	34	2.5	3	6.25	9	7.5
(5)	23	34	1	3	1	9	3
(6)	43	43	4.5	6.5	20.25	42.25	29.25
(7)	45	43	7.5	6.5	56.25	42.25	48.75
(8)	45	23	7.5	1	56.25	1	7.5
(9)	43	34	4.5	3	20.25	9	13.5
(10)	45	43	7.5	6.5	56.25	42.25	48.75
Total			55	55	379	378	342

$$\rho = \frac{\sum R_X R_Y - \frac{(\sum R_X)(\sum R_Y)}{n}}{\sqrt{\left[\sum R_X^2 - \frac{(\sum R_X)^2}{n}\right]\left[\sum R_Y^2 - \frac{(\sum R_Y)^2}{n}\right]}}$$

$$\rho = \frac{342 - \frac{55 \times 55}{10}}{\sqrt{\left[379 - \frac{55^2}{10}\right]\left[378 - \frac{55^2}{10}\right]}}$$

$$\rho = \frac{342 - 302.5}{\sqrt{(379 - 302.5)(378 - 302.5)}}$$

$$\rho = \frac{39.5}{\sqrt{76.5 \times 75.5}} = \frac{39.5}{76}$$

$$\rho = 0.520$$

Q9. Describe Phi Coefficient and Biserial Correlation.
Ans. Refer to Chapter-2, Q.No.-11 and Q.No.-12

Section–C

Write short notes on any two of the following in about 100 words each:
Q10. Kendall's Tau
Ans. Refer to Chapter-2, Q.No.-14
Q11. Wilcoxon Matched Pair Signed Rank Test
Ans. Refer to Chapter-4, Q.No.-8
Q12. Multiple Correlation
Ans. Refer to Chapter-2, Q.No.-18

Statistics in Psychology : MPC-006
December, 2016

Note : *(i) All sections are compulsory.*
(ii) Use of simple calculator be permitted.

SECTION-A

Note: Answer any two of the following questions in about 500 words each:

Q1. Discuss the concept of Normal Curve. Describe properties of Normal Probability Curve.

Ans. Refer to Chapter-3, Q.No.-1

Q2. Define Non-parametric Statistics. Describe the assumptions and use of non-parametric tests.

Ans. Refer to Chapter-1, Q.No.-1

Q3. A research was carried out to find if significant difference exists in the self concept of early, middle and late adolescents. The scores obtained on self concept are given below. Using ANOVA indicate if the groups differ on self concept significantly.

Group I (Early)	Group II (Middle)	Group III (Late)
14	8	7
15	13	5
13	14	7
12	22	6
11	14	8
10	24	8
9	12	10
5	15	8
3	20	6
4	15	6

Critical value: 5.49 at 0.01 level of significance.
3.35 at 0.05 level of significance.

Ans. $H_o : \mu_1 = \mu_2 = \mu_3$

The mean of self-concept of early, middle and late adolescents is statistically equal and there is not any difference.

H_1: Mean of self-concept of at least one out of early, middle and late adolescents is not statistically equal.

In this example,
k=3 (i.e. self-concept of early, middle and late adolescents)

n=10 (i.e. each group is having 10 observations)
N=30 (i.e. the total numbers of observations)
Here,

$df_{between} = k - 1 = 3 - 1 = 2$

$df_{within} = N - k = 30 - 3 = 27$

$df_{total} = N - 1 = 30 - 1 = 29$

S.No.	Group I (Early)		Group II (Middle)		Group III (Late)	
	X_1	X_1^2	X_2	X_2^2	X_3	X_3^2
(1)	14	196	8	64	7	49
(2)	15	225	13	169	5	25
(3)	13	169	14	196	7	49
(4)	12	144	22	484	6	36
(5)	11	121	14	196	8	64
(6)	10	100	24	576	8	64
(7)	9	81	12	144	10	100
(8)	5	25	15	225	8	64
(9)	3	9	20	400	6	36
(10)	4	16	15	225	6	36
Σx	96	1086	157	2679	71	523
Mean $(\overline{X})$	9.6		15.7		7.1	
$(\Sigma x)^2$	9216		24649		5041	
$\Sigma(\Sigma x)$	96+157+71=324					
$\Sigma(\Sigma x^2)$	1086+2679+523=4288					

$SS_B = \sum \frac{(\Sigma x)^2}{n} - \frac{(\Sigma(\Sigma x))^2}{N}$

$= \left(\frac{96^2}{10} + \frac{157^2}{10} + \frac{71^2}{10} \right) - \left(\frac{(96+157+71)^2}{30} \right)$

=3890.6 - 3499.2
=391.4

$SS_w = \left(\Sigma(X_1^2) - \frac{(\Sigma x_1)^2}{n} \right) + \left(\Sigma(x_2^2) - \frac{(\Sigma x_2)^2}{n} \right) + \left(\Sigma(x_3^2) - \frac{(\Sigma x_3)^2}{n} \right)$

$= \left(1086 - \frac{96^2}{10} \right) + \left(2679 - \frac{157^2}{10} \right) + \left(523 - \frac{71^2}{10} \right)$

=164.4+214.1+18.9
=397.4

$$MS_B = \frac{SS_B}{df_B} = \frac{391.4}{2} = 195.7$$

$$MS_W = \frac{SS_W}{df_W} = \frac{397.4}{27} = 14.72$$

F Ratio $= \frac{MS_B}{MS_W} = \frac{195.7}{14.72} = 13.296$

Source of Variation	Sum of Squares	Degree of Freedom	Mean Square	F Ratio
Between Sample	391.4	2	195.7	13.296
Within Sample	397.4	27	14.72	
Total	788.8	29		

Critical values of F=5.49 at 0.01 level of significance
Critical values of F=3.35 at 0.05 level of significance
Since it is observed that F(calculated) > F(critical), at 0.01 and 0.05 level of significance, it is then concluded that the null hypothesis is rejected.
Therefore, there is enough evidence to claim that there is significant difference in self-concept of early, middle and late adolescents as not all 3 population means are equal, at α = 0.01 and 0.05 significance level.

Q4. Compute regression equation for X and Y based on the data given below:

Individuals	X	Y
A	2	10
B	7	12
C	8	3
D	3	10
E	5	10

Ans.

S.No.	X	Y	X^2	Y^2	XY
(1)	2	10	4	100	20
(2)	7	12	49	144	84
(3)	8	3	64	9	24
(4)	3	10	9	100	30
(5)	5	10	25	100	50
Total	25	45	151	453	208

Here,

n = 5, $\bar{X} = \frac{\Sigma X}{n} = \frac{25}{5} = 5$ $\bar{Y} = \frac{\Sigma Y}{n} = \frac{45}{5} = 9$

$(\Sigma X)^2 = 25 \times 25 = 625$ $(\Sigma Y)^2 = 45 \times 45 = 2025$

Regression Equation- 'X' on 'Y'

$$S_x = \sum X^2 - \frac{(\sum X)^2}{n} = 151 - \frac{625}{5} = 26$$

$$Cov_{XY} = \sum XY - \frac{(\sum X)(\sum Y)}{n} = 208 - \frac{25 \times 45}{5} = -17$$

$$b = \frac{Cov_{XY}}{S_x} = \frac{-17}{26} = -0.654$$

$$a = \overline{Y} - b\overline{X} = 9 - (-0.654 \times 5) = 12.269$$

$$\hat{Y} = a + bX$$

$$\hat{Y} = 12.269 - 0.654X$$

SECTION-B

Note: Answer any four of the following questions in about 300 words each:

Q5. Define hypothesis testing. Discuss general procedure for testing a hypothesis with the help of suitable example.

Ans. Refer to Chapter-1, Q.No.-18 and Q.No.-19

Q6. Calculate Mann-Whitney U-test with the help of the following data:

Group 1 : 40, 17, 46, 51, 45
Group 2 : 12, 18, 20, 15, 17

Ans.

Group 1	Rank	Group 2	Rank
40	7	12	1
17	3.5	18	5
46	9	20	6
51	10	15	2
45	8	17	3.5
$\sum R_1$	37.5	$\sum R_2$	17.5

$$U = n_1 \cdot n_2 + \frac{n_1(n_1+1)}{2} - \sum R_1 \qquad U' = n_1 \cdot n_2 + \frac{n_2(n_2+1)}{2} - \sum R_2$$

$$U = 5 \times 5 + \frac{5(5+1)}{2} - 37.5 \qquad U' = 5 \times 5 + \frac{5(5+1)}{2} - 17.5$$

$$U = 25 + 15 - 37.5 = 2.5 \qquad U' = 25 + 15 - 17.5 = 22.5$$

$$U = 2.5 \text{ and } U' = 22.5$$

Q7. Compute Chi-square for the following data:

Gender	Answers given	
	Correct	Incorrect
Males	50	60
Females	40	30

Ans.

Gender		Answer Given		Total	χ^2
		Correct	Incorrect		
Male	O	50	60	110	
	E	55	55		
	O-E	-5	5		
	$(O-E)^2$	25	25		
	$(O-E)^2/E$	0.45	0.45		0.9
Female	O	40	30	70	
	E	35	35		
	O-E	5	-5		
	$(O-E)^2$	25	25		
	$(O-E)^2/E$	0.71	0.71		1.42
Total		90	90	180	2.32

$$\chi^2 = \sum \frac{(O-E)^2}{E} = 2.32$$

Q8. Compute Spearman's Rank Correlation for the following data:

Data 1 : 44, 45, 45, 34, 43, 23, 54, 34, 67, 45
Data 2 : 12, 21, 32, 12, 12, 15, 26, 12, 16, 12

Ans.

S. No.	X	Y	Rank X	Rank Y	$(\text{Rank X})^2$	$(\text{Rank Y})^2$	(Rank X)(Rank Y)
(1)	44	12	5	3	25	9	15
(2)	45	21	7	8	49	64	56
(3)	45	32	7	10	49	100	70
(4)	34	12	2.5	3	6.25	9	7.5
(5)	43	12	4	3	16	9	12
(6)	23	15	1	6	1	36	6
(7)	54	26	9	9	81	81	81
(8)	34	12	2.5	3	6.25	9	7.5
(9)	67	16	10	7	100	49	70

(10)	45	12	7	3	49	9	21
Total			55	55	382.5	375	346

$$\rho = \frac{\sum R_X R_Y - \frac{(\sum R_X)(\sum R_Y)}{n}}{\sqrt{\left[\sum R_x^2 - \frac{(\sum R_x)^2}{n}\right]\left[\sum R_y^2 - \frac{(\sum R_y)^2}{n}\right]}}$$

$$\rho = \frac{346 - \frac{55 \times 55}{10}}{\sqrt{\left[382.5 - \frac{55^2}{10}\right]\left[375 - \frac{55^2}{10}\right]}}$$

$$\rho = \frac{346 - 302.5}{\sqrt{(382.5 - 302.5)(375 - 302.5)}}$$

$$\rho = \frac{43.5}{\sqrt{80 \times 72.5}} = \frac{43.5}{76.16}$$

$$\rho = 0.571$$

Q9. Describe point biserial correlation and tetrachoric correlation.

Ans. Refer to Chapter-2, Q.No.-10 and Q.No.-12

SECTION - C

Note: Write short notes on any two of the following in about 100 words each:

Q10. Kruskal-Walli's ANOVA Test
Ans. Refer to Chapter-4, Q.No.-12

Q11. Levels of measurement
Ans. Refer to Chapter-4, Q.No.-1

Q12. Wilcoxon Matched Pair Signed Ranks Test
Ans. Refer to Chapter-4, Q.No.-8

Statistics in Psychology : MPC-006
June, 2017

Note : *(i) All sections are compulsory.*
(ii) Use of simple calculator be permitted.

Section–A
Answer any two of the following questions in about 450 words each:

Q1. Define and differentiate between Parametric and non-parametric statistics.
Ans. Refer to Chapter-1, Q.No.-1

Q2. Explain step by step the calculation of point biserial correlation and phi coefficient and indicate their uses.
Ans. Refer to Chapter-2, Q.No.-10 and Q.No.-11

Q3. Explain linear and non-linear relationship. Find out the degree of relationship between the 2 data given below using Spearman's Rho.

	A	B	C	D	E	F	G	H	I	J
Data 1:	22	23	29	20	25	27	30	34	37	35
Data 2:	35	39	22	40	31	45	30	28	25	20

Ans. Refer to Chapter-2, Q.No.-4
Let Data 1 be X and Data 2 be Y

	X	Y	Rank X	Rank Y	D = (Rank X-Rank Y)	D²
A	22	35	2	7	-5	25
B	23	39	3	8	-5	25
C	29	22	6	2	4	16
D	20	40	1	9	-8	64
E	25	31	4	6	-2	4
F	27	45	5	10	-5	25
G	30	30	7	5	2	4
H	34	28	8	4	4	16
I	37	25	10	3	7	49
J	35	20	9	1	8	64
Total			55	55	0	292

$$\rho = 1 - \frac{6\sum D^2}{n(n^2-1)}$$

$$= 1 - \frac{6 \times 292}{10(100-1)}$$

$$= 1 - \frac{1740}{990} = 1 - 1.77, \rho = -0.77$$

Hence, there is high negative relationship between the given sets of data.

Q4. A research was carried out to find the effectiveness of three techniques of stress management. The data collected from three different groups on stress scale are given below. Find out using ANOVA if the obtained differences are significant.
Group A (Technique 1): 2, 4, 5, 6, 7
Group B (Technique 2): 3, 2, 3, 2, 4
Group C (Technique 3): 3, 6, 2, 4, 7
Critical Value: 0.05 level of significance = 19.41
0.01 level of significance = 99.46

Ans. In this example,
k = 3 (i.e. three techniques of stress management)
n = 5 (i.e. each group is having 5 observations)
N = 15 (i.e. the total numbers of observations)
$H_o : \mu_1 = \mu_2 = \mu_3$

The effectiveness of three techniques of stress management is statistically equal and there is not any difference.

H_a : There is significant difference in the effectiveness of three techniques of stress management.

$df_{between} = k - 1 = 3 - 1 = 2$
$df_{within} = N - k = 15 - 3 = 12$
$df_{total} = N - 1 = 15 - 1 = 14$

S. No.	Group A (Technique 1)		Group B (Technique 2)		Group C (Technique 3)	
	x_1	x_1^2	x_2	x_2^2	x_3	x_3^2
(1)	2	4	3	9	3	9
(2)	4	16	2	4	6	36
(3)	5	25	3	9	2	4
(4)	6	36	2	4	4	16
(5)	7	49	4	16	7	49
Σ	24	130	14	42	22	114
Σx^2	24 × 24 = 576		14 × 14 = 196		22 × 22 = 484	
Σ (Σx)	24 + 14 + 22 = 60					
Σ (Σx²)	576 + 196 + 484 = 1256					

$SS_B = \sum \frac{(\Sigma x)^2}{n} - \frac{[\Sigma x)]^2}{N}$

$= \left(\frac{24^2}{5} + \frac{14^2}{5} + \frac{22^2}{5} \right) - \left(\frac{(24+14+22)^2}{15} \right)$

= 251.2 − 240

= 11.2

$SS_W = \left(\Sigma(x_1^2) - \frac{(\Sigma x_1)^2}{n} \right) + \left(\Sigma(x_2^2) - \frac{(\Sigma x_2)^2}{n} \right) + \left(\Sigma(x_3^2) - \frac{(\Sigma x_3)^2}{n} \right)$

$$= \left(130 - \frac{24^2}{5}\right) + \left(42 - \frac{14^2}{5}\right) + \left(114 - \frac{22^2}{5}\right)$$
$$= 14.8 + 2.8 + 17.2$$
$$= 34.8$$

$$MS_B = \frac{SS_B}{df_B} = \frac{11.2}{2} = 5.6$$

$$MS_W = \frac{SS_W}{df_W} = \frac{34.8}{12} = 2.9$$

$$F\ Ratio = \frac{MS_B}{MS_W} = \frac{5.6}{2.9} = 1.93$$

Source of Variation	Sum of Squares	Degree of Freedom	Mean Square	F Ratio
Between Sample	11.2	2	5.6	1.93
Within Sample	34.8	12	2.9	
Total	46	14		

Since it is observed that F (observed) <F (critical), for 0.01 and 0.05 level of significance, it is then concluded that the null hypothesis is accepted.

Therefore, there is enough evidence to claim that there is no statistical significance difference in the effectiveness of three techniques of stress management for all three different groups on stress scale, at the $\alpha = 0.01$ and 0.05 significance level.

Section–B

Answer any four of the following questions in about 250 words each:

Q5. Describe the four levels of measurement and indicate the data for which they are used.
Ans. Refer to Chapter-4, Q.No.-1

Q6. Compute Mann – Whitney U test for the following data:
Data 1 : 10, 24, 14, 15, 30, 17, 29
Data 2 : 20, 12, 16, 18, 36, 38, 50
Ans.

S.No.	Data 1	Rank	Data 2	Rank
(1)	10	1	20	8
(2)	24	9	12	2
(3)	14	3	16	5
(4)	15	4	18	7
(5)	30	11	36	12
(6)	17	6	38	13
(7)	29	10	50	14
(8)	ΣR_1	44	ΣR_2	61

$$U = n_1 \cdot n_2 + \frac{n_1(n_1+1)}{2} - \sum R_1 \qquad U' = n_1 \cdot n_2 + \frac{n_2(n_2+1)}{2} - \sum R_2$$

$$U = 7 \times 7 + \frac{7(7+1)}{2} - 44 \qquad U' = 7 \times 7 + \frac{7(7+1)}{2} - 61$$

$$U = 49 + 28 - 44 = 33 \qquad U' = 49 + 28 - 61 = 16$$

$$U = 33 \text{ and } U' = 16$$

Q7. For question 'How often do you exercise?', the replies given by males and females were categorised as frequently, occasionally, rarely and never. Is there any association between gender and frequency?

	Frequently	Occasionally	Rarely	Never
Males	10	5	4	6
Females	20	10	3	2

Critical Value: for 0.01 level of significance = 11.345
For 0.05 level of significance = 7.815

Ans. Null Hypothesis: There is NO association between the gender and frequency for the replies for question, 'How often do you exercise?'

		Gender		Total	χ^2
		Male	Female		
Frequently	O	10	20	30	
	E	12.50	17.50		
	O−E	−2.50	2.50		
	$(O-E)^2$	6.25	6.25		
	$(O-E)^2/E$	0.50	0.36		0.86
Occasionally	O	5	10	15	
	E	6.25	8.75		
	O−E	−1.25	1.25		
	$(O-E)^2$	1.56	1.56		
	$(O-E)^2/E$	0.25	0.18		0.43

Rarely	O	4	3	7		
	E	2.92	4.08			
	O−E	1.08	−1.08			
	$(O-E)^2$	1.17	1.17			
	$(O-E)^2/E$	0.40	0.29			0.69
Never	O	6	2	8		
	E	3.33	4.67			
	O−E	2.67	−2.67			
	$(O-E)^2$	7.11	7.11			
	$(O-E)^2/E$	2.13	1.52			3.66
Total		25	35	60		5.63

$$\sum x^2 = 5.63$$

At 0.01 level of significance, Calculated Chi-Square Value (5.63) is less than Critical chi-square table value (11.345), so Null hypothesis is accepted.

Whereas, at 0.05 level of significance Calculated Chi-Square Value (5.63) is more than Critical chi-square table value (7.815), so Null hypothesis is accepted.

Hence, we can say that there is NO association between the gender and frequency for the replies for question, 'How often do you exercise?' at 0.01 and 0.05 level of significance.

Q8. Compute Kendall's tau for the following data:

	A	B	C	D	E
X	4	7	8	9	3
Y	3	4	7	8	9

Ans.

	A	B	C	D	E
X	4	7	8	9	3
Y	3	4	7	8	9

	A	B	C	D	E
R_x	2	3	4	5	1
R_y	1	2	3	4	5

R_x	1	2	3	4	5
R_y	5	1	2	3	4

R_y	5	1	2	3	4	Total
	5	-	-	-	-	-4
		1	+	+	+	+3
			2	+	+	+2
				3	+	+1
					4	0
					Grand Total (S)	2

$$\tau = \frac{2S}{[n(n-1)]}$$

$$\tau = \frac{2 \times 2}{[5(5-1)]}$$

$$\tau = \frac{4}{20}, \quad \tau = 0.20$$

Q9. Describe the properties of Normal Probability Curve.

Ans. Refer to Chapter-3, Q.No.-1

SECTION-C

Write short notes on any two of the following in about 100 words each:

Q10. Errors in Hypotheses testing.

Ans. Refer to Chapter-1, Q.No.-22

Q11. Correlation and Causality

Ans. The correlation does not necessarily imply causality. But, if the correlation between two variables is high then it might indicate the causality. If X and Y are correlated, then there are three different ways in which the relationship between two variables can be understood in terms of causality.

(1) X is a cause of Y.

(2) Y is cause of X.

(3) Both, X and Y are caused by another variable Z.

However, causality can be inferred from the correlations.

Regression analysis, path analysis, structural equation modeling, are some examples where correlations are employed in order to understand causality.

Q12. Interactional effect

Ans. The interactional effect means joint effect of the two or more variables acting together on a dependent or criterion variables. In case of insignificant interactional effect of the two or more predictors or independent variables on a criterion or dependable variable. The two-way analysis variance is a useful technique in experimental psychology as well as in experimental education especially in the field of teaching and learning. It is frequently used in field experiments or true experiments, when we use factorial designs specifically. Without considering the interaction between the different variables in a study, there is no use of two way or three way analysis of variance.

Statistics in Psychology : MPC-006
December, 2017

Note : *(i) All sections are compulsory.*
(ii) Use of simple calculator be permitted.

SECTION - A

Answer any two of the following questions in about 450 words each:

Q1. Define nonparametric statistics and discuss its advantages and disadvantages.
Ans. Refer to Chapter-1, Q.No.-1 and Q.No.-2

Q2. Discuss multiple correlation. Explain partial correlation with suitable example.
Ans. Refer to Chapter-2, Q.No.-18 and Q.No.-15

Q3. Define correlation. Find out if relationship exists between the data given below with the help of Pearson's Product Moment Coefficient of Correlation.

	A	B	C	D	E	F	G	H	I	J
Data 1:	2	3	4	7	8	9	2	3	4	8
Data 2:	10	7	8	2	3	1	10	10	7	2

Ans. Refer to Chapter-2, Q.No.-1

	Data 1 (x)	Data 2 (y)	xy	x^2	y^2
A	2	10	20	4	100
B	3	7	21	9	49
C	4	8	32	16	64
D	7	2	14	49	4
E	8	3	24	64	9
F	9	1	9	81	1
G	2	10	20	4	100
H	3	10	30	9	100
I	4	7	28	16	49
J	8	2	16	64	4
Total	$\sum x=50$	$\sum y=60$	$\sum xy=214$	$\sum x^2=316$	$\sum y^2=480$

$$r_p = \frac{n(\Sigma xy)-(\Sigma x)(\Sigma y)}{\sqrt{\left[n\Sigma x^2-(\Sigma x)^2\right]\left[n\Sigma y^2-(\Sigma y)^2\right]}}$$

$$r_p = \frac{n(\Sigma xy)-(\Sigma x)(\Sigma y)}{\sqrt{\left[n\Sigma x^2-(\Sigma x)^2\right]\left[n\Sigma y^2-(\Sigma y)^2\right]}}$$

$$= \frac{2140-3000}{\sqrt{[3160-2500][4800-3600]}}$$

$$= \frac{-860}{\sqrt{660 \times 1200}} = \frac{-860}{889.9} = -0.97$$

$r_p = -0.97$

Thus, there is a perfect negative linear relationship.

Q4. A research was carried out to find if significant difference exists in motivation of three groups of employees after they received three different training programmes. Compute ANOVA for the data given below:

Group A (Training 1): 2, 3, 2, 3, 5
Group B (Training 2): 5, 5, 5, 10, 10
Group C (Training 3): 10, 10, 2, 3, 5
Critical value: 0.05 level of significance = 19.41
         0.01 level of significance = 99.46

Ans. Same as June-2017, Q.No.-4

SECTION - B

Answer any four of the following questions in about 250 words each:

Q5. Discuss normal curve. Explain divergence from normal distribution, indicating the causes for the same.

Ans. Refer to Chapter-3, Q.No.-1 and Q.No.-4

Q6. Compute Mann - Whitney U test with the help of the following data:

Data 1: 13, 16, 40, 47, 56, 70
Data 2: 34, 12, 25, 39, 64

Ans. Same as June-2017, Q.No.-6

Q7. Male and female participants responded with strongly agree, agree, undecided, disagree and strongly disagree to a health related attitude questionnaire. The data is given below, compute chi square.

	strongly agree	agree	undecided	disagree	strongly disagree
Males	1	4	7	8	5
Females	3	2	6	4	5

Critical Value: for 0.01 level of Significance = 13.277
for 0.05 level of Significance = 9.488

Ans. Same as Chapter-4, Q.No.-11 (Practical Problem)

Q8. Compute Kendall's tau for the following data:

	A	B	C	D	E	F
X	2	7	1	5	8	10
Y	4	5	6	8	10	9

Ans. Same as Chapter-2, Q.No.-14

Q9. Explain null hypothesis with an example. Discuss errors in hypothesis testing.

Ans. Refer to Chapter-1, Q.No.-23 and Q.No.-22

SECTION - C

Write short notes on any two of the following in about 100 words each:

Q10. Regression equation.
Ans. Refer to Chapter-2, Q.No.-19

Q11. Measuring divergence from normal curve.
Ans. Refer to Chapter-3, Q.No.-4

Q12. Ratio and Interval data.
Ans. Refer to Chapter-4, Q.No.-1

"Our greatest glory is not in never falling, but in rising every time we fall".
-Confucius

WE'D LOVE IT IF YOU'D LIKE US!

/gphbooks

We're now on Facebook!

Like our page to stay on top of the useful, greatest headlines & exciting rewards.

Our other awesome Social Handles:

gphbooks
For awesome &
informative videos
for IGNOU students

9350849407
Order now
through WhatsApp

gphbooks
We are
in pictures

gphbook
Words you get
empowered by

Statistics in Psychology : MPC-006
June, 2018

Note : *(i) All sections are compulsory.*
(ii) Use of simple calculator be permitted.

SECTION – A

Answer any two of the following questions in about 450 words each:

Q1. What is inferential statistics? Discuss in detail Hypothesis Testing.

Q2. Explain the concept and theoretical base of normal curve. Elucidate the properties of normal probability curve.

Q3. Define outliers. Compute only Spearman's Rho for the following data:

data A	5.0	5.9	6.0	5.7	5.6	5.5	4.9	3.6	4.0
Data B	53	50	49	55	63	60	64	69	70

Q4. Compute ANOVA for the following data :

Group 1	3	2	2	2	3	3	2	2	2
Group 2	1	1	1	2	2	1	1	1	1
Group 3	2	2	4	4	4	4	2	3	3

Critical value: 19.45 at 0.05 level of significance
99.46 at 0.01 level of significance

SECTION – B

Answer any four of the following questions in about 250 words each:

Q5. Discuss classification as a technique for organising the data.

Q6. Compute Mann Whitney U test for the following data:
Group A : 54, 76, 80, 69, 68, 52, 42, 49
Group B : 74, 72, 70, 56, 62, 45, 50, 48

Q7. Compute chi square for the following data:

	Respones		
	Agree	Disagree	Total
Male	20	30	50
Female	30	70	100
Tatal	50	100	150

Critical value : 3.841 at 0.05 level of significance
6.635 at 0.01 level of significance

Q8. Compute regression equation for X and Y based on the following data:

Individuals

	A	B	C	D	E
X	2	3	2	5	8
Y	3	2	4	1	10

Q9. Describe various levels of measurement with suitable examples.

SECTION – C

Write short notes on any two of the following in about 100 words each:

Q10. Type I and Type II errors

Q11. Phi Coefficient

Q12. One-tailed and Two-tailed hypothesis tests

Statistics in Psychology : MPC-006
December, 2018

Note : *(i) All sections are compulsory.*
(ii) Use of simple calculator be permitted.

SECTION - A

Answer any two of the following questions in about 450 words each:

Q1. Differentiate inferential from descriptive statistics. Describe steps in setting up the level of significance.

Q2. Discuss the rational for using non-parametric statistics and describe its advantages and disadvantages.

Q3. Explain partial correlation. Compute Spearman's Rho for the following data:

Data A	60	54	59	44	49	48	40
Data B	55	60	69	70	67	66	54

Q4. Compute ANOVA for the following data:

Group 1	2	2	3	3	2	4	2	3	2
Group 2	3	2	2	2	3	3	2	2	2
Group 3	3	3	3	4	4	4	1	1	1

Critical value: 19.41 for 0.05 level of significance
                99.46 for 0.01 level of significance

SECTION – B

Answer any four of the following in about 250 words each:

Q5. Compute t teAt for the data given below:
Group A : 10, 4, 3, 2, 4, 2, 5, 10, 5, 5
Group B: 4, 6, 8, 2A 1, 12, 13, 10, 10
Critical value: 2.10 at 0.05 level of significance
                    2.88 at 0.01 level of significance

Q6.. Compute Mann Whitney U test for the following data:
Group A: 100, 86, 94, 85, 69, 70, 82, 74, 64, 59
Group B: 96, 92, 90, 84, 80, 78, 76, 65, 62, 50

Q7. Compute Chi square for the following data:

	\ responses		
Male	Agree	Disagree	Not decided
	20	10	20
Female	10	20	30

Critical value:
5.991 at 0.05 level of significance
9.210 at 0.01 level of significance

Q8. Discuss the importance and application of standard error of mean.

Q9. Discuss factors causing divergence in normal curve.

SECTION – C

Write short notes on any two of the following in about 100 words each:

Q10. Point biserial correlation.
Q11. Linear regression.
Q12. Two ways Analysis of Variance.

 ## Why Students Choose GPH Books

- Syllabus covered as prescribed by Universities/Boards/Institutions.
- Easily understandable language and format that help students prepare for exam in short period of time.
- Published with exam-oriented approach, hence prepared in question-answer format which provides students the instant understanding of a correct answer.
- Maximum solved previous year question papers included which help students to understand unique examination structure and equip them better for exam.
- Both semesters' question papers (June-December) are included with solutions.
- Instant updation of data as and when any change occurs.
- Use of recycled paper.
- Handy books and reasonable prices.
- For every book sold, we contribute for society/institution/NGOs/underprivileged

Feedback is the breakfast of Champions.

Ken Blanchard

You can Help other students.
"Inform any error or mistake in this book."

We and Universe
will reward you for Your Kind act.

Email at : feedback@gullybaba.com
or
WhatsApp on 9350849407

Statistics in Psychology : MPC-006
June, 2019

Note : *(i) All sections are compulsory. Use of simple calculator be permitted.*

SECTION–A

Answer any two of the following questions in about 450 words each.

Q1. Explain descriptive statistics. Describe graphical presentation of data.
Ans. Refer to Chapter-1, Q.No.-7 and Q.No.-12 (Pg. No.-11, 22)

Q2. Discuss Spearman's rank-order correlation with suitable example.
Ans. Refer to Chapter-2, Q.No.-13 (Pg. No.-67)

Q3. Describe standard error. Compute t test for the following data:

Data 1:	8,	4,	2,	1,	6,	7,	2,	3,	2,	5
Date 2:	10,	15,	20,	21,	9,	30,	31,	19,	10,	15

Critical value = 2.10 at 0.05 level
2.88 at 0.01 level

Ans. Refer to Chapter-3, Q.No.-6(v) (Pg. No.-111) and Same as Dec-2018, Q.No.-5 (Pg. No.-255)

Q4. What is tetrachoric correlation ? Compute Kendall's tau for the following data :

	A	B	C	D	E
Variable X:	3	1	2	4	5
Variable Y:	4	5	3	2	1

Ans. Refer to Chapter-2, Q.No.-12 (Pg. No.-66) and Same as June-2017, Q.No.-8 (Pg. No.-245)

SECTION–B

Answer any four of the following questions in about 250 words each.

Q5. Explain hypothesis testing. Describe errors in hypothesis testing.
Ans. Refer to Chapter-1, Q.No.-18 and Q.No.-22 (Pg. No.-37, 42)

Q6. Compute Mann-Whitney U test for the following data:
   Group 1 : 32, 93, 19, 40, 46, 71, 63, 98, 47, 49, 52
   Group 2 : 89, 21, 82, 91, 85, 84, 103, 101, 100, 107, 110
Ans. Same as Dec-2016, Q.No.-6 (Pg. No.-238)

Q7. Compute Chi-square for the following data:

Opinion

	Agree	Undecided	Disagree
Male	10	13	11
Female	15	12	14

Ans. Same as June-2016, Q.No.-7 (Pg. No.-233)

Q8. Discuss the use of non-parametric tests.
Ans. Refer to Chapter-1, Q.No.-2 (Pg. No.-3)

Q9. Explain in detail Wilcoxon matched pair signed rank test with suitable example.
Ans. Refer to Chapter-4, Q.No.-8 (Pg. No.-164)

SECTION—C

Write short notes on any two of the following in about 100 words each.

Q10. Semipartial Correlation.
Ans. Refer to Chapter-2, Q.No.-17 (Pg. No.-75)

Q11. Factors causing divergence in normal curve.
Ans. Refer to Chapter-3, Q.No.-4 (Pg. No.-109)

Q12. Meaning of Variance.
Ans. Refer to Chapter-3, Q.No.-16 (Pg. No.-119)

Statistics in Psychology : MPC-006
December, 2019

Note : *(i) All sections are compulsory. Use of simple calculator be permitted.*

SECTION–A

Answer any two of the following questions in about 450 words each.

Q1. Explain the meaning of inferential statistics. Describe hypothesis testing.

Q2. Discuss in detail partial correlation with suitable example.

Q3. Describe the basic assumptions in testing of significance of difference between two sample means. Compute t value for the following data:

Data 1:	2,	3,	4,	2,	5,	3,	4,	2,	2,	3
Date 2:	3,	4,	5,	5,	5,	2,	2,	4,	4,	6

Critical Value =
2.10 at 0.05 level of significance
2.88 at 0.01 level of significance.

Q4. Compare between Rho and Tau. Compute Kendall's tau for the following data:

	A	B	C	D	E
Variable X:	3	2	4	1	5
Variable Y:	5	1	2	3	4

SECTION–B

Answer any four of the following questions in about 250 words each.

Q5. Explain the meaning and concept of levels of significance Describe the steps in setting up the level of significance.

Q6. Compute Mann Whitney U test for the following data:
Group 1 : 19, 25, 17, 27, 30, 16, 44, 50,
Group 2 : 12, 36, 10, 37, 13, 46, 57, 63, 70

Q7. Compute chi-square for the following data :

	Agree	Disagree
Male	12	14

| Female | 13 | 20 |

Q8. Define non-parametric statistics and discuss its assumptions.

Q9. Explain divergence in normality with the help of suitable diagrams.

SECTION—C

Write short notes on any two of the following in about 100 words each.

Q10. Measures of Dispersion
Q11. Concept of Normal Curve
Q12. Kruskal-Wallis ANOVA test

Statistics in Psychology : MPC-006
June, 2020

Note : *(i) All sections are compulsory. Use of simple calculator be permitted*

SECTION-A

Answer any two of the following questions in about 450 words each:

Q1. Define parametric statistics and describe its assumptions, advantages and disadvantages.
Ans. Refer to Chapter-1, Q.No.-1

Q2. Explain linear and nonlinear relationship with suitable diagrams. Discuss the steps in computing Pearson's product moment correlation.
Ans. Refer to Chapter-2, Q.No.-4

Equations for Pearson's Product Moment Coefficient of Correlation: Having revised the concepts, we shall now learn to compute the Pearson's Correlation Coefficient.

Formula

Since we have already learned to compute the covariance, the simplest way to define Pearson's correlation is...

$$r = \frac{Cov_{XY}}{S_X S_Y} \quad \quad \ldots (1)$$

Where,

the Cov_{XY} is covariance between X and Y,

S_X is standard deviation of X

S_Y is standard deviation of Y.

Since, it can be shown that Cov_{XY} is always smaller than or equal to $S_X S_Y$, the maximum value of correlation coefficient is bound to be 1.

The sign of Pearson's r depends on the sign of Cov_{XY}.

If the Cov_{XY} is negative, then r will be negative and

if Cov_{XY} is positive then r will be a positive value.

The denominator of this formula ($S_X S_Y$) is always positive. This is the reason for a − 1 to + 1 range of correlation coefficient. By substituting covariance equation $\left(\text{Cov}_{XY} = \dfrac{\Sigma(X-\bar{X})(Y-\bar{Y})}{n}\right)$ for covariance we can rewrite equation 1 as

$$r = \dfrac{\dfrac{\Sigma(X-\bar{X})(Y-\bar{Y})}{n}}{S_X S_Y} \qquad \ldots(2)$$

By following a simple rule, $a \div b \div c = a \div (b \times c)$, we can rewrite equation 2 as follows.

$$r = \dfrac{\Sigma(X-\bar{X})(Y-\bar{Y})}{nS_{X_r}S_Y} \qquad \ldots(3)$$

Q3. Compute t test for the following data:
Group-A 2, 3, 5, 4, 1, 5, 10, 4, 6, 10
Group-B 7, 10, 5, 8, 4, 6, 12, 13, 2, 3
Ans. Refer to Dec-2018, Q.No.-5

Q4. Compute one way ANOVA for the following data and indicate if groups differ on the variable:

F value = $\begin{array}{cc} P<0.5 & P<0.1 = \\ 3.35 & 5.19 \end{array}$

Group A: 2, 3, 4, 2, 3, 2, 2, 2, 3, 3
Group B: 2, 4, 5, 5, 5, 2, 3, 5, 5, 2
Group C: 2, 3, 4, 2, 5, 2, 2, 3, 2, 3
Ans. Same as June-2017, Q.No.-4

SECTION-B

Answer any four of the following questions in about 250 words each.

Q5. Discuss frequency distribution in terms of grouped and ungrouped data. Elucidate the types of frequency distribution.
Ans. Refer to Chapter-1, Q.No.-9

Types of Frequency Distribution: There are various ways to arrange frequencies of a data array based on the requirement of the statistical analysis or the study. A couple of them are discussed below:

(i) Relative frequency distribution: A relative frequency distribution is a distribution that indicates the proportion of the total number of cases observed at each score value or internal of score values.

(ii) Cumulative frequency distribution: Sometimes investigator may be interested to know the number of observations less than a particular value. This is possible by computing the cumulative frequency. A cumulative frequency corresponding to a class-interval is the sum of frequencies for that class and of all classes prior to that class.

(iii) Cumulative relative frequency distribution: A cumulative relative frequency distribution is one in which the entry of any score of class interval expresses that score's cumulative frequency as a proportion of the total number of cases.

Q6. Differentiate between partial and part correlation with suitable example.
Ans. Refer to Chapter-2, Q.No.-15 and Q.No.-17

Q7. Compute Mann Whitney U for the following data:
Group 1: 23, 21, 7, 14, 10, 13, 25, 29, 48, 55
Group 2: 20, 8, 15, 9, 45, 12, 40, 47, 50, 51
Ans. Same as Dec-2018, Q.No.-6

Q8. Discuss the step by step procedure for Kendall's Rank Order Correlation.
Ans. Refer to Chapter-4, Q.No.-14

Q9. Compute Chisquare for the following data:

	Male	Female
Literate	10	30
Illiterate	20	40

Ans. Same as Dec-2016, Q.No.-7

SECTION- C

Write short notes on any two of the following in about 100 words each:

Q10. Sampling error.
Ans. Refer to Chapter-3, Q.No.-6(iv)

Q11. Assumptions underlying the Analysis of Variance.
Ans. Refer to Chapter-3, Q.No.-21

Q12. Nominal data.
Ans. Refer to Chapter-4, Q.No.-1

Statistics in Psychology : MPC-006
February, 2021

Note : *(i) All sections are compulsory. Use of simple calculator be permitted*

SECTION A
Answer any two of the following questions in about 450 words each:

Q1. Describe measures of central tendency. Elucidate advantages and disadvantages of descriptive statistics.
Ans. Refer to Chapter-1, Q.No.-14 and Refer to Chapter-1, Q.No.-7

Q2. What is Normal distribution? Discuss its importance and characteristics.
Ans. Refer to Chapter-3, Q.No.-3

Q3. Compute t test for the following data:
Group A: 2, 3, 4, 5, 2, 7, 5, 4, 3, 2
Group B: 3, 2, 7, 2, 6, 5, 5, 5, 4, 3
Ans. Refer to Dec-2018, Q.No.-5

Q4. Compute one-way ANOVE for the following data and indicate if the three groups differ on the variable,
$P < .05 = 3.35$
$P < .01 = 5.49$
Group A: 2, 3, 2, 2, 2, 5, 5, 5, 5, 5
Group B: 3, 3, 3, 2, 2, 4, 4, 4, 2, 2
Group C: 3, 5, 4, 4, 2, 3, 2, 4, 5, 5
Ans. Same as June-2017, Q.No.-14

SECTION B
Answer any four of the following questions in about 250 words each:

Q5. Discuss merits and demerits of Two-way Analysis Variance.
Ans. Refer to Chapter-3, Q.No.-23

Q6. Discuss Point and Interval estimation.
Ans. Refer to Chapter-1, Q.No.-17

Q7. Compute Mann-Whitney U test for the following data:
Group A: 7, 18, 20, 34, 23, 28, 27, 48, 43, 55
Group B: 16, 8, 37, 31, 35, 40, 42, 50, 52, 44
Ans. Same as Dec-2018, Q.No.-6

Q8. Compare Pearson's 'r' with Kendall's 'Tau'.
Ans. Refer to Chapter-2, Q.No.-7 and Q.No.-14

Q9. Compute chi-square for the following data.

	Low socio-economic status	High socio-economic status
Male	20	25
Female	60	35

Ans. Same as Dec-2016, Q.No.-7

SECTION C

Write short notes on any two of the following in about 100 words each:

Q10. Histogram
Ans. Refer to Chapter-1, Q.No.-12

Q11. Interactional effect
Ans. Refer to June-2017, Q.No.-12

Q12. Assumptions underlying Regression
Ans. Refer to Chapter-2, Q.No.-23

Statistics in Psychology : MPC-006
June, 2021

Note: *(i) All sections are compulsory. (ii) Use of simple calculator be permitted.*

SECTION-A

Answer any two of the following questions in about 450 words each.

Q1. Describe the four major statistical techniques for organising the data.

Ans. There are four major statistical techniques for organising the data. These are:
- (1) **Classification:** Refer to Chapter-1, Q.No.-8, Q.No.-9 and Q.No.-10
- (2) **Tabulation:** Refer to Chapter-1, Q.No.-11
- (3) **Graphical Presentation:** Refer to Chapter-1, Q.No.-12
- (4) **Diagrammatical Presentation:** Refer to Chapter-1, Q.No.-13

Q2. Discuss the concept, properties and characteristics of normal probability curve with the help of a suitable diagram.

Ans. Refer to Chapter-3, Q.No.-1

Q3. Explain Phi coefficient. Compute Pearson's product moment correlation for the following data:

Individuals	A	B	C	D	E	F	G	H	I	J
Data X	5	5	4	4	4	3	2	2	6	5
Data Y	6	6	4	4	4	5	5	5	4	7

Ans. Refer to Chapter-2, Q.No.-11 and Same as Dec.-2017, Q.No.-3

Q4. Compute one-way ANOVA for the following data:

Group A	4	5	5	5	3	3	3	4	4	4
Group B	5	5	6	5	6	3	4	7	7	7
Group C	6	5	6	3	8	8	7	5	3	9

Critical Value:
3.35 at 0.05 level
5.49 at 0.01 level.

Ans. Same as June-2017, Q.No.-4

SECTION–B

Answer any four of the following questions in about 250 words each.

Q5. Differentiate between parametric and non-parametric statistics.
Ans. Refer to Chapter-1, Q.No.-1

Q6. Compute Mann-Whitney U-test for the following data:
Group A : 60, 22, 27, 31, 35, 47, 56, 40, 55
Group B : 20, 29, 24, 39, 34, 41, 49, 50, 51
Ans. Same as Chapter-4, Q.No.-1 (Solved Practical Problems)

Q7. Compute Chi-square for the following data:

	Responses	
	Yes	No
Male	20	15
Female	20	20

Ans. Same as Chapter-4, Q.No.-13 (Solved Practical Problems)

Q8. Elucidate interactional effect. Discuss the merits and demerits of two-way ANOVA.
Ans. Refer to June-2017, Q.No.-12 and Chapter-3, Q.No.-23

Q9. Describe the levels of measurement with suitable examples.
Ans. Refer to Chapter-4, Q.No.-1

SECTION–C

Write short notes on any two of the following in about 100 words each:

Q10. Decision errors.
Ans. Refer to Chapter-1, Q.No.-24 (ii)

Q11. Characteristics of variance.
Ans. Refer to Chapter-3, Q.No.-16

Q12. Multiple regression.
Ans. Refer to Chapter-2, Q.No.-18

Statistics in Psychology : MPC-006
December, 2021

Note : (i) All sections are compulsory. (ii) Use of simple calculator be permitted

SECTION–A

Answer any two of the following in about 450 words each:

Q1. Discuss the applications of normal distribution curve. Describe divergence from normality with suitable diagram and discuss the factors causing divergence.
Ans. Refer to Chapter-3, Q.No.-2 and Q.No.-4

Q2. Elucidate the definition and assumptions of non-parametric statistics and describe its use.
Ans. Refer to Chapter-1, Q.No.-1 and Chapter-4, Q.No.-2

Q3. Explain biserial correlation. Compute Pearson's product moment correlation for the following data:

	Data X	Data Y
A	10	12
B	12	13
C	13	5
D	11	12
E	9	13
F	8	15
G	12	10
H	5	10
I	10	10
J	10	10

Ans. Refer to Chapter-2, Q.No.-12 and Q.No.-10

Q4. Compute one-way ANOVA for the following data:

Group 1	Group 2	Group 3
2	4	5
3	5	5
3	5	5
2	5	4
2	2	4
3	4	5
3	4	5
2	5	4

2	5	4
2	5	5

CV = 3.35 at 0.05 level
5.49 at 0.01 level.
Ans. Same as June-2017, Q.No.-4

SECTION–B

Answer any four of the following questions in about 250 words each.

Q5. Compute Mann-Whitney U-test for the following data:

Data A	Data B
5	4
23	17
20	18
11	8
27	29
24	13
40	30
37	33
45	50
31	

Ans. Same as Chapter-4, Q.No.-1 (Solve Practical Problems)

Q6. Compute Chi-square for the following data:

	Responses		
	Yes	No	Undecided
Male	10	10	10
Female	20	10	10

Ans. Same as Chapter-4, Q.No.-13 (Solve Practical Problems)

Q7. Define and describe coefficient of correlation. Discuss the characteristics and measures of correlation.

Ans. Correlation Coefficient

The correlation between any two variables is expressed in terms of a number, usually called as correlation coefficient. The correlation coefficient is denoted by various symbols depending on the type of correlation. The most common is 'r' (small 'r') indicating the Pearson's product-moment correlation coefficient.

The representation of correlation between X and Y is r_{xy}.

The range of the correlation coefficient is from –1.00 to + 1.00.

It may take any value between these numbers including, for example, – 0.72, – 0.61, – 0.35, + 0.02, + 0.31, + 0.98, etc.

If the correlation coefficient is 1, then relationship between the two variables is perfect.

This will happen if the correlation coefficient is – 1 or + 1

As the correlation coefficient moves nearer to + 1 or − 1, the strength of relationship between the two variables increases.

If the correlation coefficient moves away from the + 1 or − 1, then the strength of relationship between two variables decreases (that is, it becomes weak).

So correlation coefficient of + 0.87 (and similarly − 0.82, − 0.87, etc.) shows strong association between the two variables. Whereas, correlation coefficient of + 0.24 or − 0.24 will indicate weak relationship. Figure 1 indicates the range of correlation coefficient.

|—+—+—+—+—+—+—+—+—+—+—+—+—+—+—+—+—+—+—+—|
−1.0 −0.9 −0.8 −0.7 −0.6 −0.5 −0.4 −0.3 −0.2 −0.1 0 0.1 0.2 0.3 0.4 0.5 0.6 0.7 0.8 0.9 1.0

Fig.1 : The Range of Correlation Coefficient

You can understand the strength of association as the common variance between two correlated variables. The correlation coefficient is NOT percentage.

So correlation of 0.30 does NOT mean it is 30% variance.

The shared variance between two correlated variables can be calculated. Let me explain this point. See, every variable has variance. We denote it as S_x^2 (variance of X). Similarly, Y also has its own variance $\left(S_y^2\right)$. In the previous block you have learned to compute them. From the complete variance of X, it shares some variance with Y. It is called covariance.

The Figure 2 below shown below explains the concept of shared variance. The circle X indicates the variance of X. Similarly, the circle Y indicates the variance of Y. The overlapping part of X and Y, indicated by shaded lines, shows the shared variance between X and Y. One can compute the shared variance.

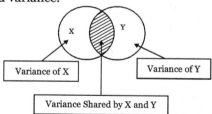

Fig.2 : Covariance indicates the degree to which X shares variance with Y

To calculate the percentage of shared variance between X and Y (common variance), one needs to square the correlation coefficient (r). The formula is given below:

Percentage of common variance between X and $Y = r_{xy}^2 \times 100$

...(1)

For instance, if the correlation between X and Y is 0.50 then the percent of variation shared by X and Y can be calculated by using equation 1 as follows.

Percentage of common variance between X and $Y = r_{xy}^2 \times 100 = 0.50^2 \times 100 = 0.25 \times 100 = 25\%$

It indicates that, if the correlation between X and Y is 0.50 then 25% of the variance is shared by the two variables, X and Y. You would note that this formula is applicable to negative correlations as well. For instance, if $r_{xy} = -0.81$, then shared variance is:

Percentage of common variance between X and Y $= \times 100 = -0.81^2 \times 100 = 0.6561 \times 100 = 65.61\%$

Measurements of Correlation

Correlation coefficient can be calculated by various ways. The correlation coefficient is a description of association between two variables in the sample. So it is a descriptive statistics. Various ways to compute correlation simply indicate the degree of association between variables in the sample. The distributional assumptions are not required to compute correlation as a descriptive statistics. So it is not a parametric or nonparametric statistics.

The calculated sample correlation coefficient can be used to estimate population correlation coefficient.

The sample correlation coefficient is usually denoted by symbol 'r'.

The population correlation coefficient is usually denoted by symbol 'ñ'.

It is Greek letter rho(ñ), pronounced as row (Spearman's correlation coefficient is also symbolised as rho.

- When the population correlation coefficient is estimated from sample correlation coefficient.
- Then the correlation coefficient becomes an inferential statistic.
- Inference about population correlation (ñ) is drawn from sample statistics (r).
- The population correlation (ñ) is always unknown.
- What is known is sample correlation (r).
- The population indices are called as parameters and the sample indices are called as statistics.
- So ñ is a parameter and r is a statistics.

While inferring a parameter from sample, certain distributional assumptions are required. From this, you can understand that the descriptive use of the correlation coefficient does not require any distributional assumptions.

The most popular way to compute correlation is 'Pearson's Product Moment Correlation (r)'. This correlation coefficient can be computed when the data on both the variables is on at least equal interval scale or ratio scale.

Apart from Pearson's correlation there are various other ways to compute correlation. Spearman's Rank Order Correlation or Spearman's rho (r_s) is useful correlation coefficient when the data is in rank order.

Similarly, Kendall's tau (ô) is a useful correlation coefficient for rank-order data.

Biserial, Point Biserial, Tetrachoric, and Phi coefficient, are the correlations that are useful under special circumstances.

Apart from these, multiple correlations, part correlation and partial correlation are useful ways to understand the associations (Please note that the last three require more than two variables).

Characteristics of a Correlation

Correlations have three important characteristics. They can tell us about the direction of the relationship, the form (shape) of the relationship, and the degree (strength) of the relationship between two variables.

(1) **The Direction of a Relationship:** The correlation measure tells us about the direction of the relationship between the two variables. The direction can be positive or negative.

   (i) **Positive:** In a positive relationship both variables tend to move in the same direction: If one variable increases, the other tends to also increase. If one decreases, the other tends to also.

   In the example above, GPA and MathSAT are positively related. As GPA (or MathSAT) increases, the other variable also tends to increase.

   (ii) **Negative:** In a negative relationship the variables tend to move in the opposite directions: If one variable increases, the other tends to decrease, and vice-versa.

   The direction of the relationship between two variables is identified by the sign of the correlation coefficient for the variables. Positive relationships have a "plus" sign, whereas negative relationships have a "minus" sign.

(2) **The Form (Shape) of a Relationship:** The form or shape of a relationship refers to whether the relationship is straight or curved.

   (i) **Linear:** A straight relationship is called linear, because it approximates a straight line. The GPA, MathSAT example shows a relationship that is, roughly, a linear relationship.

   (ii) **Curvilinear:** A curved relationship is called curvilinear, because it approximates a curved line. An example of the relationship between the Miles-per-gallon and engine displacement of various automobiles sold in the USA in 1982 is shown below. This is curvilinear (and negative).

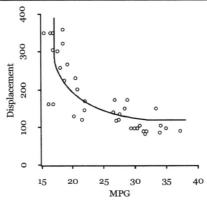

(3) The Degree (Strength) of a Relationship: Finally, a correlation coefficient measures the degree (strength) of the relationship between two variables. The measures we discuss only measures the strength of the linear relationship between two variables. Two specific strengths are:

(i) **Perfect Relationship:** When two variables are exactly (linearly) related the correlation coefficient is either +1.00 or –1.00. They are said to be perfectly linearly related, either positively or negatively.

(ii) **No Relationship:** When two variables have no relationship at all, their correlation is 0.00.

There are strengths in between –1.00, 0.00 and +1.00. Note, though that +1.00 is the largest positive correlation and –1.00 is the largest negative correlation that is possible.

Q8. Describe the measures of central tendency and measures of dispersion.

Ans. Refer to Chapter-1, Q.No.-14 and Q.No.-15

Q9. Explain step by step procedure for computation of Kruskal Wallis ANOVA with an example.

Ans. Step by step procedure for Kruskal Wallis Anova

(1) Rank all the numbers in the entire data set from smallest to largest (using all samples combined); in the case of ties, use the average of the ranks that the values would have normally been given.

(2) Total the ranks for each of the samples; call those totals T_1, T_2, . . ., T_k, where k is the number of groups or populations.

(3) Calculate the Kruskal-Wallis test statistic,

$$H = \left[12 / N(N+1)\right]\left[\Sigma\left((\Sigma R)^2 / n\right)\right] - 3(N+1)$$

N = the total number of cases
n = the number of cases in a given group

$(\Sigma R)^2$ = the sum of the ranks squared for a given group of subjects
(4) Find the *p*-value.
(5) Make your conclusion about whether you can reject H_0 by examining the p-value.

Example of a Small Sample

In a Study, 12 participants were divided into three groups of 4 each, they were subjected to three different conditions, A (Low Noise), B (Average Noise), and C (Loud Noise). They were given a test and the errors committed by them on the test were noted and are given in the table below.

Participant No.	Condition A (Low Noise)	Participant No.	Condition B (Average Noise)	Participant No.	Condition C (Loud Noise)
1	3	5	2	9	10
2	5	6	7	10	8
3	6	7	9	11	7
4	3	8	8	12	11

The researcher wishes to know whether these three conditions differ amongst themselves and there are no assumptions of the probability. To apply Kruskal Wallis test, following steps would be taken:

Step 1: Rank all the numbers in the entire data set from smallest to largest (using all samples combined); in the case of ties, use the average of the ranks that the values would have normally been given.

Condition A	Ranks T1	Condition B	Ranks T2	Condition C	Ranks T3
3	2.5	2	1	10	11
5	4	7	6.5	8	8.5
6	5	9	10	7	6.5
3	2.5	8	8.5	11	12
	ΣT1 = 14		ΣT2 = 26		ΣT3 = 38

Step 2: Total the ranks for each of the samples; call those totals T1, T2, ..., Tk, where k is the number of populations.
T1 =14
T2 =26
T3=38

Step 3: Calculate H

$$H = \left[12/N(N+1)\right]\left[\Sigma\left((\Sigma R)^2/n\right)\right] - 3(N+1)$$

N = 12
n = 4

$$(\Sigma R)^2 = (14 + 26 + 38)^2 = 6084$$

$$H = \left[12/12(12+1)\right]\left[(14^2/4) + (26^2/4) + (38^2/4)\right] - 3(12+1)$$

H= [12/156] [49 + 169 + 361] – 39
H= (0.076 × 579) – 39

H = 44.525 − 39
H = 5.537

Step 4: Find the p-value.

Since the groups are three and number of items in each group are 4, therefore looking in table H (k=3, sample size of 4,4,4) it can be seen that the critical value is 5.692 ($\alpha = 0.05$).

Step 5: Make your conclusion about whether you can reject Ho by examining the p-value.

Since the critical value is more than the actual value we accept the null hypothesis that all the three conditions A (Low Noise), B (Average Noise), and C (Loud Noise), do not differ from each other, therefore, in the said experiment there was no differences in the groups performance based on the noise level.

SECTION–C

Write short notes on any two of the following in about 100 words each:

Q10. Degrees of Freedom
Ans. Refer to Chapter-3, Q.No.-9

Q11. Interactional Effect
Ans. Refer to June-2017, Q.No.-12

Q12. The Regression Equation
Ans. Refer to Chapter-2, Q.No.-19

NOTES

CPSIA information can be obtained
at www.ICGtesting.com
Printed in the USA
BVHW052341300623
666614BV00010B/937